SAMURAI
AN ILLUSTRATED HISTORY

A Nanbokucho period samurai commander, in this case wearing the oyoroi *short armor. His* utsubo *quiver is covered with a white cloth. His helmet has a parasol-like* shikoro, *tall* kuwagata *or horns, and extremely back-folded* fukigaeshi.

SAMURAI
AN ILLUSTRATED HISTORY

MITSUO KURE

COMPENDIUM

LONDON

Editor's note

In this text most Japanese nouns have been *italicized*. Exceptions are 'samurai,' professional warrior; 'daimyo,' provincial baron; 'shogun,' military dictator; and 'bakufu,' the shogun's government; and proper names of places, persons and religious movements, which are capitalized. Rather than constantly repeating e.g. 'the Takeda family (or clan),' we have often used in this sense the form 'the Takeda.' Japanese names are given throughout in the traditional form, i.e. family name first and given name second.

The reconciliation of exact dates between the Japanese and modern Western calendar is notoriously difficult (for instance, according to the Japanese calendar the month of March 1599 was repeated twice). Many English language references are unclear as to the sources of dates quoted. Generally this text follows Japanese sources, e.g. the date of the battle of Sekigahara is given as September 15, 1600 rather than 21 October.

Illustrations

Photographs of various historical reenactments were taken in many locations in Japan during the 1990s. Uncredited photographs are © the author; photographs from other sources are individually credited. The detailed line drawings of costume, armor, etc., which appear throughout the book and are credited (SY), are by Dr Sasama Yoshihiko, and are reproduced by courtesy of the Kashiba Shobo Publishing Company.

Editor: Martin Windrow

Designer: Frank Ainscough @ Compendium

Maps: Peter Harper

This edition published in 2001 by
Compendium Publishing
1st Floor
43 Frith Street
London W1D 4SA

ISBN 1 902579 38 0

Printed in China through Colorprint Offset

A CIP Catalogue record for this book is available from the British Library

CONTENTS

PREFACE

For about 700 years the samurai were the leading class in Japanese society. Yet the date of the emergence of this class into history is still a matter of controversy. Did they originate in a military aristocracy, or from among paid professional warriors? Was their birthplace in Kyoto, or Kanto? Such fundamental questions still exercise scholars, and many facts which have been accepted as a matter of course are now exposed to the suspicious eyes of the researcher. In this book I have tried to touch upon these new questions as they effect our view of the samurai. Naturally, all aspects of samurai history cannot be covered in this limited space; but it is my hope that readers may find enough in these pages to suggest a new image of the samurai, modifying a picture which has been distorted by romanticism.

It is a truism that history is written by winners, and in Japan, as in Europe, the ruler often manipulated the record; even contemporary documents should be assessed with some care. Edo period prints, drawings, and paintings on room partitions vividly depict samurai life and warfare, but these 19th-century sources are not a reliable guide to the historical facts of the medieval age. Only some scrolls surviving from the Kamakura period may be relied upon as convincing depictions of scenes from the lives and battles of 13th- and 14th-century samurai. I have included here some old pictures which have become famous from an artistic point of view, but I have drawn attention to their credibility, or lack thereof, as historical documents. On the other hand, I am also glad to publish here—by courtesy of the Kashiwa Shobo Publishing Company—several dozen exact illustrations by Dr. Sasama Yoshihiko, whose deep knowledge of samurai culture is a guarantee of these images.

Japanese armor has been well preserved in shrines, because samurai used to present it to these precincts in prayer for or thanks following victory (although in emergencies it was not unknown for them to take it back to use again). Another reason that historical Japanese armor has been preserved in relatively good condition, in spite of the humid climate, is that they were coated with lacquer, which gives almost the same protection as a modern 'high tech' glass fiber compound; the only danger is from exposure to sunlight. I have included here many photographs of original well-conserved armor. Readers who wish to see how these types of armor appear in action should refer to my previous book *The Samurai Recreated in Colour Photographs* (The Crowood Press, UK; ISBN 1 86126 335 X).

The weapons of the samurai are described only to the extent that readers will not become confused by over-detailed explanations and variations. The Japanese are very fond of establishing 'schools'; they have invented many distinct martial arts, and even schools for different techniques of shooting the matchlock arquebus. Rather than pursuing precision to confusing lengths, let it suffice that there were many ways of handling weapons.

Castles are symbols of the samurai period still seen in the middle of major Japanese cities. But when the imperial government was restored in 1869 all castles were ordered destroyed, and only a handful survived. Apart from these few, the castles that today's tourists see are reconstructions built with modern techniques. Fortifications in the mountains are long destroyed and forgotten, and only archaeological evidence remains. Unlike the more ancient remains, the excavation of medieval fortifications has been rather neglected in Japan, and requires serious study in the future.

Mitsuo Kure

INTRODUCTION
WHO WERE THE SAMURAI?

The samurai were a class of people who served the aristocracy with arms. The word first appeared in a document of the Heian period; before that time such people had been called *mono-no-fu* or *bushi*. *Mono* means 'thing' and *fu* means 'man'; that is, men who deal with things—'things' in this case meaning weapons. The word *bushi* means 'man of arms.' Another document from the Heian period, listing various professions, includes *bushi* along with other specialists such as men of letters, doctors, singers, dancers and others.

As a recent study has pointed out, they were neither landowners nor armed farmers; from the beginning they were professional warriors. The central government at Kyoto learned by experience, during their attempts to overcome the stubborn resistance of the *emishi* or 'barbarians' who controlled northern Honshu, that the old army consisting of drafted soldiers was not of much use. These 'barbarians' were very effective mounted warriors, and in order to subdue them the Kyoto government had to rearrange its forces. The government hired men from the Kanto area who were skilled at shooting bows from the saddle.

Why did the Kanto area yield such good horsemen? During the 6th and 7th centuries AD there were many wars on the Korean peninsula in which the Japanese monarchy in Kyoto involved itself. After the fall of the Japanese colony of Mimana in 562, and of the Paekche dynasty in 660, many people from Korea took refuge in Japan. They were so many, indeed, that the Kyoto government became uneasy about their influence, and transferred these immigrants to the eastern lowlands of Kanto (now in the Tokyo area). Among these immigrant communities there were some who traditionally raised horses; there may even have been the descendants of nomads from central Asia. It is not a large step from the settlement of these horse-archers to the idea that they were the forefathers of the *mono-no-fu*. This kind of speculation seems an attractive explanation for the growth of the samurai, but there are still many contradictions—among them the facts that the samurai used a long bow instead of the short recurved type typical of Asian nomads, and rode uncastrated stallions instead of geldings.

In the Nara period, the government conscripted men of 20 to 30 years of age from the provinces of Japan. Each province had a corps consisting of 1,000 soldiers and officers called *gunki* which was attached to the *kokushi*, the provincial governor. However, this system was abolished in 792 (with some few exceptions); and a new system—*kondeisei*—was introduced. Under this reorganization, intended to reduce the burden of military service on the farmers whose work underpinned the entire economy, the government drew upon young men from the richer families who were skilled at riding horses and shooting the bow.

Were these later to become the samurai? Considering that the original samurai battle tactics were based on horse archery, and that before this period we have no evidence of cavalry in Japanese history, it is appropriate to assume that these troops were distinct from the previous emperors' conventional soldiers and were the origin of the samurai.

Another document describes certain people called *kugutsu*, who wandered Japan like gypsies. They supposedly entertained the people with puppet shows and acrobatics where they stopped, and their women earned a living by prostitution. They had one other remarkable attribute, however—they were good horse-archers. It is not hard to imagine a commander afflicted by *emishi* raids hiring *kugutsu* as mercenaries; but did they use the long bow?

It is interesting to note that the *emishi* had a very high reputation as horse-archers.[1] It was not only through contact on the battlefield, but also through trade and social communication with the *emishi* that changes came about in the fighting methods of Kyoto government troops. Later the government used captured or pacified *emishi* as mercenaries to defend Kyushu from imminent Chinese and Korean invasion.

In the course of the continuing discussion over the origins of the samurai, some researchers have recently argued that they lie with military aristocracy in the service of the Kyoto government. They analyze contemporary documents to support the theory that the samurai were created at the emperor's court.[2] It is quite true that the word *samurai* means, literally, 'in service.' But we should bear in mind the fact that Kanto and northern Tohoku were the places which produced good horses; and where good horses grow, so do good horsemen. It is not surprising that a strong corps of samurai would soon enter the pages of history from the Kanto area.

It may be added that a study of *oyoroi* style armor soon makes clear that it was invented in the field, not at the emperor's peaceful court. Many elements—the *sode* (armored sleeve), *nodowa* (throat guard), *wakidate* (right flank guard), and others—were added one after another, progressively protecting more and more weak points which must have been identified through combat experience.

(1) *shoku nihonkoki*
(2) *Bushi no seiritsu, Bushizo no soshitsu*, by Takahashi Yoshiaki (1999)

Until the 8th century AD the Nara government applied a military service law called ritsuryosei, *based on Chinese practice, by which they drafted men from 20 to 30 years of age to serve in a provincial corps. The structure of such a 1,000-man corps in the Heian period is indicated here. (SY)*

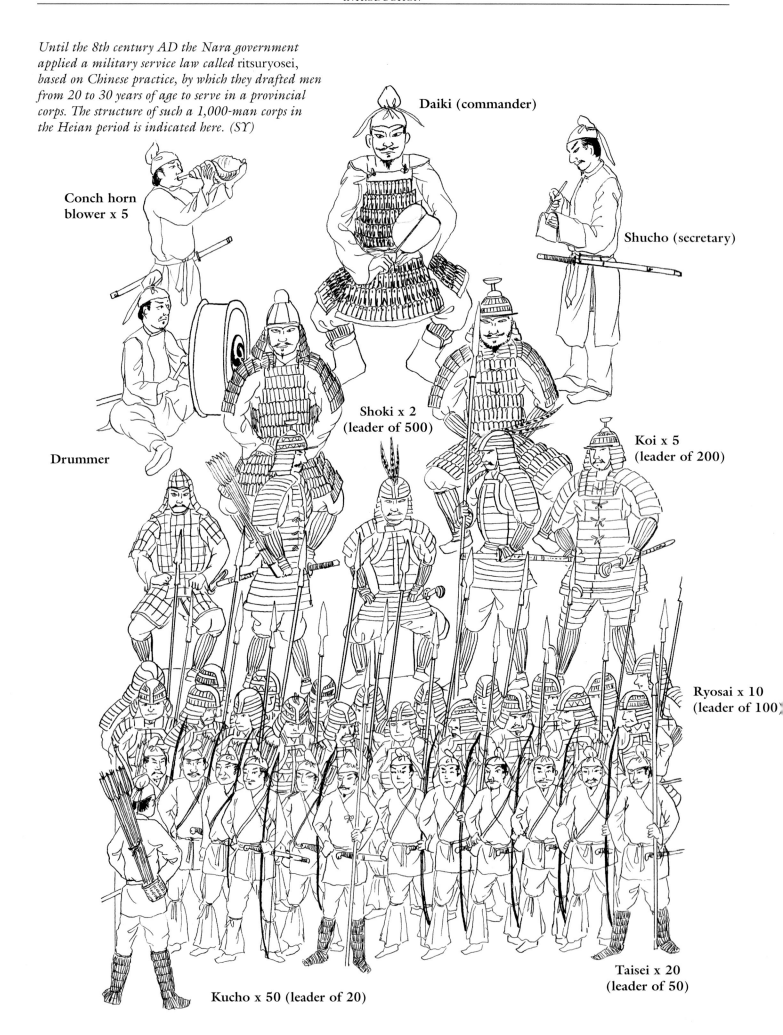

Daiki (commander)

Shucho (secretary)

Conch horn blower x 5

Drummer

Shoki x 2 (leader of 500)

Koi x 5 (leader of 200)

Ryosai x 10 (leader of 100)

Taisei x 20 (leader of 50)

Kucho x 50 (leader of 20)

PART 1:
THE CENTURIES OF
THE SAMURAI

CHAPTER 1:
THE RISE OF THE WARRIOR CLASS

After AD 794, when the Japanese imperial capital moved from Nara to Kyoto, the aristocracy enjoyed some 150 years of prosperity under the imperial regime. However, the local governors—*kokushi*—sent out by the regime oppressed the population of the provinces. Heavy taxation provoked many attempted revolts; it also obliged small farmers to attach themselves to powerful local families, who amassed ever greater holdings. There was mutual tension between the court-based aristocrats of the Kyoto government and the increasingly wealthy provincial landowning class, who were not themselves considered aristocrats. (This distinction would remain of central importance throughout the period covered by this book.)

From the beginning of the 10th century, these provincial landowners began to organize private armies. They hired to their service numbers of professional warriors, and recruited and trained soldiers from among the farmers, artisans and townspeople. These forces made them increasingly important in their regions, and increasingly confident in their dealings with the aristocracy. Up to this period, military service and 'policing' had been entirely the prerogative and responsibility of the central government. Judges appointed by Kyoto were charged with settling disputes; if the conduct of one party was held to be illegal, the judge punished that family and took all its properties for himself. It is unsurprising that the reality of the situation was often far removed from the ideal.

Once their private armies gave them a degree of local independence, wealthy magnates sought to extend or defend their estates in frequent petty wars. In the great rice-growing area of the Kanto Plain, far to the east of Kyoto, there were constant skirmishes, night raids, ambushes and robberies. Against the background of such an environment it is to be expected that a new and less romantic evaluation

Scene from the Early Nine Years War campaign. In 1051 the Abe family rebelled in Mutsu (Tohoku region), and Minamoto Yoriyoshi and his son Yoshiie were sent north to suppress the rising. General Yoriyoshi is third from the left, and Yoshiie second from the left; Yoshiie's helmet has tall horn-like ornaments. This scroll is presumed to have been made in the 13th or 14th century, and the painter shows Kamakura period armor. (Tokyo National Museum)

of the nature of the samurai is generally accepted today. They were a kind of 'mafiosi,' who fought for family, land and plunder, but scarcely for honor.

Violent competition was also the rule within the highest levels of society. The noble families of the aristocratic class surrounding the imperial court jockeyed and fought for relative advantage. The authority of the emperor himself was weakened by the maneuvering of the maternal side of the imperial family. Among the court families the Fujiwara became the most powerful, manipulating imperial authority through a regency; so confident did they become that Fujiwara Michinaga sang in a poem that 'My world is like a full moon and will never wane'.

All wealth depended on the income of rice-growing land; the court families drew their resources from their manorial estates in the countryside, and enjoyed privileges by which they evaded taxation. Their local estates were managed by magistrates, whose authority was enforced by private armies. At the bottom of the pyramid were the farmers; they suffered heavy taxation and yearned for protection against the demands of the great estates.

Rebellion in the Johei—Tengyo period
In 935 the governor in Kanto, Taira Masakado, killed his uncle Kunika. By 939 he had seized power over the whole region and proclaimed himself the New Emperor.

Taira Masakado on the march; in the war of AD 935-940 his forces dominated the Kanto area. His soldiers consisted of two kinds: jurui *and* banrui. *The former were Masakado's loyal retainers who served him to the end; the latter were mainly peasant farmers who usually returned home after a battle, and would not serve during the rice planting and harvest seasons. They were not reliable, and often fled if things seemed to be turning against them. On the flag are four characters: fire, thunder, heaven and god. (SY)*

Meanwhile, in the other direction from Kyoto, on the Inland Sea, Fujiwara Sumitomo organized pirates and local naval forces to pursue his own revolt. These major risings against the central government initially reduced the court aristocracy to praying for the assistance of the gods; but in time other militarized families crushed both revolts, in which the samurai class had played an important role. Seen as attempts by the samurai class to challenge the aristocracy, these risings were historically premature. The samurai families were self-seeking and chronically disunited, and no grouping was strong enough to maintain its power for long against the others which the imperial regime enlisted to oppose them. Nevertheless, these rebellions showed the way of the future; it was becoming obvious who had the real potential power.

For a while the frequency of local revolts seems to have diminished. At the same time, however, out in the provinces the relationships between lords and their vassals were beginning to develop a new character. Bonds of family loyalty, rather than mere employment, were strengthening between the rich local families and their retainers.

The most important of the samurai clans were called the Heishi and the Genji; the Heishi (or Heike) were descended from the Kanmu Emperor, and the Genji from the Seiwa Emperor. Members of the Heishi were known by the family name of Taira, while samurai related to the Genji were named Minamoto. (The simultaneous use of different names came from different readings of the original Chinese characters used in written Japanese; Heishi and Genji are the Chinese readings of the characters for Taira and Minamoto.) The Taira power base was Kanto, while the Genji were influential in Osaka.

In 1028, Taira Masakado's cousin Taira Tadatsune rebelled in Kanto. The reaction of the court was very slow, and it was four months before a punitive force was sent against the rebels. After a four-year struggle Minamoto Yorinobu was called from Yamanashi to serve with the imperial pacification forces, and eventually Tadatsune surrendered to him. After this incident, connections between the Genji clan and the samurai families of Kanto became strong.

At the court in Kyoto, influential samurai families were called for guard duty at the emperor's and other nobles' residences. The word '*samurai*' derives from the word '*saburau*' meaning in the service of or in attendance on a noble. Certain samurai families thus began to have strong connections with noble families; but a samurai's position in the world of the court was very inferior, and they were generally despised by the aristocracy.

The wars of the years Zenkunen and Gosannen

The northern part of Honshu—Tohoku—was originally beyond the power of the Kyoto government. In 1051 a

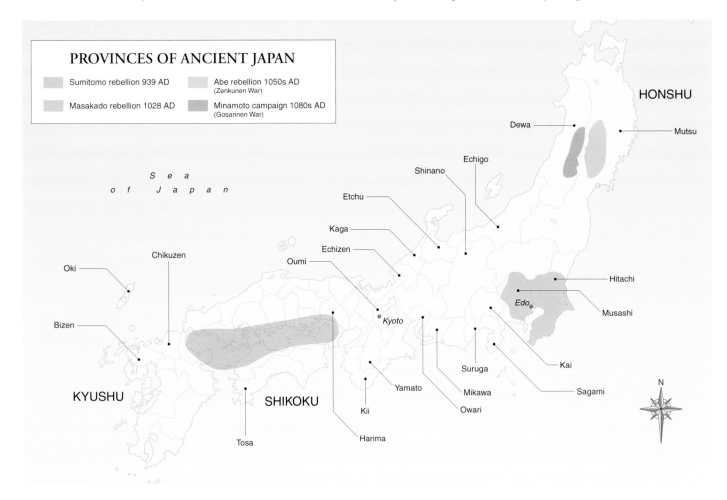

PROVINCES OF ANCIENT JAPAN

Sumitomo rebellion 939 AD

Masakado rebellion 1028 AD

Abe rebellion 1050s AD (Zenkunen War)

Minamoto campaign 1080s AD (Gosannen War)

Top: *A banquet before battle. Minamoto Yoriyoshi (far right), Yoshiie (centre), and their retainers, already wearing their armor, feast before taking the field. (Tokyo National Museum)*

Above: *The rebel Sadatoki sent a message to Yoriyoshi that as it was the day of the chrysanthemum festival (9 September), they should drink chrysanthemum sake and enjoy looking at the flowers. This was a trick, and his army attacked Yoriyoshi's. They fought all day, but neither side won a decisive advantage. Note the details of the drum at top centre, and the mantlets at bottom right—again, these were painted in the Kamakura period. (Tokyo National Museum)*

descendant of the *emishi* barbarians, Abe Yoriyoshi of Mutsu, rose in revolt against the emperor. The court appointed a son of Minamoto Yorinobu, Yoriyoshi, as general of a punitive force to march north. Abe Yoriyoshi soon surrendered; but after several months he again rebelled, provoked by Minamoto Yoriyoshi's oppression of the Abe family. This time it took Yoriyoshi and his son Yoshiie six years to suppress the Abe rebellion; their operations were hindered by the cold climate, deep winter snow, lack of sufficient troops and horses, and difficulties over food supplies. Finally, Yoriyoshi allied with Kiyowara Takenori in Dewa, and entirely as a result of his intervention, this Early Nine Years War was brought to a victorious conclusion. The court gave Kiyowara Takenori the title of tutelary general, and he succeeded to the territorial holdings of the defeated Abe family.

This outcome of the war was not favorable for the Minamoto, and from then on they sought an opportunity to destroy the Kiyowara family. Twenty-one years later, in 1083, when Yoriyoshi's son Minamoto Yoshiie was serving as the general of Mutsu (Iwate), he intervened in a Kiyowara family conflict and destroyed them. However, the court took the view that this had been the prosecution of a private quarrel, and Yoshiie was granted no reward. The giving of gifts to retainers after a war was very important. The primary connection between a lord and his retainer depended on how much land the former granted the latter in return for his services; it was the income from riceland which allowed the retainer to equip himself and give his time to his master's service.

Since he received no lands from the court for his victory, Minamoto Yoshiie was obliged to give away parcels of his own estates to his followers. In any event, this deed made his name famous; many other samurai families donated land to him, and wanted to become his retainers. Nevertheless, from the viewpoint of the court aristocracy the Minamoto family were still regarded merely as organized gangsters.

Above: *An encounter during the* Gosannen *campaign of the 1080s: Minamoto Yoshiie (right) attacks enemies hiding in tall grass; their attempted ambush was betrayed when he noticed small birds flying up from the field. The use of the bow from the saddle against foot soldiers was called* oimono-uchi *or 'the chasing shot'. (Tokyo National Museum)*

Below: *Death of Seuwari Shiro during the* Gosannen *war, 1083. Ashamed at being called a coward, he ate a large meal of rice and drank much* sake *before charging the enemy; but he was shot in the throat, and the food spilled out from the wound as he died miserably. (Tokyo National Museum)*

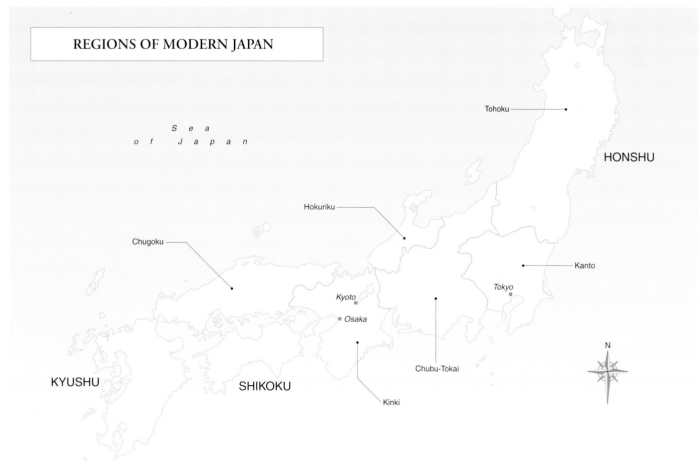

REGIONS OF MODERN JAPAN

Tohoku

*S e a
o f   J a p a n*

HONSHU

Hokuriku

Chugoku

Kanto

Tokyo

Kyoto

Osaka

Chubu-Tokai

KYUSHU

SHIKOKU

Kinki

N

ARMOR OF THE 5TH TO 10TH CENTURIES AD

Japanese armor from this earliest age—identified as the 'Ancient Tumulli' period—can only be reconstructed by study of the terra cotta figurines and other grave goods recovered from ancient royal tombs, which provide much material for speculation. Generally the armors of this period show strong Chinese influence, and we rarely find any of the specifically Japanese characteristics so marked in later periods.

These Tumulli Period Japanese armors were characterized by lamellar construction, the c.800 lamellae being connected by leather laces. They resemble Chinese Tang and Song style lamellar armors, and are termed in Japan the *keiko* style. The wearer put this armor on over the head like a poncho, the front and rear panels being fastened together at the sides. The individual lamellae, termed *sane*, were the basic element of Japanese armor. The shape of the *sane* differed from that employed in Roman scale armors (*lorica squamata*) and later European equivalents, being elongated and pierced with multiple holes for lacing together in several directions, forming nearly rigid 'boards'. This style of armor was probably invented by Mongolian or other steppe nomads who normally fought on horseback. Whether the Japanese ruling class of this period originally migrated from the northern Asian mainland, or native Japanese borrowed or imported foreign fighting techniques and styles of equipment, is still a controversial question.

By the 8th century the *sane* became smaller and narrower, and it took some 1,500 lamellae to construct an armor covering the torso and hips. This was apparently found too time-consuming a method, and a new manufacturing technique was adopted, again following Chinese Tang models. This involved attaching the scales individually to a base garment rather than to one another, which not only saved time but was preferred by northern nomad peoples for its greater protection from the cold climate.

Another important style of Japanese armor was the so-called short armor or *tanko*, which consisted of a riveted combination of segments and transverse plates. Its

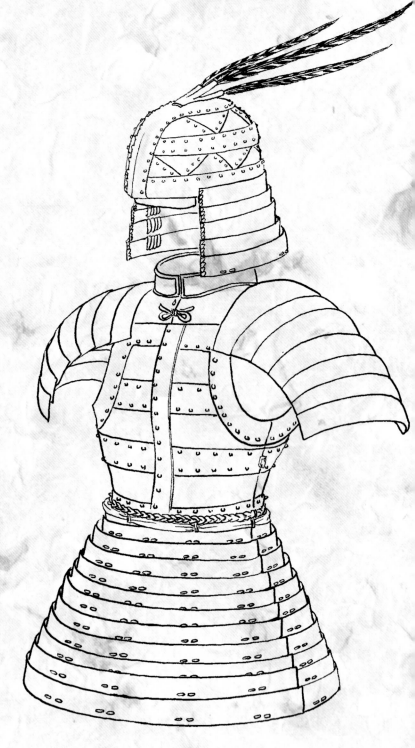

Tanko *or short armor, which had been called* mijika-yoroi *in ancient times (4th-5th centuries AD); and* shokaku *helmet, with a frontal 'beak' added to a basically hemispherical helmet to act as 'spaced armor'. This combination was common, but in some cases* keiko *cuirasses and* shokaku *helmets have been excavated together. (SY)*

characteristic difference from similar foreign cuirasses was the presence of large shoulder plates; these suggest that in this period soldiers were concerned to protect themselves from blows struck from the rear. Obviously they also needed protection from the front, but excessively large plates in this area would presumably have hindered the necessary free movement of the arms.

There were two distinct types of helmets in ancient Japan, which corresponded with the *keiko* and *tanko* styles of armor. Associated with the former was the *mabizashi* or horizontally peaked helmet, and with the latter, the 'beaked' helmet or *shokaku*. The *mabizashi* was constructed of small *sane* with a circumambient plate incorporating the frontal

peak; this had the same function as that found on Roman helmets, to give protection against direct downward or diagonal blows to the front of the head. By contrast, some *shokaku* helmets—characterized by the large protruding 'parrot's beak' at the front of the bowl—were constructed from riveted triangular segment plates and a circumambient belt. This *shokaku* was easier, and thus quicker and cheaper to construct, and became popular; later it was often found associated with *keiko* armor. Both styles of helmet were augmented with attached skirt-like cheek and neck guards made from *sane*.

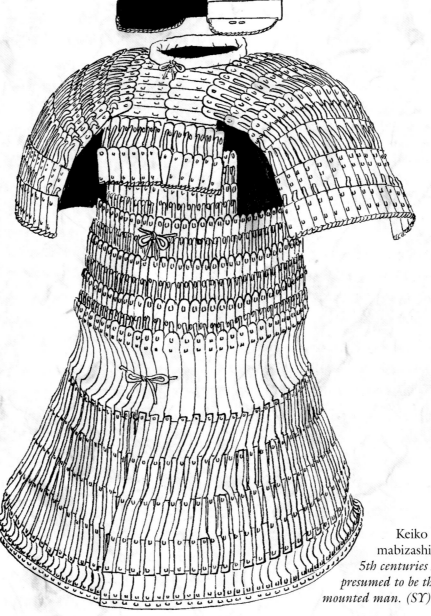

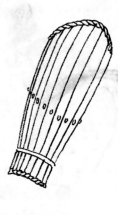

Keiko *lamellar armor with* mabizashi *peaked helmet (4th–5th centuries AD). This is presumed to be the harness of a mounted man. (SY)*

CHAPTER 2:
THE PROSPERITY OF
THE HEISHI

During the Nara period (AD 710-784) and the Heian period (AD 794-1192) the western part of Japan was ruled by the imperial government, at first from Nara and later from Kyoto, where the Kanmu Emperor removed it in 794 to escape the exaggerated influence of the great religious establishments of Nara. At the summit of the system was the emperor, and the aristocracy formed the bureaucracy which governed in his name. All land was held to belong to the state. Provincial officials were appointed by the government to collect the rice taxes (the *koku* was the standard measure of rice, about five bushels, or enough to feed one person for a year). The north-east part of Japan, especially the territories lying far north of the Kanto area, was effectively a 'no man's land,' where the *emishi* often revolted against the servants of the Kyoto government.

Rice taxes were often a heavy burden upon the farmers. Many *kokushi* became rich by embezzling the tax income, and in the later Heian period their greed provoked sporadic revolts in various areas. On the other hand, the wealthy aristocracy gave some measure of protection to the farmers on their manorial estates. Rather than suffer exploitation by local officials, farmers sought to attach themselves to these estates, which consequently increased in size. The accumulation of private property was basically against the established system, or *ritsuryosei*; the increase of private property meant a decrease in state property. The 'retired emperor' Go-Shirakawa often ordered the abolition of aristocratic estates and their re-absorption into the national patrimony.

The institution of the 'retired emperor' was a feature of the late Heian period, which achieved a degree of separation between the constrained, ceremonial aspect of the imperial role and the opportunities for executive initiative. Emperors were strongly associated with conservative customs and had not been able to adapt their role to an age of change. Consequently an emperor might formally abdicate his ceremonial position and pass it to his son. Taking the title of *joko*, he in fact assumed active powers in political society—sometimes controversially, since this was a period of flux. Ostensibly he became 'cloistered'—*ho-o*; but in reality he lived in a part of the *gosho* or imperial residence. These apartments and offices were called the *In*; and from them many retired emperors issued laws which carried as much authority as the orders of the actual emperor.

Left: Kyoto, December 1159: a coup led by Minamoto Yoshitomo forces the Nijo Emperor to escape from the gosho, his imperial residence, in an ox carriage, disguised as a lady. The warriors checking the carriage are all armed with bows. (Heishi Monogatari scroll, Tokyo National Museum)

Below: Kyoto, December 1159: Minamoto Yoshitomo and Fujiwara Nobuyori make a surprise attack on the Sanjo palace of the retired emperor (Joko), Go-Shirakawa, and set fire to it. At the center right of the picture two warriors are beheading a fallen enemy; the practice of taking heads was well established, and lasted for the next 500 years. (Heishi Monogatari scroll, TNM)

The retired emperor summoned samurai groups to guard his offices; stationed in the northern part of his residence, they were called the *hokumen-no-bushi* or 'samurai of the northern aspect'. As the power of the *joko* increased, so

Above: *Sanjo youchi, the night raid by Minamoto and Fujiwara samurai on the Sanjo palace. Trying to escape the fighting, court ladies fell into the well. (Heishi Monogatari scroll, TNM)*

Right: *After his escape from the night raid, the Nijo Emperor took refuge at Taira Kiyomori's house at Rokuwara; here Heishi samurai greet the emperor's father, Go-Shirakawa. (Heishi Monogatari scroll, TNM)*

samurai groups vied with one another for this connection with him. Being designated to this position was a mark of the favor of the imperial family. It is not surprising that within the court, tensions and conflicts arose between emperor, *joko* and *ho-o*—nor that the attendant aristocrats divided into factions, which gathered samurai groups around them. At this period all initiative still lay entirely with the court aristocracy, and the samurai families were used merely as their tools.

In 1156, the Go-Shirakawa Emperor made a surprise attack on the *Joko* Sutoku in his residence, and defeated him. The two had been in conflict over the succession and, knowing that the *joko* was preparing a coup d'etat, Go-Shirakawa attacked first. This incident, known as the *Hogen-no-ran*, caused major rifts at the court and beyond it. The extremely powerful Fujiwara family split into factions, as did the aristocrats of the *In*. The leading Taira and Minamoto samurai families were also divided: Minamoto Yoshitomo and Taira Kiyomori at first fought together and defeated Sutoku, but in the aftermath of this incident they became bitter foes. (It was not unusual for intermarriage between clans and feuds within them to produce deadly divisions within families.) The Heishi (Taira) originally ruled in Ise and Iga (Mie prefecture). When the growing military strength of the Genji (Minamoto) clan alarmed them, the Heishi approached the now-retired Go-Shirakawa, seeking to influence him against their rivals.

In December 1159 Taira Kiyomori travelled to the Kumano shrine; and the next month Minamoto Yoshitomo and Fujiwara Nobuyori launched a coup, isolating the Nijo Emperor and capturing his father, the ex-emperor Go-Shirakawa. Kiyomori hurried back to Kyoto, and gathered his forces. The teenage emperor was spirited away from the imperial residence in an ox-cart, disguised as a woman, and Go-Shirakawa also escaped from the Minamoto. The Taira defeated the rebels, who were killed in battle or executed. Minamoto Yoshitomo's infant children were spared and sent into exile, one of them, his son Yoritomo, to Izu (Kanagawaken). It was Yoritomo who would later become the first samurai to establish his own regime as shogun.

The Heishi now seemed to enjoy great security and prosperity. Their economic base was trade with Song China. They dominated the Inland Sea and the route to China north of Saigoku (Kyushu), and their control of maritime trade brought them great riches.

In 1167, Taira Kiyomori was appointed *daijodaijin* (prime minister), the highest position among the court nobility. He gave his daughter Tokusi in marriage to the Takakura Emperor, and his success seemed to be at its zenith. This risen samurai did not use his power to reform the old system of aristocratic government, simply using it and adopting the style of the nobility.

CHAPTER 3:
THE STRUGGLE BETWEEN THE GENJI AND HEISHI

During the 1160s and 1170s the 'cloistered emperor' Go-Shirakawa remained a Machiavellian figure in the background. At first he used the military predominance of the Heishi to put down a number of insurgents; but as time passed he became hostile to the excessive influence of these Taira upstarts. In 1177 a plot against the Heishi was revealed. The nobles—from Go-Shirakawa's entourage—and a priest involved in the conspiracy were executed. Relations between the Heishi and Go-Shirakawa had reached their nadir; Taira Kiyomori arrested the former emperor and abolished the institution of the *In*. This provocative step gave further impetus to the anti-Heishi movement. There followed the long, bloody confrontation between the Taira and Minamoto armies in 1180-85 known as the Genpei War (from the first syllables of the names Genji and Heishi in their Chinese readings).

In 1180 the elderly Minamoto Yorimasa, who was still a member of the Heishi court, was encouraged by Go-Shirakawa's passed-over son Prince Mochihito to take up arms against them. Before he could assemble an army his small force was attacked at a bridge over the Ujigawa River and wiped out; Mochihito was killed and Yorimasa committed *seppuku* (*harakiri*). (Incidentally, this practice first appears in the documentary record only ten years before this date.) The prince's proclamation calling for the destruction of the Heishi lived on and now reached scattered Genji families, however. The first man to rise against them was Minamoto Yoshitomo's son Yoritomo, with help from Hojo Tokimasa; but they were soon defeated at Ishibashiyama in August 1180. Yoritomo fled to Chiba, where he raised more vassals; and by October he and his followers had entered Kamakura, declaring it his base city. Kamakura is on the sea coast and surrounded on the other three sides by mountains, making it extremely difficult

to attack. Yoritomo's father Yoshitomo had lived there, and it was a place of special significance for the Genji family. Yoritomo's younger brother Yoshitsune escaped from the Kurama Mountains (Kyoto) and joined his army.

In September 1180, Yoritomo's cousin Minamoto Yoshinaka rose in response to Prince Mochihito's proclamation. He raised an army in the mountain country of Kiso, where he had grown up (and whose name he preferred to use, rather than Minamoto). Kiso Yoshinaka was a brave soldier and an able general. In June 1183 he defeated a Taira army at Kurikara, and in August he entered Kyoto shortly after the Taira leaders had fled for Kyushu, taking with them the infant Antoku Emperor. This was as much of a shock to Minamoto Yoritomo, still at Kamakura, as it was to the Taira in general.

Kiso Yoshinaka had no interest in the complex intrigues of the court, and his army busied itself in looting the citizens of the capital indiscriminately. A pursuit of the Taira forces into their own country on the Inland Sea ended in defeat at Mizushima that November. Having captured the capital the country-bred Yoshinaka seemed to have little idea what to do with it, and relations with his cousin Minamoto Yoritomo became worse. The ex-emperor Go-Shirakawa urged Yoritomo to march on Kyoto himself to

Top left: *The oldest image of 12th century samurai of the Heian period is found in the Ban Dainagon scroll made in 1164. In this scene four samurai wear* oyoroi *armor and carry bows. They are not allowed to carry swords while on police duty in Kyoto city as they are only the private guards of the chief constable or* kebiishi. *He is the rider at centre right, wearing white and red; note that he wears a sword as the symbol of his police powers. (Idemitsu Museum)*

Above: Iza Kamakura—*the 'rush to Kamakura'. The Kamakura bakufu maintained the roads to Kamakura from all over the Kanto area in order to allow the samurai to assemble rapidly. (SY)*

Left: *A samurai receives a message from his master during the Kamakura period. Once he was summoned to the muster he had to join the army as soon as possible; even if he was eating, he had to put down his chopsticks and saddle up immediately. His servants would follow him to the place of assembly later, bringing his armor, weapons and other horses.*

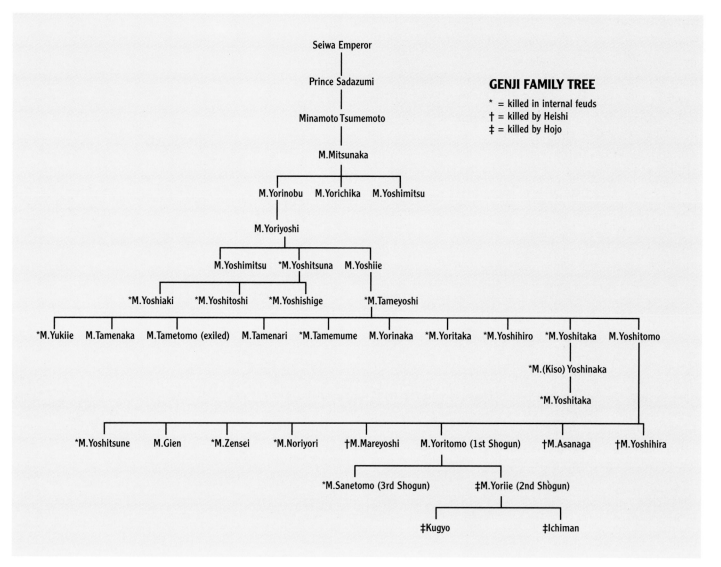

GENJI FAMILY TREE

* = killed in internal feuds
† = killed by Heishi
‡ = killed by Hojo

Seiwa Emperor

Prince Sadazumi

Minamoto Tsumemoto

M.Mitsunaka

M.Yorinobu   M.Yorichika   M.Yoshimitsu

M.Yoriyoshi

M.Yoshimitsu   *M.Yoshitsuna   M.Yoshiie

*M.Yoshiaki   *M.Yoshitoshi   *M.Yoshishige   *M.Tameyoshi

*M.Yukiie M.Tamenaka M.Tametomo (exiled) M.Tamenari *M.Tamemume M.Yorinaka *M.Yoritaka *M.Yoshihiro *M.Yoshitaka M.Yoshitomo

*M.(Kiso) Yoshinaka

*M.Yoshitaka

*M.Yoshitsune M.Gien *M.Zensei *M.Noriyori †M.Mareyoshi M.Yoritomo (1st Shogun) †M.Asanaga †M.Yoshihira

*M.Sanetomo (3rd Shogun)   ‡M.Yoriie (2nd Shogun)

‡Kugyo   ‡Ichiman

Mounted soldiers surrounded by retainers. In 1185 the famous warrior Kumagai Jiro Naozane fought against the Heishi at Ichinotani in Kobe with his son and banner bearer, his group consisting only of only three: in this period they counted only mounted samurai, and foot soldiers were not counted as soldiers. When contemporary writers referred to a force of 200, they meant there were about 600 soldiers including foot. A samurai always needed reserve horses, because the oyoroi *armor more or less limited him to fighting on horseback; if his horse was injured or killed his retainers brought him a reserve. The man (foreground) carrying a* naginata *wears his master's helmet; he will pass it to him when the battle begins. In some cases, retainers wore their master's armor over their own on the march, passing it over if an emergency occurred. In the Sengoku period muster rolls they counted not only samurai but also* ashigaru, *laborers and supply porters, so the real fighting constituent of a force counted for less than a third of the total. (SY)*

expel his cousin; but Yoritomo—no great general, but a match for any man in guile—sent his heroic younger brother Yoshitsune instead. Early in 1184 Yoshitsune defeated his cousin's forces at the Ujigawa River, and Kiso Yoshinaka was killed while trying to reach Awazu.

While the Genji families had been fighting one another, the Heishi had been rebuilding their strength, and now the Taira army returned to Fukuhara (Kobe) and encamped there. In March 1184 Yoshitsune won his second great victory at Ichinotani, penetrating a very strong position by brilliantly audacious cavalry tactics. The Heishi withdrew to Yashima on the Inland Sea, where they were again defeated, but their naval strength prevented Yoshitsune's army making any further gains. Yoshitsune spent a year building up his naval force to match that of the enemy, and the final sea battle took place in April 1185 off a beach called Dan-no-ura. It ended in defeat for the Heishi; and many on the losing side committed suicide by throwing themselves into the sea rather than be taken—among them the baby emperor, drowned in his mother's arms. Some see the deliberate deaths of these educated, cultured nobles as symbolic of the end of one age and the beginning of another—the age of the samurai warlords.

Although the Genpei War is presented as a conflict between the Taira and Minamoto families, the real distinction between the sides was not that simple. At the beginning of the struggle the Hojo family and other samurai groups had belonged to the Heishi camp, and their duty was to keep an eye on the exiled Minamoto Yoritomo in Izu. But when Yoritomo raised his flag the majority of his forces were provided by Heishi families. Indeed, Yoritomo had married Hojo Masako—from a Heishi vassal family—and relied on Heishi samurai groups instead of Genji families in northern Kanto. The Genji or Minamoto families were always discordant and quarrelsome, and bloody conflicts within the clan were nothing unusual. Thus, after the destruction of the Heishi regime at Kyoto, the Heishi families in the Kanto area supported the Kamakura bakufu—the first samurai government.

The Kamakura bakufu

Minamoto Yoritomo took the advice of influential family vassals and stayed at Kamakura rather than moving his base to Kyoto. His gifts had always been for strategic planning, and now he concentrated on building a structure of government to control the samurai. Originally, the term *bakufu*—derived from a Chinese word—meant the general's headquarters during an expeditionary campaign. Now it would be used to mean the seat of the military government, and by extension, the government itself: 'Kamakura Headquarters' gives roughly the right resonance in English.

In 1180 Yoritomo founded the *monchujo*, a court governing the financial affairs of the samurai, and in 1184

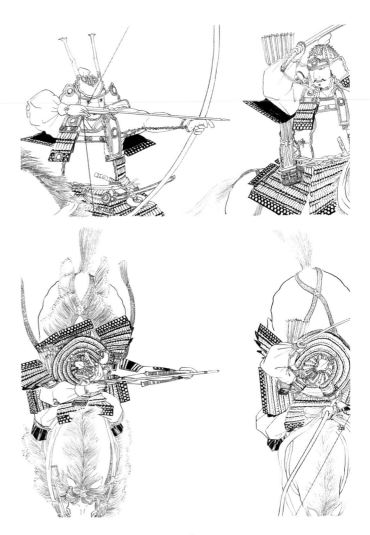

The reason why early samurai preferred to face their left side to the enemy when approaching him: they could draw the bow to the maximum. In a hand-to-hand mêlée, of course, presenting the right side allowed use of the sword unhindered by the horse's head. (SY)

the *kumonjo*, the bakufu's ministry of finance, appointing Wada Yoshimori as its head. In 1192 Yoritomo was declared *seiitai shogun*, an archaic temporary title meaning 'commander in chief for suppression of barbarians'; but in effect the *shogun* now became a permanent, and hereditary, military dictator, parallel to the nominal emperor and wielding much greater actual power.

The vassals who followed Yoritomo relied on their personal relationships with him. In reward for their long campaigns on his behalf and in return for a continuing obligation of military service, their titles to their lands, new or inherited, had been secured or confirmed by Yoritomo. This granting and confirmation of land holdings to samurai had formerly been in the sole gift of the emperor. Now the situation changed: the relationship of endorsement and obligation between the shogun and his feudal vassals or 'franchised samurai'—*gokenin*—was secured on terms laid down by the bakufu. Yoritomo's older samurai were made

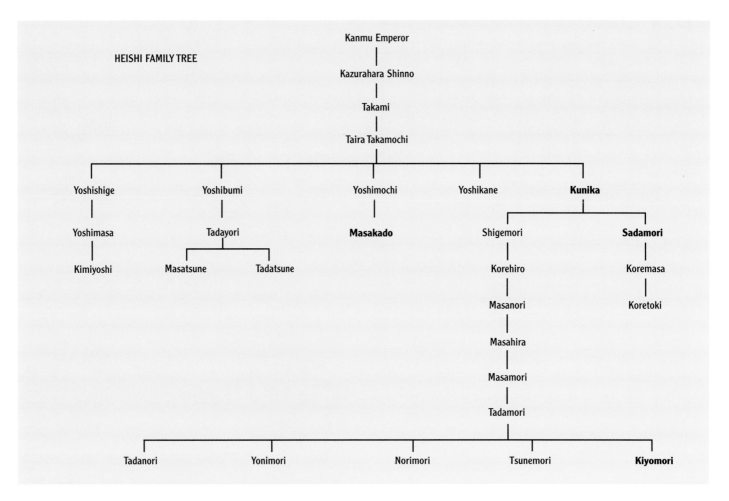

HEISHI FAMILY TREE

Kanmu Emperor

Kazurahara Shinno

Takami

Taira Takamochi

Yoshishige — Yoshibumi — Yoshimochi — Yoshikane — **Kunika**

Yoshimasa

Kimiyoshi

Tadayori

Masatsune — Tadatsune

Masakado

Shigemori — **Sadamori**

Korehiro — Koremasa

Masanori — Koretoki

Masahira

Masamori

Tadamori

Tadanori — Yonimori — Norimori — Tsunemori — **Kiyomori**

uneasy by this reform, which shifted their obligation from the person to the institution; they preferred a personal assurance from him.

The fall of Yoshitsune

Minamoto Yoshitsune is a favorite figure of Japanese legends (one of the most extreme stories being that he actually became Genghis Khan of the Mongols). After Yoshitsune's victory over the Heishi he returned to Kyoto and was given a place at the Ho-o Go-Shirakawa's court. Yoshitsune gave land to his retainers in reward for their efforts during the war; he even tried to send his army to pacify rebellious samurai in Kyushu. Yoritomo regarded this as a violation of his prerogatives; the right to give land to samurai in recognition of their service belonged solely to the leader of samurai, Yoritomo. Yoshitsune was a talented general and his tactics were unusual among contemporary samurai leaders. For a long time he had been raised in the Kurama Mountains, and his closest retainers were mountain people,

Left: This oyoroi *of the late Heian period belonged to Kono Michinobu, the general of Mishima naval forces, who followed Minamoto Yoshitsune in the 'Genpei' or Genji-Heishi war. The* sane *are mixed leather and metal. The side panels of the skirt defenses—*kusazuri*—are longer than the frontal and rear ones to give thigh protection while riding. (Oyamazumi Shrine)*

monks and outlaws. His surprise attacks on the Taira armies are rational (if reckless) to modern eyes, and seem vindicated by their success. However, to 12th century samurai, who had a deeply conservative attachment to time-honored conventions of battle, they seemed distasteful. They alienated the vassals who once followed him into battle against the Heishi; and when Yoritomo moved to destroy him only a few stood by him.

Yoritomo was uneasy about the influence of the Ho-o over Yoshitsune; he feared that at any time his younger brother might rise against him with the encouragement of the wily ex-emperor. He summoned Yoshitsune from Kyoto to Kamakura, where he could be kept under constant surveillance; but he never trusted him again, nor forgave him. Yoshitsune had no choice but to persuade Go-Shirakawa to issue a call for the destruction of Yoritomo; but this came too late for him, and he fled north to Oshu (Tohoku), relying on the help of the Fujiwara family.

Yoritomo forced the imperial court to activate the *shugo* (the military and police organization) all over the country to arrest Yoshitsune, in effect declaring him an outlaw. His purpose was not only to secure the short term goal of his brother's

arrest, but also the long term one of spreading his military authority all over Japan. In 1189 Yoshitsune was attacked by Fujiwara Yoshihira, from whom he had sought protection, and was killed or committed suicide. Yoshihira's treachery brought a fitting reward; later that year he himself was attacked by Yoritomo, on the sole pretext that he had once sheltered Yoshitsune. As always, Yoritomo was thinking ahead; the real purpose of this expedition was to obtain valuable territory where gold was found.

Yoritomo's destruction of his heroic younger brother made him infamous during the much later Edo period; but it is interesting that throughout the samurai age proper his actions were apparently regarded as reasonable. Was the cause of their struggle personal jealousy on the part of the scheming Yoritomo for the dazzling young hero Yoshitsune—or was it cold statecraft?

Right: *A naval magistrate conducts the fleet. At the battle of Dan-no-ura in 1185 both sides' ships were concentrated in a narrow strait. As in Classical times in the West, ships were usually employed simply as platforms allowing soldiers to fight each other with their usual weapons. At Dan-no-ura the Genji general Minamoto Yoshitsune is supposed to have jumped from one ship to another eight times when hard pressed by an enemy samurai.*

ARMOR OF THE HEIAN PERIOD (LATE 8th TO 12th CENTURIES AD)

Right: In the 8th century the Nara government seems to have altered the armor style from the tanko *and* keiko *to the* men-okoyori *of plates attached to a fabric garment, presumably for ease of production. No archaeological remains survive, however. (SY)*

In the 8th century the Imperial Nara government ordered the abandonment of the manufacture of the two earlier types of armor because of their heavy weight and complexity of manufacture. Surviving documentation states that the Japanese government imported armor from Tang Dynasty China, and that the government made 200-250 armors for the forces guarding the southern part of the country. The description of these armors resembles contemporary Chinese equipment. According to the document, they were to be 'garment' armors, i.e. made from rectangular leather armor plates sewn on to cotton garments. Due to the decomposition of organic materials, no surviving remains of this style have so far been excavated.

Despite the lack of archaeological material from this transitional period to confirm the documentary evidence, we may of course speculate as to the process of transformation of armors and helmets towards the later *oyoroi* style. The 'beaked' helmet evolved into the *ikaboshi kabuto,* a helmet of radial segment construction with large, visible rivet heads. The front part of the cheek guards was turned outwards and backwards, becoming the wing-like *fukigaeshi.* The left side of the *keiko* cuirass was permanently closed, the armor being fastened at the right side only. This inherently weaker fastening side was protected by an additional plate called the *waidate.*

The armor which protected the collarbones and fronts of the armpits became transformed into separate hanging plates, both originally termed *sendan-no ita,* meaning that they were attached in front of the cuirass. Later they were allotted Chinese characters which had the same sound but different meanings: the larger right hand plate remained *sendan-no ita,* while the longer, narrower left hand plate was called *kyubi-no ita* (*kyubi* meaning a pigeon's tail, which it supposedly resembled). The different shape and construction of these two plates reflected their functions. The *sendan-no-ita* was larger but of more flexible construction; in the early days samurai fought with the bow from horseback, and shooting a bow both required more freedom of movement for the right arm and exposed more of the right armpit.

The *oyoroi* style of armor had its merits when it was used for fighting on horseback. Its primary purpose was to give

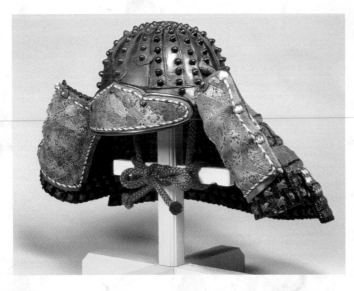

Above: Late Heian period helmet, with characteristic large, protruding rivet heads. The neck guard hangs at a relatively vertical angle, another indication of an earlier piece. (Itsukushima Shrine)

Below: Heian period oyoroi: *an akaito odoshi armor— laced with red braid. This example was repaired in the Meiji period, when* waki-no-ita *or side armor was added to it—in the Kamakura period this had not yet been invented. (Tokyo National Museum)*

protection from the enemy's arrows. On the helmet the large hanging neck guard, *shikoro*, gave protection at the rear and the *fukigaeshi* survived as a remnant of the cheek guard. The hanging shoulder defenses, *sode*, were large panels which covered the arm almost to the elbow, fulfilling the function of the shield which samurai did not carry. Inside them the front of the shoulder/armpit area was protected by the *sendan-no ita* and *kyubi-no ita* described above. For convenience when riding the tassets or thigh protectors, *kusazuri*, suspended from the bottom of the cuirass, were divided into four panels. The total weight of the armor was about 60lbs (about 27–28kg); the burden on the shoulders was lightened by the saddle, which supported the bottom of the armor when mounted. If the samurai had to fight on foot, however, this full harness was far too heavy for prolonged combat.

The *sane* scales were made of hardened leather or metal, and coated with lacquer to protect them from the very humid Japanese summer climate; metal lamellae rusted and broke easily if they got wet. Their size became gradually smaller. In the mid-Heian period (c.10th century AD) the standard size was 3 x 1.2ins (roughly 7.5 x 3.0cm); by the mid-Kamakura period (c.13th century AD) this had been reduced to 2.75 x 0.95ins (7.0 x 2.4cm). Each scale was pierced by two or three rows of small holes to take the laces which fastened it to its neighbors. In some cases metal and leather *sane* were used alternately to build up armor panels, or metal scales were used only for the most important defensive parts. The scales were always laced together so as to overlap each other, so that much of the area of the resulting panels offered more than one layer of protection. If the overlapping was done in such a way as to form three layers, such armor was called *tatenashi*—'no need for a shield'.

Samurai wore an *eboshi* style cap, over which they put on a helmet. In the top of the helmet bowl there was a hole about 4cm across, which not only provided ventilation, but helped to steady the helmet when the top-knot of the warrior hairstyle was drawn up through it—this was important, since at first the helmet had no inside liner and was only fixed to the head by the chin cord and top-knot. However, in the Kamakura period (13th–14th centuries) samurai began to wear their hair in a loose style, and the practical point of the hole disappeared. Moreover, this sizeable gap in the apex of the helmet bowl was vulnerable to arrows when the samurai charged with the head tilted forward. Eventually the hole was abandoned, and by the Muromachi period (15th century) it survived only as an ornament attached to the outside of the helmet.

On the whole, during this period armors were made long— there was an expression, to 'wear the armor long.' However, a gradual change in styles of combat demanded revisions.

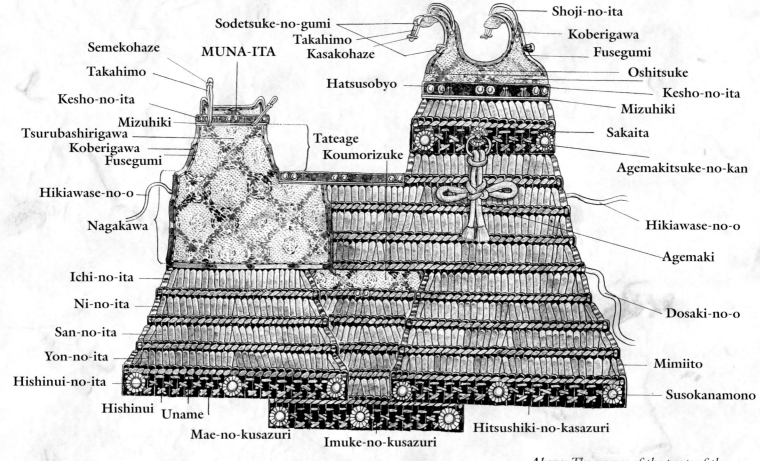

Sodetsuke-no-gumi
Takahimo
Kasakohaze
Semekohaze
Takahimo
MUNA-ITA
Hatsusobyo
Kesho-no-ita
Mizuhiki
Tsurubashirigawa
Koberigawa
Fusegumi
Tateage
Koumorizuke
Hikiawase-no-o
Nagakawa
Ichi-no-ita
Ni-no-ita
San-no-ita
Yon-no-ita
Hishinui-no-ita
Hishinui
Uname
Mae-no-kusazuri
Imuke-no-kusazuri

Shoji-no-ita
Koberigawa
Fusegumi
Oshitsuke
Kesho-no-ita
Mizuhiki
Sakaita
Agemakitsuke-no-kan
Hikiawase-no-o
Agemaki
Dosaki-no-o
Mimiito
Susokanamono
Hitsushiki-no-kasazuri

Above: *The names of the parts of the* oyoroi *cuirass. (SY)*

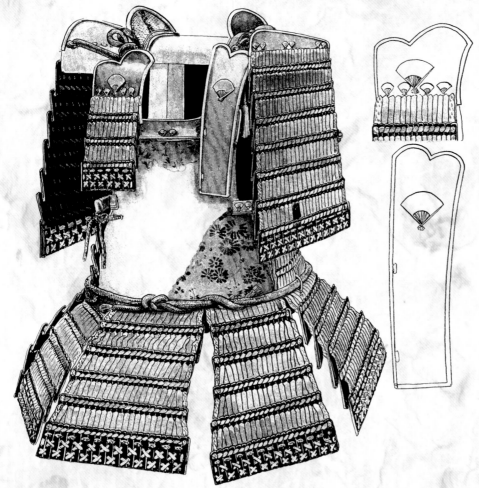

Left & right: *Front, rear and details of a* do maru *of the late Heian period. At this time the* do maru *was used by lower ranking soldiers, but this example shows us elaborate ornament and very long* sode, *as well as seven* kusazuri, *all of which indicate that the armor was made for a higher class samurai. (SY) (Oyamazumi jinja shrine)*

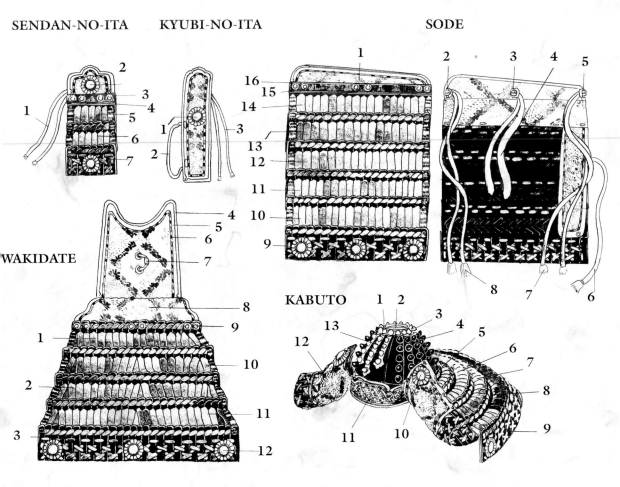

SENDAN-NO-ITA

KYUBI-NO-ITA

SODE

WAKIDATE

KABUTO

SENDAN-NO-ITA
1 Tsukeo
2 Kanmuri-no-ita
3 Kesho-no-ita
4 Mizuhiki
5 Ichi-no-ita
6 Ni-no-ita
7 Hishinui

KYUBI-NO-ITA
1 Suemon
2 Hikae-no-o
3 Tsukeo

WAKIDATE
1 Ichi-no-ita
2 San-no-ita
3 Hishinui-no-ita
4 Fukurin
5 Koberigawa
6 Fusegumi
7 Tsubo-no-o
8 Komorizuke
9 Hatsusobyo
10 Ni-no-ita
11 Yon-no-ita
12 Susokanamono

SODE
1 Kanmuri-no-ita
2 Kan
3 Kan
4 Shitsuka-no-o
5 Kan
6 Mizunomi-no-o
7 Kakeo
8 Ukeo
9 Hishui-no-ita
10 Go-no-ita
11 Yon-no-ita
12 San-no-ita
13 Ni-no-ita
14 Ichi-no-ita
15 Mizuhiki
16 Kesho-no-ita

KABUTO
1 Tehen-no-za
2 Tehen-no-ana
3 Aoiza
4 Hoshi
5 Ichi-no-ita
6 Ni-no-ita
7 San-no-ita
8 Yon-no-ita
9 Hishinui-no-ita
10 Suemonkanamono
11 Mabisashi
12 Fukigaeshi
13 Shinodare

Above, & key at right: The supplementary pieces of the oyoroi *armor, and helmet. (SY)*

CHAPTER 4:
THE HOJO REGENCY

Above: When about to enter battle, after praying for victory, and the ceremonial eating and drinking of ritual foods, the commander stood and shouted, 'Ei, ei?' ('Are you ready, are you ready?'); and his retainers answered with 'Oh!' ('Yes!'). Today this is misunderstood in Japan; politicians addressing election gatherings often shout 'Ei, ei, oh!' all by themselves. (SY)

In spite of the structural changes which henceforward favored the samurai class, the bakufu did not dare to damage the aristocracy or the powerful temples in Kyoto. Their manorial estates still represented large tracts of land and many productive farmers. Neither did Yoritomo make any attempt to abolish the imperial court; he merely made himself independent from it in his wielding of executive power. In the conventional view of Japanese history, Yoritomo's appointment as shogun marks the transformation from an aristocratic to a samurai regime; but careful study reveals that the real turning point came in the later Hojo regency period.

Jokyu-no-ran (the Joko rebellion)

After the sudden death of Yoritomo in a riding accident in 1199, his teenage son Yoriie became shogun in 1202. He relied on his wife's Hiki family to control the bakufu; but Yoritomo's widow Masako and her father Hojo Tokimasa felt this was a challenge to them. Some of the *gokenin* thought Yoriie's policies dangerous to them, because he often disregarded their vested rights. Consequently Masako and the chief vassals removed Yoriie from power, agreeing that all decisions would henceforth be made by conference. Before long the Hojo family assassinated Yoriie; his brother Sanetomo became the third shogun, but he in his turn was killed by Yoriie's son. The Hojo family now seized the bakufu. Originally tracing their family to a government official sent by the Heishi to Izu, their social rank was so low that they could provide neither the head of a samurai family nor a shogun. They therefore determined to install a man of noble birth as a puppet shogun while wielding the real power themselves through a regency. The intrigues surrounding this succession led to the Jokyu-no-ran.

Left: *Typical Kamakura period scene of samurai on the march, made colorful and varied by the different braids used for lacing their armor. The rider carrying the white flag is the only man distinguished by antler-like helmet decorations or* kuwagata. *(Kiyomizudera engi, TNM)*

Below left & right: *Reconstruction of the gear of a Kamakura period fighting man—*do maru *armor, and the type of face guard called a* happuri.

Opposite: *Kamakura period samurai leader mounting his horse, from the right side—they did not want to hit the horse's shoulder with the sword hilt. Small details had superstitious importance. If the horse urinated or whinnied before the rider mounted, this could be disregarded; but if it did so after his foot had touched the stirrup, he had to unfasten and re-fasten both the horse's girth and his armor belt.(SY)*

Above: *Kamakura period samurai are surprised by an enemy attack, and hastily try to put on their oyoroi armor; note, at right, men taking armor from a wooden chest. (Onegi Saburo ekotoba, TNM)*

The snuffing out of Yoritomo's blood line caused unrest among the *gokenin*. The Hojo family asked the *Joko* Go-Toba to name one of his relatives to lead the bakufu as a shogun. Thinking that the destruction of the bakufu was imminent, Go-Toba refused, and called on the samurai of Kyushu, the major temples in Kyoto, and his household *hokumen-no-bushi* and *saimen-no-bushi* to tear down the bakufu. Against his expectations, only a few samurai rallied to him. The Hojo family called their *gokenin* to Kamakura, and Yoritomo's widow Masako made a famous speech to them: 'Yoritomo's favor was higher than a mountain and deeper than the sea. Now the imperial court issues an unreasonable order to destroy us; but you should remember Yoritomo's great generosity, and defend the shogun's position. If you prefer to obey the orders of the *In*, leave now . . . '. The Hojo force departed Kamakura with just 18 horsemen; but by the time they arrived in Kyoto there were said to be more than 10,000. Of course, contemporary historians may have exaggerated this figure; but the essential meaning is clear— the authority of the bakufu had now become more important than that of the emperor or the *joko*. After several skirmishes the bakufu forces were victorious. The samurai who had sided with the losers were punished; and three retired emperors—Go-Toba, Sutoku, and Tsuchi-mikado—were exiled

In 1224, after the death of Hojo Yoshitoki—Yoritomo's widow Masako's brother—his son Yasutoki became regent,

and ordered that bakufu policy should once more be decided by conference. In 1232 the bakufu promulgated a new code of law—*gosei baishi kimoku*—to govern the affairs of the *gokenin*. Until then only the imperial court could issue laws. Through the new code the bakufu appeared to criticize the complexity and obsolescence of the old system, and to declare the independence of the samurai world. Of course, this law was applicable to neither the aristocracy in Kyoto nor the temples and important shrines. But the spirit of the law influenced the later samurai code; the essential elements included the importance of loyalty to a master, and of a son paying filial duty to his father; that a wife should follow her husband, and a master should promote the safety and prosperity of the farmers.

This code derived from the declared everyday values of the samurai, which in reality had long become more or less meaningless; a distinction should be drawn between actual medieval behavior and the later so-called samurai code of the Edo period, which was created by ideologues of the Tokugawa government. In reality, in medieval Japan sons killed their fathers, brothers attacked their brothers, wives betrayed their husbands and hosts their guests, and the forces of the bakufu destroyed those of the emperors and did not hesitate to depose them. The samurai of the Middle Ages still fought for property, lands and money, and only rarely for honor.

ARMOR OF THE 12TH TO 14TH CENTURIES

Although the *oyoroi* style of armor seems to have flourished from the late Heian to the Kamakura period, changes in the methods and tactics of fighting necessitated a process of gradual revision.

The wing-like *fukigaeshi*, the front parts of the *shikoro* neck guard on the helmet, became sharply up-turned to give a better view to the sides and to prevent them hampering the drawing of the bowstring. When a samurai wanted to deliver a sword slash the enemy's up-turned *fukigaeshi* presented a real obstacle, forcing him to make his cut at a shallow angle and robbing him of the greater impact of a blow straight downwards.

In any case, on the battlefields of this period the sword was normally used single-handed from the saddle, and can rarely have delivered a fatal wound to an armored opponent. If samurai used all their arrows without successfully dispatching their enemy, they approached one another to continue the combat with sword slashes; but, being usually well protected by armor, this often led to a brief bout of wrestling on horseback, soon followed by a fall to the ground. On the ground they tried to stab unprotected areas of each other's bodies with the dagger—*wakizashi*; but a samurai's retainers would naturally rush to help their master, and combat degenerated into an ugly hand-to-hand mêlée. In such situations the box-like *oyoroi* cuirass was simply a potentially fatal encumbrance.

Below: A Kamakura period samurai putting on oyoroi *armor (1); right to left, top to bottom:* Kosode *under-garment and* oguchi-hakama *undertrousers. Fastening the samurai's* eboshi *cap. Putting on the gloves; in emergencies only the right glove was worn, enabling the samurai to use his bow. (SY)*

Below: Putting on oyoroi *armor (2); right to left, top to bottom: The loose-sleeved* hitatare *jacket and* hakama *trousers. Fastening the lower legs of the* hakama. *Putting on the* suneate *greaves, left leg first, above the socks; and* tsuranuki *deerskin shoes. Gathering and fastening the right sleeve only. (SY)*

Left & right: Late Kamakura period oyoroi: this shiraito odoshi armor—laced with white braid—shows the cuirass becoming shorter and the lower part getting narrower. The design on the tsurubashiri, the leather covering of the cuirass, shows Fudo Myoo or Acalanatha. The top view of the helmet associated with this armor shows the rivets becoming smaller, as is the top hole—where the top-knot of the hairstyle used to be pulled out. The fukigaeshi are turned sharply backwards so as not to hinder visibility. (Hinomisaki Shrine)

Below: *Putting on* oyoroi *armor (3). Top right: During the late Kamakura period* haidate *thigh protectors were worn. Top left: Putting on the armored left sleeve* kote; *the wide left jacket sleeve got in the way of using the bow, so it was tucked down under the* obi *sash. Bottom right & left: Putting on the* waidate *right flank plate, and* nodowa *throat guard. (SY)*

Below: *Putting on* oyoroi *armor (4); right to left, top to bottom: Putting on the cuirass, with its* sode *shoulder guards, over the head and fastening the* takahimo. *Fastening the* sotei-no-o *waist belt, and over it the* obi. *Inserting the dagger,* koshigatana. *(SY)*

Above: *Details of* oyoroi *armor typical of the Nanbokucho period.*

Below: *Putting on* oyoroi *armor (5); right to left, top to bottom: Attaching the sword,* tachi, *and quiver full of arrows. A retainer puts the helmet on his master's head and a page fastens the chin cords; note the reel of spare bowstring on the left hip. With bow and fan in hand, the samurai general is ready to review his men. (SY)*

As mentioned before, the not inconsiderable weight of the harness fell on the shoulders; furthermore, the lower edge of the cuirass hit the pelvis. To get around this problem, armorers narrowed the lower part of the chest plate and fitted it more closely to the body, fastening it with a cloth sash, which distributed the weight better. The *sane* became smaller to reduce the depth of the chest armor for greater ease of movement; the *oyoroi* became on average some 3.9ins (10cm) shorter during the Nanbokucho period (1336–92). This revision, in turn, required giving greater protection to the upper thighs; and samurai began to wear thigh defenses called *haidate* attached apron-fashion beneath the hanging *kusazuri* skirt of the cuirass.

Usually, the helmet consisted of 15 triangular segment plates fastened by rivets; but later the plates became narrower, construction of a helmet taking as many as 32 segments. The overlapping of these plates gave a thicker, layered protection; the rivets became smaller, and moved from the rims to the centers of the plates. The hole in the top became smaller and finally, as already mentioned, it was discarded altogether and replaced by an ornamental metal disc. The *shikoro* neck guard, which hung fairly vertically from the rim of the helmet bowl in the Heian period, gradually spread out transversely, like a parasol, to allow easier movement of the head. To compensate, armorers then introduced a partial face mask called a *menpo*. (Cheek protection had first been seen in the late Heian period in a form termed *happuri*, which hung from the forehead over the cheeks; another style called *hampo* covered the jaw and cheeks.)

CHAPTER 5:
THE MONGOL INVASIONS

In 1268, 1271 and 1274 the Mongol emperor of China, Kublai Khan, sent envoys to Japan with thinly disguised demands for the payment of tribute. The Japanese imperial court had been of the opinion that China was a great country and worthy of respect. Whether or not the message was couched in arrogant terms, the response was determined by the nature of the recipient—a new, ambitious samurai government. The newborn bakufu had no experience of foreign diplomacy, and their information came largely from expatriate Chinese Buddhist priests. The Kamakura regime generally welcomed priests who escaped from Song China, and some became very influential, especially the Zen sect and the Japan-based Nichiren sect. We may assume that the samurai government was strongly influenced by the opinion of Chinese priests on the Mongolians. The founder of the Nichiren sect preached that the Mongol invasion of China was a sign of the degeneration of the world. If the bakufu had really appreciated the overwhelming power of the Mongols their decision might have been different.

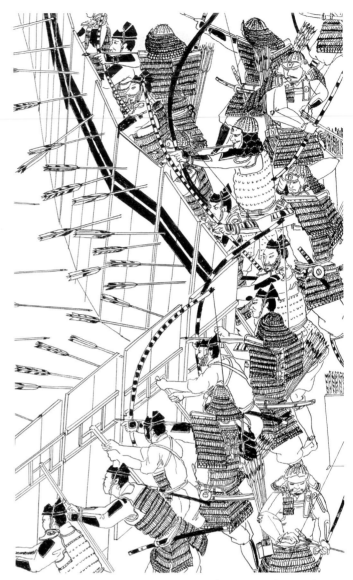

Above: *After the opening ceremony, the troops advanced behind portable mantlets, shooting their bows until they ran out of arrows. It was sometimes known for a strong archer to penetrate a mantlet with a large arrow. (SY)*

Left: *Kyushu, autumn 1274: Takenaga Sueaki attacks Mongol forces during the first invasion. He charges the Mongol line, but his horse is hit by arrows and terrified by explosives. At first the Mongols' tactics took the samurai by surprise, but after a few encounters they began to deal with them more successfully. (Moko shurai ekotoba, Kunaicho Museum)*

Left: What remains of the defensive wall above Hakata Bay beach on Kyushu. These defenses originally stretched for some 20km. Their construction varies from place to place; one stretch is entirely of stones, another of sand in-fill between two stone faces.

Below: Reconstruction of the kind of wooden portable mantlet which the retainers carried in the advance during battles of the late Heian to Kamakura periods, while the samurai shot arrows in the gaps between them.

Understandably, at the imperial court in Kyoto the aristocracy considered accepting the Mongol demands for tribute; but the young regent Hojo Tokimune was determined to refuse. He called upon all samurai to set aside their differences in defense of the country, and watch was kept in northern Kyushu. Meanwhile Kublai Khan ordered the Koreans to build him 900 ships for an invasion of Japan.

In October 1274 the Mongols set sail, apparently ignorant of the fact that this was the Japanese typhoon season. The Japanese had no sea-going naval tradition, and were unable to interfere with the crossing. The Mongols made a landing on Tsushima Island, half way between Korea and Kyushu, and a few days later on neighboring Iki Island. Their numbers overwhelmed the defenders; the two deputy *shugo* in command, So Sukekuni and Tairano Kagetaka, died with their men.

Landing in Hakata Bay in northern Kyushu, the Mongols were met by strange warriors. One young horseman came out from their line and yelled something incomprehensible; then he shot a whistling arrow, and charged towards the Mongol ranks, only to fall instantly under a shower of Mongol arrows. To the samurai it was a rule that someone must begin a battle by introducing himself by name and shooting a whistling arrow. This ceremony might even have been a very ancient Mongol custom; but if so, it had been long forgotten.

The difference of fighting styles between the two armies dismayed the samurai, who were accustomed to fairly rigid conventions governing the behavior of warriors. The Mongols were disciplined, skilled in controlled tactical maneuvers, fought en masse, and were utterly ruthless, butchering every soul in their path. Their use of explosive devices called *testouhou* also alarmed both the samurai and their horses to the point of panic.

After suffering severe losses, the Kyushu samurai retreated inland to Dazaifu, the center of government in Kyushu,

where they prepared to make a last stand behind some ancient fortifications while hoping against hope for the arrival of reinforcements. However, it seems that despite their advantages the Mongol commanders had been shaken by the bravery of the individualistic samurai attacks. Another factor was the low morale of the Korean troops who had been forced to join their conquerors' expedition (it was claimed that the Korean shipwrights had built fragile vessels, and had even deliberately sabotaged them). Aware that Japanese reinforcements might arrive at any time, and unwilling to risk being caught by a night counterattack on strange ground, they retreated to their ships. That night heavy rain and storm winds struck the fleet in Hakata Bay; and the next morning the probing samurai found no Mongol ships in sight. They had withdrawn, with the loss of more than 200 ships and

KOREA

Masan

MONGOLIAN INVASION ROUTE
1274 AD

*Up to 900 ships,
26,000 men*

S e a   o f   J a p a n

TSUSHIMA

SHIKANOSHIMA

IKI

Hakata

TAKASHIMA

Dazaifu

KYUSHU

13,500 soldiers. After this abortive invasion Kublai Khan sent several more envoys to Japan, but in vain.

By 1279 the Mongols had extended their conquest over southern China, which delivered into Kublai's hands the whole army and the considerable navy of the Song dynasty; he immediately ordered the Chinese to construct 600 warships. With another invasion attempt was inevitable, the regent Hojo Tokimune ordered the construction of a defensive wall along the shores of northern Kyushu. The samurai had to contribute to this project according to their wealth. Many of the Kyushu samurai called out for this duty were not *gokenin*, but former Heishi warriors who were independent from the bakufu organization. The wall was made of earth and stones, two meters high on a base three meters thick. This was hardly the Great Wall of China; but

it was enough to obstruct the invaders—particularly the Mongol cavalry—as they tried to deploy inland from the landing beaches.

Kublai Khan's forces were divided into an Eastern and a Southern army. The former, consisting of 900 ships with about 25,000 Mongol, Korean and Chinese soldiers and 15,000 sailors, embarked in eastern Korea in July 1281. The Southern fleet—perhaps four times as strong—was to rendezvous with the first squadron off Iki Island. The Eastern force again landed on Tsushima and Iki Islands, but pressed on to Kyushu without waiting for reinforcements. The troops attempted to land on Shiga Island, at the tip of the northern arm of Hakata Bay, but met fierce resistance from the soldiers of the *shugo* Otomo Yasuyori and Adachi Morimune. Thwarted in their attempt to establish a

Kyushu, 1281: Takenaka Sueaki passes in front of Kikuchi Jiro Takefusa, who defends the newly-built wall against the second Mongol invasion. Sueaki is recorded as telling Takefusa that he was about to attack the enemy ships, and asking him, if he survived, to tell their general that Sueaki had fought bravely. This scroll was made for Takenaka Sueaki, who wanted the Kamakura bakufu to reward him for his part in the war and instructed the painter to show his prowess. Made under the supervision of the samurai who actually fought in the campaign, it is therefore a reliable source for the arms and armor of this period. (Moko shurai ekotoba, Kunaicho Museum)

beachhead, the Mongols anchored close offshore—only to suffer repeated day and night attacks by Japanese warriors in light craft, who formed daring boarding parties and set many ships on fire.

The fleet moved westwards to Takashima Island near Hirato, where the defenses were thought to be thin. Anchored off Takashima Island to replenish their stores and treat their wounded, they suffered further from the weather. July is the rainy season in Japan. The hot, wet, cramped conditions on board the ships rotted the rations, and some 3,000 Mongols—their morale weakened by the frustration of continuous battle without success—died of sickness.

The squadron waited a month on their rotting, stinking ships for the arrival of the Southern fleet.

In mid-August the integrated fleet finally assembled off Iki Island and moved on Kyushu. A Japanese force embarked from Hakata Bay and made repeated and damaging attacks on the Mongols' ships throughout the night of 19/20 August. On 22 August the Southern fleet's attempt to land was foiled by the intervention of what became known to the Japanese as the 'divine wind'—a typhoon which sank perhaps 4,000 vessels and drowned some 30,000 men. Intact at Hirato, the Eastern fleet did not suffer severely. Now the generals quarreled over whether they should continue their expedition. The mainly Mongol generals of the Eastern army demanded that they continue; the Chinese leaders of the Southern army were unwilling. The Chinese commander transferred to a safe ship, leaving his army and returning to China. Thousands of troops, left behind on Takashima Island, were hunted down by the samurai. All Mongols and Koreans were killed, but the Chinese were not executed.

After this invasion Kublai Khan planned several more attempts, but they all came to nothing due to the distraction of rebellions by his Chinese and Vietnamese subjects. He ordered the raising of one army in Korea, but had to abandon the plan because of mass desertion. For forty years Kublai Khan wanted to conquer the 'islands of gold', but his dream was never accomplished.

WEAPONS OF THE SAMURAI: THE BOW

Immediately after shooting the bow from the saddle; the archer's body must never sway while he is riding the running horse.

The reason why the bow traditionally held the first place among the weapons of the samurai was that in the earliest period of importance of this warrior class being a good archer was the primary qualification of a samurai. As described in a previous chapter, when the samurai first appeared in history he was described as a 'man of the bow.'

The most primitive bow was made from branches of the *azusa*, *mayumi* and *keyaki*. The power of these bows was not great, and consequently they were made long in order to maximize their cast. Even in the late Heian period major bows were still made of these materials.

In that period, however, an improved technique was also introduced. Scraping the rounded frontal surface (the 'back') of the bow stave and gluing on a bamboo strip made the bow more elastic and powerful (*fuetake yumi*). The next step, not surprisingly, was to sandwich the wooden stave between two pieces of bamboo (*sanmai uchi no yumi*). But this was only the beginning of the process of improvement. Glued composite bows still broke easily after some years of use; so bowyers reinforced them with cane, knotted and tied around the bow stave (*tomaki no yumi* or *shigeto*). The length of the bow varied between about 71 to 98 inches (180 and 250cm). The *shigeto* was asymmetric, with 36 turns of cane reinforcement above the grip and 28 below it; but the reverse was found in a later period. In theory the cane bow was painted with lacquer and the string was not

to be white; in practice, of course, there were many variations of cane reinforcement.

The changes in the method of warfare during the Sengoku period led to a decrease in the length of the bow. The samurai organized trained companies of non-samurai foot archers, who needed a shorter weapon for easy handling; consequently the stave was shortened to 78ins (198cm) and reinforced with five turns of cane, each knot being one *shaku* or about 11.8ins (30cm) apart.

For greater power, composite bows were made from several wood and bamboo strips glued together (*higoyumi*), and these recorded an accurate range of 33 *ken* (c.144 yards, 132m) in a flat trajectory. This distance comes from the length of the corridor in Renge-ohin (Sanjusangendo) temple, where there is an annual festival every year; participants have to shoot arrows down the corridor at a target.

The length of the arrows was expressed in units of fist and finger widths. The longest arrows were recorded as 23 fists and 3 fingers long, and the average as 12 fists—but of course fist sizes varied. They had either three or four fletchings. Various shapes of arrowhead reflected their intended purpose: to pierce armor, break through portable shields, cut armor lacing, make a larger wound, and so on. Whistling arrows had been used in ancient China and imported to Japan; called the *kabura* or 'turnip,' the head was hollowed out to produce a sound in flight. If they hit

an enemy on the helmet they would cause concussion, of course, but *kabura-ya* were mainly used in ceremonies. At the start of engagements samurai generals would shoot them towards the enemy to announce the opening of battle. (They did this during the Mongol invasions of Japan; naturally, the practical Mongols mocked this ceremony.)

The ancient Japanese believed that weapons, such as the sword and bow, had special spiritual functions apart from simply killing people. The samurai were as superstitious as their contemporaries among the aristocrats of medieval Europe. At the imperial court, the night guard used to carry bows; as they patrolled the courtyards they made the bow string sound, as this was thought to drive away evil spirits.

The bowstring was originally made from a plant called *karamushi* or *ramie* but later from hemp. Samurai always carried one or two spare strings coiled and hanging at their left hip. The lacquered string was always used in combination with a lacquered bow.

The effective range of the bow when shot from the saddle was only between 33 to 50ft (10 and 15m), and a fully armored samurai could be killed only when shot in an exposed point of the face or torso. It was to protect themselves from arrows that the Japanese developed the *oyoroi* style of armor. But of course, history records some bowmen of legendary strength. At Heijinoran, Minamoto

Tametomo—a famously strong archer—was defending the imperial court when he shot an arrow into an enemy's chest which passed though him and killed the man behind. Another story describes him defeated in battle and exiled to an island. The enemy, afraid of his prowess, sent a force to kill him, but Tametomo shot at their boats with his big bow and sank some of them. (Whether this tale is merely exaggerated or pure fiction, it shows the respect in which powerful bow-shooting was held.)

Top left: Ebira *or openwork quiver.*

Above & right: Yabusame *practice—the school of horse archery. In both practice runs and the real performance the rider carries three or four arrows at his hip; they are drawn backwards, as if he were taking them from a quiver. He has to shoot three targets in one run of about 200m.*

Top left: Yabusame *Master Kaneko Ienori, who heads the Takeda style school in Kamakura. He showed his skill in using the bow and lance from the saddle in Kurosawa's film* The Seven Samurai.

Top right: *Bows and arrows; the nearest bow is a shigeta, massively reinforced with split cane. All these practice arrows have 'turnip' or kabura heads.*

Left: *A horse used for yabusame. Today Japanese horses are bred from European bloodstock; original Japanese horses, called* Kiso koma, *are found only in a limited area. In yabusame performances thoroughbreds are rarely used; they run too fast to give the archer time to shoot his three targets.*

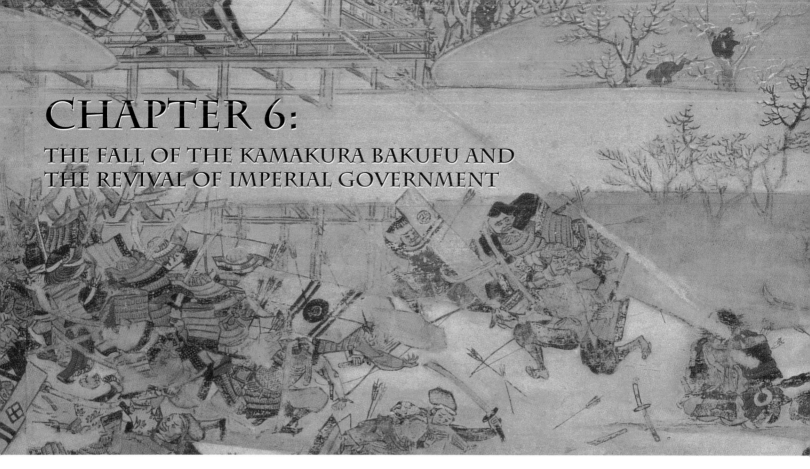

CHAPTER 6:
THE FALL OF THE KAMAKURA BAKUFU AND THE REVIVAL OF IMPERIAL GOVERNMENT

After the Mongol invasions the bakufu strengthened their grip over the samurai of Kyushu in the name of national defense. Previously they had not been controlled directly by Kamakura; during the war against the Mongols they had been willing to join the bakufu army, both for the chance of short term reward and the prospect of advantageous longer term connections. It may be noted that few of the *gokenin* of the Kanto area, who formed the core of the bakufu forces, joined the defensive army during the crisis; some even tried to cheat their way out of sending their obligatory contingents to Kyushu.

In the aftermath of the 1281 invasion the bakufu's power reached its zenith. Under the regency of the Hojo family the regime successfully expanded their rule to Kyushu, and kept the aristocracy in Kyoto under effective surveillance. But the smaller *gokenin* families were suffering poverty. The war against the Mongols had emptied the regime's coffers and brought no booty, so the usual rewards after victory were small or neglected altogether. When samurai were ordered to join the army, they had to meet the expenses of providing for their retainers from their own means, and if they received no reward after the campaign the less wealthy families faced bankruptcy. In an attempt to avert this crisis the bakufu issued a special law forbidding them to pawn their land and cancelling their previous debts. In fact this palliative law turned out to be disastrous for them—thereafter no moneylender dared to lend money to poor samurai for fear of having the debt cancelled by government decree.

Enter the *akuto*
In Kinai (the Kyoto and Osaka area) bandits called *akuto* now entered history. These were a mixture of warrior

A Kamakura period battle from the scroll Honen shonin eden. *Honen was a son of Urushima Tokikuni, a samurai; when he was young, enemies attacked their house and his father was fatally wounded. Before dying his father urged Honen not to seek revenge, because hate only produced hate. Honen became a founder of a new Buddhist sect which preached that through praying to Namu Amida Butsu anybody could reach heaven. This Jodo-shin-shu movement became influential in the 15th century under the leadership of Rennyo. (Chion-in)*

monks, temple workers, criminals, bankrupted samurai and unemployed mercenaries. At first they were described as wearing strange clothes, such as the woman's *kimono*, and not the *eboshi*—the samurai's characteristic formal cap; their swords were carried in faded scabbards, and they travelled furtively so as not to be seen by the public. Groups of 20 to 30 of these freebooters began to attack moneylenders or storehouses.

In this area there were many large temples, whose riches rivaled those of the emperor. The temples and manorial estates often fought each other over boundary disputes; normally, according to long custom, the bakufu did not intervene in such quarrels. The *akuto* associated with the temples sometimes even approached the imperial palace to make demands, taking with them a sacred carriage; no one dared to stop them for fear of being punished by the gods or Buddha, and on occasion they even violently forced their way into the emperor's residence.

These bandits were useful to the powerful temples or the rich managers of manorial estates, who hired them as private guards. To the bakufu they were merely outlaws, and orders were often issued to the provincial governors to control them. It is speculated that one reason why the bakufu

Top: Kamakura period foot soldier wearing haramaki *armor; here the* gyoyo *shoulder protectors are located in their original position.*

Above: Kamakura period samurai in camp clothes.

Opposite: Kamakura period foot soldier, carrying kaburaya *in his* ebira.

planned to attack Korean harbors to counter the preparations for the Mongolian invasion was in order to catch all the *akuto* in Japan and send them to Korea as an expeditionary force—though this imaginative operation never materialized.[1]

After a few years these bandits had formed fairly organized groups, employed by the major temples and even by provincial governors (*jito*). They swaggered through the streets wearing flamboyant clothes and flashing, gold-trimmed armor, uncaring of traditional authority; for them money was everything.

* * *

In 1284, when the regent Hojo Tokimune died, another internal struggle troubled the bakufu. Taira Yoritsuna, who supported Tokimune's son Hojo Sadatoki, destroyed an old vassal named Adachi Yasumori. After this incident the council system of the bakufu was abolished, and the open dictatorship of the Hojo family began. Now the power of the bakufu exceeded that of the aristocratic Kyoto government, and the imperial system was in real peril of extinction.

After the Jokyu rebellion at the beginning of the 13th century the bakufu had located a kind of police department, the *Rokuhara tandai*, at Rokuhara to watch over the Kyoto regime and the imperial court; but the bakufu had never as a rule intervened in quarrels among the court aristocracy. When there was a fierce struggle over the imperial succession between the Jimyoji and Daikakuji sects, however, the bakufu finally reconciled them to an agreement that emperors should be enthroned alternately from each sect.

Nevertheless, when the Go-Daigo Emperor came to the throne in 1318 he founded a new government and issued many laws to reform obsolete systems, becoming famous as an active emperor. He secretly called for the provincial samurai to destroy the bakufu; but this plot was immediately uncovered, and he was exiled to Oki Island. Eventually, in 1333, Kusunoki Masashige rebelled against the Kamakura bakufu in response to the Go-Daigo Emperor's call. It is interesting to note that the emperor was related to some lower class samurai such as Kusunoki Masashige, and that the people who supported his movement were initially suspected of being *akuto* bandits. Perhaps he thought to change the samurai world by forging connections with the people at the lower levels of society.[2]

Whether or not Masashige was an *akuto* leader, what is certain is that he was a dealer in emery powder who had become rich through trade; and his tactics were not those of traditional samurai warfare. He constructed a fort in the mountains protected by many traps, and held it for some time. Once he judged that a battle was going against him he did not hesitate to escape from the field, and he often employed guerrilla warfare tactics. After the fall of his fort

he disappeared, only to emerge somewhere else and resume the fight. Gradually increasing numbers of samurai started to respond to the emperor's call and began attacking the bakufu. In 1333 Ashikaga Takauji, a descendant of Minamoto Yoshiie, was ordered by the bakufu to destroy the imperial army in Kyoto; but instead he turned aside and destroyed the bakufu's police department at Rokuhara.

Nitta Yoshisada raised forces in Kozuke (Kanto) and marched on Kamakura. He came from a not very important family of samurai, but his ancestor was supposed to have belonged to the Genji clan. Since the Hojo were Heishi, he may have hoped to restore the Genji cause—or perhaps he just wanted to become famous. Hojo forces counterattacked Yoshisada's army, but lost all the defensive battles, and in May 1333 Kamakura was finally laid under siege.

After the final battle at Kamakura the last regent, Hojo Takatoki, committed suicide; and the Kamakura bakufu bowed out after 150 years. But Takatoki's son Tokiyuki escaped from the inferno . . .

The Go-Daigo Emperor returned to Kyoto and founded his new government; but his policy was to revive the old system of the Heian period. Although he appointed *kokushi*, provincial government tax collectors, the military governors or *jito* appointed by the former bakufu were too strong to simply abolish. Consequently, there were two parallel government systems existing simultaneously—a situation which was unacceptable to any class except the aristocracy. Moreover, Ashikaga Takauji—destroyer of the Rokuhara police department—was not given an expected position in the new government, while many aristocrats were rewarded by the emperor. This policy predictably caused dissatisfaction among the samurai class.

When Hojo Tokiyuki, a son of Takatoki, led a rebellion in Nagano, Ashikaga Takauji—calling himself the *seiitai shogun*—led a force to put it down; but he never returned to Kyoto, nor did he respond to the emperor's order to do so. He stayed in Kamakura in order to expand his influence in the Kanto region. The Go-Daigo Emperor regarded this as an act of rebellion; he sent Nitta Yoshisada to impose his authority, but Takauji defeated him. Now Takauji went up to Kyoto to dislodge the emperor, and occupied the city. However, on the approach of an army led by Kitabatake Chikafusa, who had pursued Takauji from the Tohoku area on the emperor's orders, Takauji had to flee to Kyushu.

In less than three months Takauji rebuilt his forces and established his authority in Kyushu. Again he marched on Kyoto, from the west; and in May 1336 he defeated Kusunoki Masashige's and Nitta Yoshisada's army at Minatogawa (Kobe). Soon afterwards Takauji escorted the Kogen Emperor into Kyoto with him. The Go-Daigo Emperor escaped to Yoshino (Nara); and for nearly 60 years afterwards two rival imperial courts at Kyoto and Yoshino

existed simultaneously. Thus this period, 1336–92, was called *Nanboku-cho jidai* ('the age of the southern and northern courts').

(1) Kaitsu Ichiro: Mongolian invasion

(2) Amino Yoshihiko: *Nihon chyuseizo no saikento*

Above: *Samurai from Kusunoki Masashige's force, with the flag presented by the Go-Daigo Emperor. (Kyoto Jidaimatsuri festival)*

Opposite: *Kusunoki Masashige, a royalist in the Nanbokucho period who followed the Go-Daigo Emperor but was finally defeated by Ashikaga Takauji at Minatogawa.*

THE SOHEI

Left: Sohei *in the Enryakuji temple at Kyoto. This temple had a strong military organization, and its warrior-monks sometimes marched into the capital to press their demands. (Chion-in)*

Right: *Nanbokucho period* sohei *or warrior-monk armed with a long 'field sword'. This is too long for him to draw without the help of a comrade.*

There was a class of warriors other than samurai in Japan's history. They were called *sohei*, and they gave their allegiance to the major temples, which were important land-holders. They fought not only for their temples but also for their own profit. These forces are sometimes loosely called 'warrior monks', but this European term does not convey their exact nature; mostly they were workers in the temple's employment, or jobless people who took refuge at the temple.

In the late Heian period the power of great temples such as Kofukuji and Enryakuji in Kyoto became very great. They took their privileges and rights for granted, and sometimes sought to protect or further these by violence. Conflicts between them were theoretically settled by government intervention; but the temples kept their own trained armies, and if these judgements were unfavorable to them they did not hesitate to harass the government, or even the emperor. For example, such disputes often involved the capture of a sacred temple or intrusion on an aristocrat's residence. In that period most people were too superstitious to oppose what was ostensibly the will of the gods. Since the temples' military resources exceeded the 'police' power of the Kyoto government, the Joko Go-Shirakawa kept a private guard of samurai at his office called *hokumen no bushi* and *saimen no bushi*. In one instance, they did not hesitate to shoot arrows at a temple army which approached, complete with a sacred carriage. After the resolution of the conflict Go-Shirakawa ordered the samurai responsible punished; this concession was of course made purely in order to calm down the temples, but the samurai resented it as unjust.

One such 'warrior monk' named Benkei later became a leading vassal of Minamoto Yoshitsune. He wore a monk's cowl over his head and *do maru* armor beneath his monk's coat. The favorite weapon of such temple soldiers was the *naginata* or pole-sword, though they sometimes carried more unusual arms such as axes, hammers or saws.

In the 16th-century Sengoku period monks belonging to the Negoro temple became famous for their arquebus company. Only a few years after the Portuguese first brought firearms to Japan in the 1540s, three districts became famous for domestic arquebus production: Saiga, Negoro and Kunitomo. These regions were formerly well known for production of and trade in ironwork; now they not only manufactured guns, but supplied skilled mercenaries armed with their products. The company belonging to the Negoro temple—*Negoro-shu* or 'Negoro people'—were finally destroyed by Toyotomi Hideyoshi in 1585, but not before proving themselves a thorn in his flesh for a number of years.

Another significant group of sectarians, quite distinct from the *sohei*, were the *yamabushi*. These were the followers of En-no-gyoja, who founded a Buddhist sect which revered mountains; they lived in seclusion in mountain regions, and travelled by mountainous routes all over Japan. Because they offered a means of 'underground' communication they were hired by provincial warlords and acted as couriers; some of them became professional spies—*ninja*. Neither *sohei* nor *yamabushi* were regarded as samurai; even though some became samurai, they were considered to be of lower rank.

CHAPTER 7:
THE MUROMACHI BAKUFU

Kamakura period samurai in full oyoroi *armor, partly covered with printed decorative panels.*

In 1338 Ashikaga Takauji was appointed shogun, and established his bakufu in Muromachi, a suburb of Kyoto; and 'Muromachi Headquarters' is the name by which this 250 year regime would be known to history.

The organization of this government was similar to that of the Kamakura bakufu; Japan was once again ruled by a military dictatorship supported by important vassals and *gokenin*. In 1349, Takauji's brother Ashikaga Tadayoshi and Takauji's steward Koh Moronao started an internecine war which was ended by their deaths; after this episode Japan settled into a long period of relative stability. This was a period of great wealth and splendor, when the aristocracy beautified Kyoto with many magnificent palaces and the religious foundations with temples and gardens.

By the reign of the third Muromachi shogun, Ashikaga Yoshimitsu (1368–94) the stability of the bakufu's political and military organization was guaranteed by the support of three major families of Ashikaga retainers: the Hosokawa, Hatakeyama, and Shiba. With their assistance the shogun destroyed one by one various over-mighty provincial *shugo-daimyo*—governors who had enriched themselves and become more or less independent barons. Finally, in 1394, he integrated the separate Yoshino and Kyoto imperial courts on the condition that emperors should be chosen alternately from the Jimyoji and Daikakuji sects. (The similar agreement brokered by the Kamakura bakufu a century before had, of course, never been honored.) Thereafter, due to the influence of the Muromachi bakufu, only the former northern court enthroned emperors.

In 1392, after effectively abolishing the southern imperial court, Yoshimitsu formally resigned from the posts of shogun and *daijodaijin*. He built himself a villa at Kitayama in Kyoto (its remains are today's Kinkakuji). From this retirement home he in fact continued to control the government.

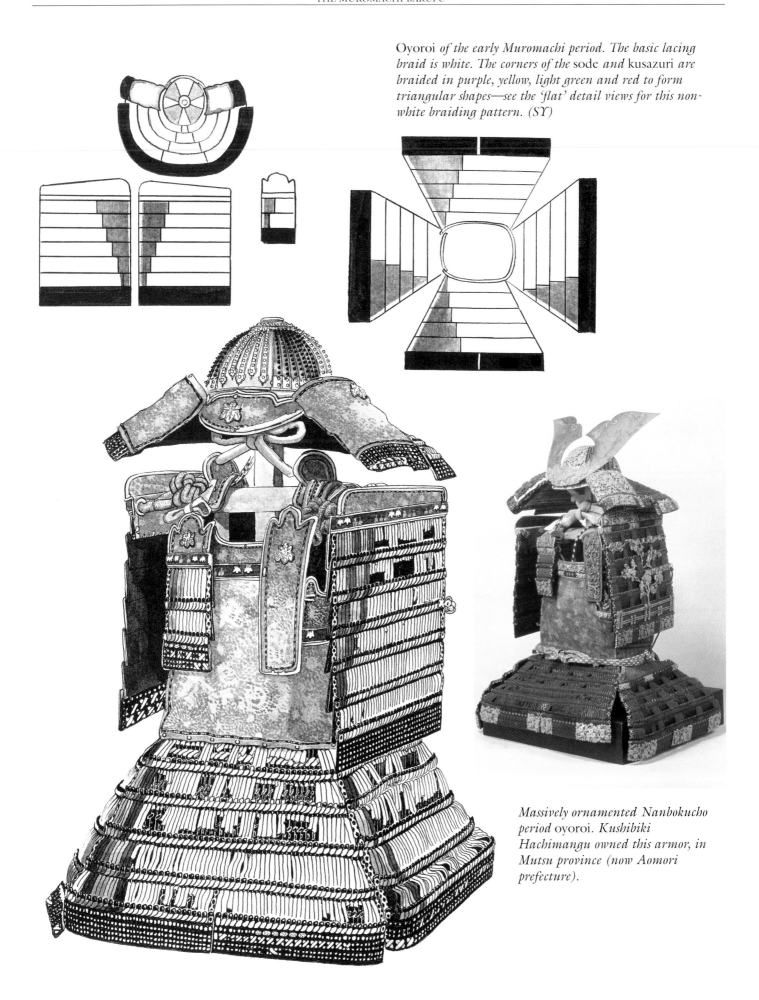

Oyoroi *of the early Muromachi period. The basic lacing braid is white. The corners of the* sode *and* kusazuri *are braided in purple, yellow, light green and red to form triangular shapes—see the 'flat' detail views for this non-white braiding pattern. (SY)*

Massively ornamented Nanbokucho period oyoroi. *Kushibiki Hachimangu owned this armor, in Mutsu province (now Aomori prefecture).*

Under the Kamakura bakufu, in spite of the Mongol invasions, government-approved trade between Yuan (Mongol-ruled) China and Japan had continued, and much Chinese currency was imported. In the late Kamakura period, however, Japanese pirates had begun marauding along the Korean and Chinese coasts. Drawn from renegade fishermen, samurai, and islanders from northern Kyushu, Iki, Tsushima and Goto Islands—as well as Chinese, Koreans and Southeast Asians—these *wako* (a kind of seaborne *akuto*) inflicted particular damage on Korean shipping and seaport towns. After the fall of the Yuan in 1382, Hung Wo established his Ming dynasty, and requested that the bakufu suppress the pirates. Responding to this, Yoshimitsu prohibited piracy and Imagawa Ryoshun, his governor in Kyushu, sent thousands of prisoners back to Korea; many lords in Kyushu followed suit. With the piracy diminishing, Yoshimitsu sent delegates to the Ming court and asked to become a subject of the Ming emperor. In return he was granted the Chinese title of 'king of Japan.' His ambition to be recognized as the head of a consolidated power structure embracing both the aristocracy and the samurai had now been attained.

Yoshimitsu secured two valuable agreements with Ming China. In return for sending tribute to the Chinese emperor he was presented with gifts—a continuing process. More importantly, he secured for Japanese ships the necessary symbols of license which were required by any vessel approved for official trading visits. Although Yoshimitsu's son, Yoshimochi, considered the exchange of tribute and gifts to be shameful to Japan and discontinued it, his successor Yoshinori soon revived the custom. Chinese trade was extremely profitable for both the shogun himself and for Japan's merchants and *daimyo* (provincial barons). Major imports from China were copper coins, wool, calligraphy and painting, while exports included swords, sulphur, copper and lacquer.

Although a number of the overambitious drew down on themselves the vengeance of the regime, from the late

Kamakura period onwards the provincial *shugo* and *jito*—essentially, the military, judicial and financial agents of government throughout the country—generally grew more powerful. These officials strengthened their connections with the local *gokenin*, the non-*gokenin* samurai, and also with the leaders of organized banditry. Such men, who combined the authority of government officials with the

Above: *A set of* oyoroi; *the construction made it easier to pack and transport than European plate armor. Note the graded colors in the lacing braid, a typical decorative feature; the braiding was seen in a huge variety of shades and patterns.*

Opposite: *Late Kamakura period samurai carrying a* naginata. *His foot is slightly out of the stirrup—this enables him to control the stirrup better.*

personal wealth of major landowners, were called *shugo-daimyo*, and they formed a consultative body in the bakufu. Their rapacity would lead to petitions for the remission of the burden of taxation; and the refusal of these petitions would provoke increasing unrest among the provincial poor. Individual outbreaks might be put down easily enough by the hired samurai of the local magnates—

Above: Rokuonji *golden pavilion, or Kinkakuji, built by the shogun Ashikaga Yoshimitsu at the end of the 14th century. In the Muromachi period the Ashikaga dynasty held complete control over the imperial court; the shogun was regarded as a king of Japan. The culture of the Muromachi period was distinctive in the way that samurai and aristocratic styles became mixed. The tea ceremony and* noh *dance were developed in this period, sponsored by rich samurai or warlords.*

samurai, armed men recruited from the upper peasantry; but the pressure would steadily build throughout the first half of the 15th century.

The bakufu directly owned about 50 large estates and was supported by their tax income. It also received commercial taxes and duties on the movement of goods; and imposed taxes on rice fields, other land holdings and houses. Due to the development of a monetary economy (as opposed to levies of rice), the regime also imposed taxes on *sake* manufacturers and warehouse owners, since they also pursued a parallel business as moneylenders.

At the beginning of the Muromachi period agricultural productivity increased based on the development of tools and methods of cultivation. A process of breaking up of the *shoen* (manorial estates) liberated farmers who had been tied to these masters, and a relatively free commerce slowly emerged in the countryside. The farming classes played their part in the contemporary social movement termed Gekokujo ('the lower overthrow the higher').

Left: In the Kamakura period the average horse height from ground to shoulder was only 130cm-140cm. The samurai preferred wild stallions for their kicking and biting in battle.

ARMOR OF THE 14TH TO 16TH CENTURIES

DO MARU AND HARAMAKI

In the early days lower class samurai had worn both *do maru* and *haramaki* style cuirasses. It has been stated that the *do maru* already existed when the *oyoroi* cuirass first appeared in the historical record. The *do maru* was a lamellar armor which fastened on the right side. Its *kusazuri* skirt differed from the *oyoroi* style in being divided into eight panels for greater ease of movement. The existence of *do maru* armors suggests that foot soldiers already played a significant part in the battles of the Heian period. In the later Heian, in the so-called 'Genpei War' of the 1180s between the Minamoto (Genji) and Taira (Heishi) clans, these lower class retainers wore *do maru* cuirasses without large *sode* shoulder guards. To avoid hindrance in handling swords and *naginata* polearms, they wore instead, hanging over the collarbones, pairs of *gyoyo*—smaller plates named after their supposed maple leaf shape. Since the *do maru* was lighter than *oyoroi*, even some samurai of the leadership class preferred it and wore it under their outer clothes like a sort of 'bulletproof vest'.

In the late Kamakura (early 14th century) and Nanbokucho periods (mid to late 14th century), it became clear that tactical changes had made the encumbering *oyoroi* obsolete. Senior samurai began to go into battle wearing *do maru* with *oyoroi*-style *sode*, and *kote* sleeve armor. In the Kamakura period foot soldiers still wore the smaller *gyoyo*, but in the Nanbokucho and Muromachi (14th-16th centuries) they attached the large *sode* characteristic of *oyoroi* harness. In this case the *gyoyo* were moved to the position in front of the armpits where the *sendan* and *kyubi* plates had been attached. The *nodowa*, gorget plate, and *menpo*, face mask, were introduced during this period. Helmets with exposed rivets, whose surface was in danger of trapping enemy weapons, were replaced by the *suji kabuto*, still of radial, segmented construction but with the rivet heads filed down and lacquered over.

Haramaki ('belly wrap') armor was made in the same way as the *do maru* but fastened down the back rather than at the right side. It was a simpler and cheaper form, and early examples were worn with the back open; but this was soon closed with a lamellar plate of about the same width as a *kusazuri* panel. *Haramaki* was never to be a major armor style, but nevertheless its production continued until the Edo period (mid-19th century).

In the Nanbokucho period, to make the production of armor easier, it was covered with leather. This *kawatsutsumi* style allowed armorers to recycle *sane* taken from the many damaged armors—the leather covering hid the patchings of mismatched scales.

Top: Iroiro odoshi haramaki—*a haramaki* cuirass laced with many-colored braid. It is seen from the rear, complete with the added defense over the fastening—this was called okubyo-ita, or 'coward board', from the conceit that no true samurai ever turned his back on the enemy. (Hinomisaki Shrine)

Above: Fusubekawatsutsumi haramaki—*front view of a* haramaki *covered with smoked leather. The basic construction of the* haramaki *was two* tateage *or torso pieces, front and rear, and a skirt of seven* kusazuri *each in five steps. The reason why so many* haramaki *were covered with leather was the increase in demand for armor in the Sengoku period: the use of recycled scales from damaged armor did not show under the leather.* (Tokyo National Museum)

Below: *Putting on the* do maru *(1); the undergarments are as worn with the* oyoroi. **Top right:** *The* do maru *is put on; the* sode *shoulder guards are already attached to it.* **Bottom left:** *The leaf-shaped* gyoyo *plates, once an alternative to* sode *for poorer soldiers, are now worn in combination with them, but moved round to the front to protect the collar bones. (SY)*

Above: *In the Nanbokucho period, 1336–92, the style of combat changed. Battles were often fought around fortresses on high ground, where mounted samurai were of little use. The lighter and more flexible do maru armor began to replace the oyoroi.* **Top right:** *For easier fighting on foot, armor became shorter, and the bow was replaced as the main weapon by those more suitable for face-to-face combat. This man has a large wooden mace reinforced with nails; his helmet bears a tall antler-like crest,* kuwagata. **Top left:** *This very long 'field sword' gave better reach and a heavier two-handed blow.* **Top left & bottom right:** *They both wear* haramaki *armor, the opening at the back reinforced with the* seita *plate, which stretches from neck to hip. Thigh protectors and greaves are worn above and below the knees. The helmet's neck guard,* shikoru, *now spreads out at a more horizontal angle, giving protection to the top of the shoulders.* **Bottom left:** *This attending page carries a dipper to give water to his master's horse. His hairstyle shows that he has not yet attained adult status. (SY)*

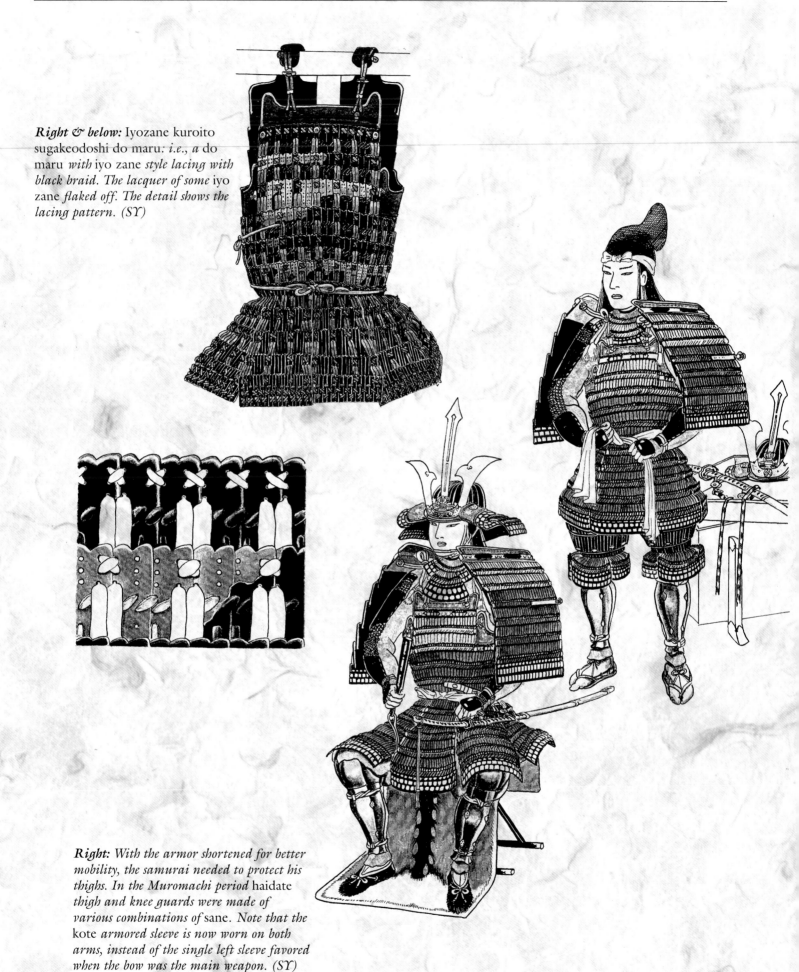

Right & below: Iyozane kuroito sugakeodoshi do maru: *i.e., a* do maru *with* iyo zane *style lacing with black braid. The lacquer of some* iyo zane *flaked off. The detail shows the lacing pattern. (SY)*

Right: *With the armor shortened for better mobility, the samurai needed to protect his thighs. In the Muromachi period* haidate *thigh and knee guards were made of various combinations of* sane. *Note that the* kote *armored sleeve is now worn on both arms, instead of the single left sleeve favored when the bow was the main weapon. (SY)*

CHAPTER 8:

THE ONIN WAR AND THE BEGINNINGS OF GEKOKUJO

By the time that Ashikaga Yoshimasa succeeded as the eighth shogun in the mid-15th century it had become obvious that the power of the provincial *shugo* class had outstripped that of the shogunate at Kyoto. Yoshimasa was not the type of ruler equipped to deal decisively with this threat. He was an aesthete, a connoisseur of art and music, and a man of letters; but he was neither a warrior nor a skillful politician. He would later spend vast sums constructing a magnificent Zen-style villa at Higashiyama; but any attempt to govern with authority which he might have been tempted to make was frustrated by the great families which effectively controlled the bakufu. He devoted himself to the life of a artistic dilettante, while around the countryside poverty-stricken farmers and other humble workers mounted periodic uprisings.

Yoshimasa wished to retire to devote himself to his cultural pleasures. Since he had no children, he named his young brother Yoshimi as his heir. Yoshimasa's wife, Hino Tomiko, came from a family to which the shogun was not otherwise related, and which he hated for their interference in his affairs. It was thus a rude shock when Tomiko unexpectedly bore a son, and vigorously advanced the claim of the infant Yoshihisa to inherit the shogunate.

Tomiko relied on the support of Yamana Mochitoyo (Sozen), one of the three ministers (*kanrei*), to make her son shogun. On the other side, Yoshimi was supported by another of the ministers, Hosokawa Katsumoto. To add to the fevered atmosphere of partisan conspiracy, the Shiwa and Hatakeyama families began their own conflicts over succession. The great rival Kyoto families called in their supporters from the countryside. In 1467, two large armies (by one probably exaggerated count, totalling as many as 250,000 soldiers) faced each other from the eastern and western districts of Kyoto. It is from this episode that Kyoto's Nishijin quarter ('west encampment') derives its name.

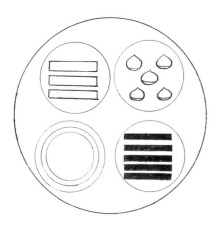

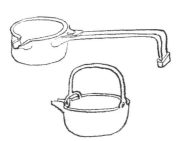

Right:
Akuto *samurai of the
Nanbokucho to
Muromachi periods, in
a leather-covered* do
maru *armor. The
helmet has a cloth*
shikoro *reinforced
with so-called 'card-
shaped' iron plates.*

Left: *The style of the ceremony differed, but a usual feature was the eating of foods whose names matched the Japanese word for victory—e.g. dried seaweed, abalone, etc. The number three was significant; the commander ate three kinds of food, and drank* sake *three times, each time in three mouthfuls. (SY)*

in the city streets. Both armies had to rely on supplies brought in from the distant provinces; the Yamana controlled seven of the eight gates, and hoped to starve the Hosokawa into submission. But by now the fighting extended beyond Kyoto, and with the breakdown of all central authority the Onin War spread like a cancer throughout much of Japan.

In the provinces the adherents of one side or the other, engaged in increasingly uncontrollable conflict. Local magnates took the opportunity to settle local scores and to enlarge their territories. Large numbers of peasant footsoldiers—*ashigaru*—were recruited, and bands of brigands preyed on the weak indiscriminately. It became increasingly difficult to follow any rational pattern in the campaigns (and it is certainly impossible to do so in a book of this size).

'The lower overthrow the higher'

One identifiable factor amongst the general bloody chaos was the element of social rebellion, identified as Gekokujo; this carried the same meaning as the historical English phrase 'the world turned upside down'. Those who promoted this movement were called Do-ikki, from *ikki*, meaning roughly 'solidarity through unity of will'. Out in the provinces the farmers, whose tax burdens and other sufferings were naturally aggravated by the war, began to rebel, often in alliance with poor local samurai, against their provincial governors—sometimes while these were absent on campaign, but not always. In an extreme case in 1485 in Yamashiro province, south of Kyoto, the united farmers and petty samurai presented an ultimatum to the warring local commanders from two branches of the Hatakeyama family, forcing both to actually withdraw from the province. They appointed 36 representatives from the districts to form a provincial government, which ruled Yamashiro for ten years.

Another important revolt grew out of a Buddhist sect called Jodo-shin-shu, which became very influential in Hokuriku (Ishikawa prefecture). Its leader, Rennyo, preached Buddha's teachings in plain language accessible to

Tension grew as incident followed incident; many citizens evacuated Kyoto, and in May 1467 the fighting began. In the first stage of what would become known as the Onin War, the Hosokawa forces ('East'), supposedly numbering some 160,000 men drawn from 24 provinces, fought mainly against the Yamana forces ('West'), who mustered about 90,000 men from 20 provinces. In September, however, Ouchi Yasuhiro's 20,000-strong army joined the West, turning the tide, and the Hosokawa army was nearly surrounded in Kyoto. Once more, another force marched up to the capital to redress the balance, joining the East and breaking their encirclement.

The fighting was initially confined to the city itself, and in the course of the first three months much of northern Kyoto was reduced to rubble and ashes strewn with unburied corpses. After warning that whichever family started the fighting would be declared outlaws, the shogun played little part in events. In October 1467, while battle raged through the burning Shokokuji Zen temple next door to his residence, Yoshimasa imperturbably continued drinking *sake*, ignoring the panic of his attendants. From April 1468 a kind of stalemate obtained across trenches dug

Samurai wearing haramaki, *'belly-wrap' armor, which was fastened at his back, with a separate section covering the vulnerable fastening. In the Muromachi period the* eboshi *hat changed to a folded shape. (SY)*

the uneducated. He taught the poor and the pious that in Buddha's world all were equal, and that it was possible to build a heaven on earth. Rennyo moved to Kaga province, where he and his followers allied themselves with petty samurai (and initially, even with the local lord, Togashi Masachika) in a movement called the Ikko-ikki—'the unified league'. This attracted huge numbers of adherents; and as they believed that death in battle was the gateway to paradise, they achieved considerable military success. In 1488 they expelled Togashi Masachika from his province and became the effective government of Kaga; eight years later they began building their great fortified monastery, Ishiyama Honganji, at the mouth of the Yodo River where Osaka Castle now stands.

* * *

Eventually, responding to the invitations of the shogun Ashikaga Yoshimasa and Yamana Sozen, Ashikaga Yoshimi returned to Kyoto from the island where he had taken refuge. He still feared for his life, however, from the near presence of the rival Hino family; and after only two weeks he fled once more, to the Koyasan Mountains. Subsequently the Yamana army (West) invited Yoshimi to be their commander-in-chief. This meant that the initial cause of the war was completely lost, since he had originally been supported by the Hosokawa family (East). The intermittent struggle for Kyoto lost much of its impetus in 1473 when both commanders, Yamana Sozen and Hosokawa Katsumoto, died within months of one another. The next year Ashikaga Yoshimasa formally abdicated and the nine-year-old Yoshihisa was proclaimed as the ninth shogun (in practice, Yoshimasa continued to rule, as indifferently as before). In 1477 the West army, now led by Ochi Masahiro, left the city. This date is taken as the end of the Onin War; but in fact the chaos and disruption which it had sparked off continued seamlessly throughout the so-called *Sengoku* or 'age of the country at war', which occupied the late 15th and entire 16th centuries. During the ten years of the Onin War the authority of the shogun had been completely destroyed; the title still had useful prestige, however, for those who needed a pretext for war— as had long been the case with the emperor.

Out in the war-torn provinces, the barons who had succeeded in holding on to their power and possessions were called '*Sengoku daimyo*'. The style of warfare had changed markedly, largely through the introduction in large numbers of the *ashigaru* or lightly armed and lightly armored foot soldier. The employment of these cheap and agile troops had been notable during the street fighting in Kyoto. They were recruited by the samurai leaders from among landless rural peasants, temple workers, unemployed townspeople and the homeless. The *ashigaru* were mainly deployed to attack the enemy's weak points or supply routes; they lacked entirely the samurai's pride in individual combat, were easily persuaded to change sides, and had no scruples about looting and burning temples and aristocrats' houses. During this long and costly war all armies relied to a great extent on *ashigaru*, since commanders were anxious to keep their main samurai forces intact.

The foot soldiers' weapons and armor were at first far from uniform. One document described a strange group of 300 people marching toward Uji Jinmeigu shrine in November 1468. They carried a lance in each hand; some wore gold helmets, others bamboo hats with long red crests. Their clothes were dirty and consisted of a single cotton *kimono* showing their hairy shins below. Since there was a rumor that a god had descended from heaven at Uji, this tattered band had taken a break from war to visit the shrine and pray for good fortune.

Although the *ashigaru* were initially recruited simply for wages, as time passed their connection with their employers became closer. They were incorporated into the daimyos' family forces as regular soldiers, and would later be supplied with uniform weapons and armor.

Opposite: Organization of an army. From the late Muromachi period the numbers of troops increased, and they were separated into special groups such as archers, spearmen, arquebusiers, etc., these groups being led by kumigashira. *If the army was large, the* kumigashira *were commanded by* monogashira. *The commands of the* monogashira *were amalgamated in* bugyo. *(SY)*

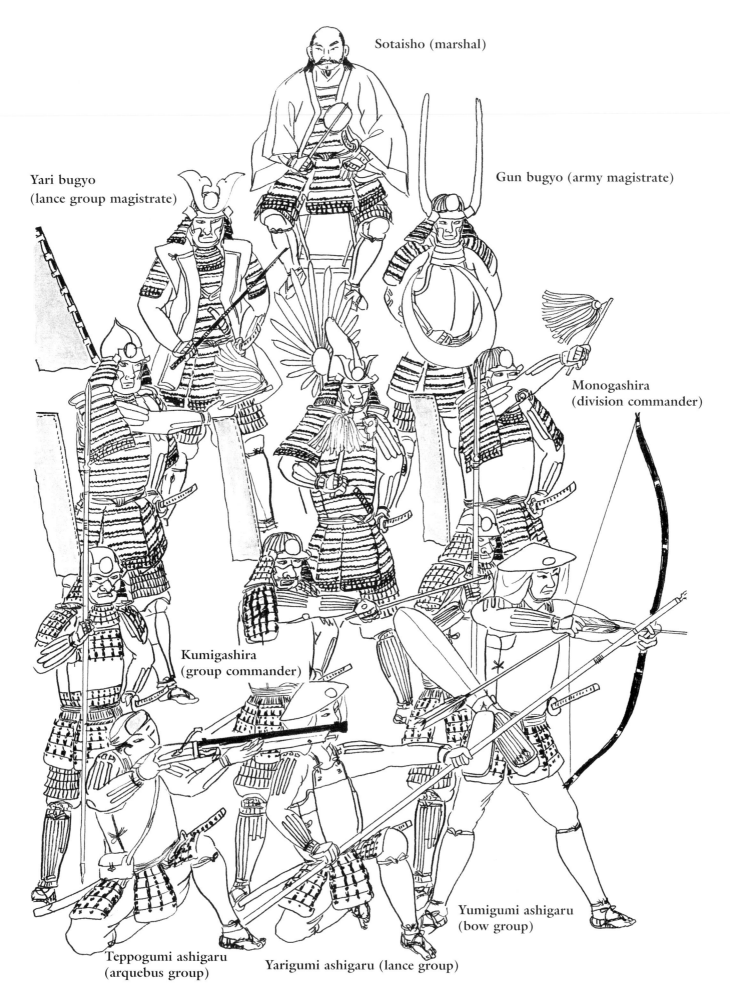

Sotaisho (marshal)

Yari bugyo
(lance group magistrate)

Gun bugyo (army magistrate)

Monogashira
(division commander)

Kumigashira
(group commander)

Yumigumi ashigaru
(bow group)

Teppogumi ashigaru
(arquebus group)

Yarigumi ashigaru (lance group)

'MODERN' ARMOR –
TOSEI GUSOKU

Above: *A cuirass of 'modern' construction but with the lower half of* sane *laced in the* kebiki odoshi *style. The braid was usually laced downwards so that the surface of the cuirass was covered. The motif of a monkey trying to catch the moon is a message to opponents – it means 'you should know your limitations...' (Osaka Castle Museum)*

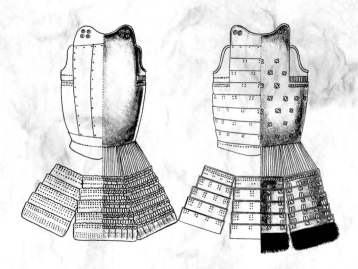

Above: *Two types of 'modern' armor, influenced by the Western styles brought into Japan by the Portuguese and Spaniards in the middle years of the 16th century: (right)* yokihagi hishitoji okegawado, *and (left)* tatehagi okegawado. *The former consists of transverse plates which are linked with thongs; the latter, of vertical plates connected by rivets, the rivet heads being filed down and the whole surface covered with lacquer. These drawings also show two types of* kusazuri *lacing. (SY)*

In the late Muromachi period (16th century), so-called 'modern armor,' originally based on the *do maru* style, appeared on the battlefield. Due to the loss of flexibility from using metal plates, the armor was separated in two, front and rear, and fastened at both sides. The *mogami do* cuirass had five horizontal plates connected by hinges and fastened at the back. This multi-hinged armor was considered very convenient to wear, and older style cuirasses were modified into this style. For ease of production the overlapped series of *sane* were abandoned in favor of larger oblong plates, *iyo sane*.

During the Sengoku period ('the age of the country at war,' late 15th to mid-16th centuries) the Portuguese introduced firearms to Japan in the form of the matchlock arquebus; this new weapon was locally copied and spread rapidly all over the country. The introduction of gunpowder weapons naturally demanded stronger armor. Meanwhile, some striking additions were being made to the panoply of the samurai on the battlefield, for two reasons. In the Sengoku period, with its almost constant warfare between shifting alliances, identification of individuals was particularly important. Warriors were especially self-conscious about their personal reputations for prowess; and commanders had to be recognizable by their followers in battle. For these reasons large crests or ornaments, in a huge variety of sometimes very impressive shapes, were added to the front of the helmet. Usually made of paper over a bamboo structure, these were not as heavy as they look, though they were still bulky. If the enemy charge seemed to threaten a commander he would pass his helmet to a retainer, escaping from the battlefield if necessary. Generals used to have spare helmets carried by their retainers, changing them if they were damaged in combat.

* * *

After the Sengoku period, with the final triumph of the Tokugawa shogunate at the beginning of the 17th century, Japan entered a period of peace which lasted almost uninterrupted for some 250 years. It is not surprising, therefore, that armor became a symbol of status and lost its functional meaning. Despite this, there was a ready demand for the great skills retained by armorers into the late Edo period. Many helmets produced at this late date and for no practical purpose, displayed a fantastic sophistication of metalwork. Just as late 17th century European commanders would have themselves portrayed in plate armor long after they had discarded its use in actual battle, so in the Edo period senior samurai often favored archaic *oyoroi* and *do maru* armors for reasons of nostalgia and respect for their family traditions.

Above: *Putting on* tosei gusoku *(1).* **Top right:** *The* etchufundoshi *loincloth was c.1.5m long.* **Top left:** *Putting on undergarments—note the button at the top.* **Centre:** *Putting on the* hakama—*note that these did not reach far down the shin.* **Bottom right:** *Putting on socks and fabric shin guards.* **Bottom left:** *Putting on* waraji *straw sandals— these gave a good grip on slippery ground. (SY)*

Above: *Putting on* tosei gusoku *(2).* **Top right:** *Putting on* suneate *greaves, here of metal 'splints' joined by ring mail.* **Top left:** *Tying on* haidate *thigh guards.* **Centre:** *Putting on a single right protective glove,* yugake. **Bottom right:** *Putting on two armored sleeves,* kote. **Bottom left:** *Putting on the* manchira, *a kind of substantial 'arming doublet' of mail with small added plates. (SY)*

Above and right: *Outside and inside of a pair of* tsubo sode, *as attached to 'modern' armor in the 16th century. These shoulder defenses now followed the curve of the upper arms instead of hanging against them in flat boards. (Tokyo National Museum)*

Left: Putting on tosei gusoku *(3).*
Top right: *Putting on the cuirass, and fastening the cords and toggles which joined the torso to the shoulder pieces.*
Bottom left: *Tying the sash,* obi; *properly adjusted, this distributed some of the weight of the armor from the shoulders to the hips. (SY)*

Right: *Putting on* tosei gusoku *(4).*
Left: *Putting on the* hachimaki *headcloth.* ***Right:*** *Several ways of attaching the swords to the sash. (SY)*

Putting on the tosei gusoku *(5).* **Right:** *The* menpo *face guard is in place; now the* nodowa *gorget is attached to it.* **Left:** *The harness is completed by the helmet, its shape here copying that of the tall cap, with a devil's face* maedate. *(SY)*

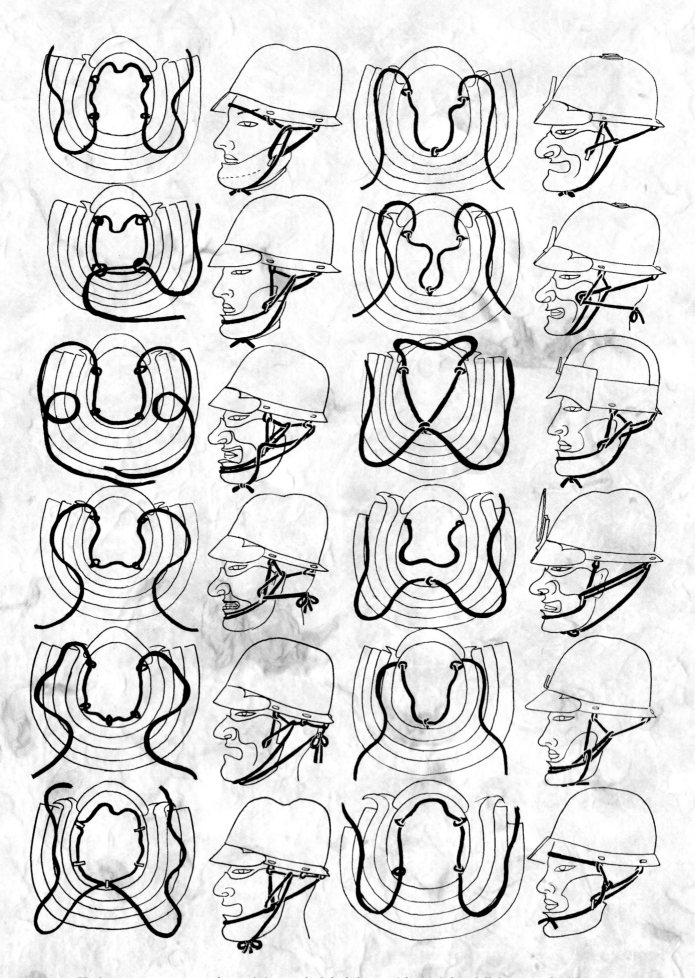

Various ways to arrange the retaining cord of the helmet, with partial or full face guards. (SY)

CHAPTER 9:
THE AGE OF BATTLES — ODA NOBUNAGA AND TOYOTOMI HIDEYOSHI

In the Kamakura period, battles began with the exchange of clouds of arrows, but during the Sengoku period volleys from massed arquebusiers marked the opening stage of most actions. Even so, this firepower could not destroy the enemy completely; the issue always had to be decided by samurai advancing to fight face to face with spears and swords. (SY)

In the late 15th century the daimyos who had survived the Onin War and the consequent unrest began to be engaged in another competitive struggle for survival and dominance, which would end only with the victory of Toyotomi Hideyoshi in 1590.

The origins of these provincial barons may be summarized in four categories:
(1) Leaders of samurai groups bound together by the *ikki* who rose to become daimyo (e.g. Mori, Matsuura).
(2) Former government-appointed *shugo* who had enriched themselves (e.g. Takeda, Imagawa, Otomo).
(3) Former subordinates—magistrates—who had driven out the local lord (e.g. Nagao, Asakura, Asai, Oda).
(4) Former unemployed samurai who made themselves daimyos (e.g. Saito, Hojo).

Whatever his origins, each daimyo needed the military support of the samurai groups within his province. The factor most important to his survival was his skill in controlling his own allies and in dividing the coalitions assembled by his enemies. In these confrontations it was not enough to be either a tactical innovator or a brave warrior.

During the early stages of this age of constant warfare the daimyos had no conception of unifying the country under a central ruler; this dream would only appear with the remarkable personality of Oda Nobunaga in the middle of the 16th century. Selfish territorial expansion was their only goal, and their domains were their whole world. Most of their battles were therefore fought around their borders and for strategic castles. Pitched battles between large armies were rare; the warlords were playing a long game, and needed to keep their own samurai and their vassals' forces as intact as possible.

The famous tales of heroic battles were mostly manipulated by historians in the later Edo period—16th-century realities were rather different. Wise daimyos preferred to win their wars without pitched battles, and plots and counter-plots played a large part in their struggles. If fighting was unavoidable they preferred the defense of fortified positions to confrontations in the open field. Generally, only the first wave of an assault was delivered with courage and determination; if that first attack was broken, collapse usually followed.

Although Japanese historians have celebrated Oda Nobunaga as an innovator of new tactics, recent studies have revealed that he was in fact rather a conventional tactician. He was described by a Western missionary as nervous, short-tempered and cruel, but his method of warfare was cautious. He should rather be appreciated as a great strategist. Until Nobunaga ordered his vassals to leave their lands and move to his castle towns, campaigns had been pursued only in the agricultural off-season. Because the petty samurai and other humble followers were busy planting rice in April and May, and also during the harvest season, a warlord could not mobilize the necessary number of soldiers for long enough to pursue major objectives. Nobunaga was the first commander who separated his soldiers from the agricultural laborers, and in so doing obtained a free hand to begin operations at any moment he chose.

By 1560, after decades of continuous fighting, a few important daimyos had emerged in the provinces who were capable of providing a focus for regional unity. Among these were the Mori family in Chugoku, the Takeda, Imagawa and

Uesugi families in Chubu, and the Hojo in Kanto. These great lords issued their own laws in their provinces, and collected taxes from the farmers through the local samurai. These local samurai had to provide their lords with numbers of soldiers according to their income. The lord and his retainers were no longer connected by the familial bonds of the Kamakura period; loyalties depended upon regional conditions at any particular time, and a warlord always had to be on his guard against betrayal by his vassals.

Another factor confronting the daimyos was the strength of religious sects. Wealthy temples such as Enryakuji, Kufukuji and Todaiji owned large estates, and often engaged in violent disputes with one another. They kept private armies enlisted from warrior monks, local samurai, temple cleaners, artisans and farmers; when the temples quarreled they sent these forces into battle, and traditionally the secular power, represented by the local *shugo* and *jito*, did not intervene. This traditional license to settle their own affairs convinced the religious foundations that they could remain independent of the newly emerging regional authority of the daimyos. However, as the daimyos followed a gradual process of consolidation in ever-larger regional power blocks, the temples would learn that their unquestioned vested rights were no longer seen as valid. For the daimyo a rich manor belonging to a major temple offered an enticing economic prize, and the prospect of absorbing its samurai into his own forces was also attractive.

The relatively new Jodo-shin-shu or Ikko-shu sect based at Ishiyama Honganji in Osaka was a unique case. The religious community did not form their own military units, but were dependent on their adherent samurai and soldiers—of which they could call on large and enthusiastic numbers. Among the men who responded to the Honganji temple's call were inhabitants of Saiga in Kii (Wakayama), an area which had long experience of both trade with China and of skilled ironwork. It was not long after the introduction of firearms to Japan by the Portuguese in the 1540s that Saiga also began to win a reputation for its arquebus-armed mercenary soldiers. These matchlock musketeers represented one of the major military assets of the Ikko-ikki movement, which also counted among its forces farmers, merchants, artisans, local samurai, pirates and temple members. They were especially influential in Kaga, Etchu, Osaka and Mikawa. In these provinces the barons could expect strong opposition to over-heavy taxation of their peasants, since many of their retainers adhered to this sect.

In 1543, a Portuguese ship bound for Ningpo from Thailand was wrecked on Tanegashima Island off southern Kyushu. It has long been said that there were two Portuguese among the survivors, who demonstrated the arquebus to the young lord of the island—the first Japanese to encounter a practical firearm (although contact with

Above: Allied arquebus men wait behind a rampart. Three lines of ramparts, ditches and palisades protected the allied position at Shitaragahara, and in the rainy season ditches were soon filled with rainwater.

Opposite and left: In 1575 at Shitaragahara (Nagashino), the allied Oda-Tokugawa army crushed the 'invincible' Takeda forces. Perhaps too much has been made of the 'decisive' use of massed arquebusiers, but they did play an important part in the early stages of the confrontation. The actual battle was fought in rain and mud, unlike this sunny re-enactment.

China must have made them familiar with pyrotechnics). However, it is speculated today that even before this incident many matchlock guns had actually been brought into Japan by pirates or merchants. The matchlock arquebus of the mid-16th century was a heavy and fairly primitive smooth-bore weapon. It had an effective range of 328ft (100m) at most, and then only at a large target such as a whole body of soldiers. On a still day the thick smoke of its discharge could be blinding. It took a long time to reload—perhaps half a minute—which might be considered a mortal defect in a battle at close quarters. In rain it could not be fired at all. In spite of these disadvantages, within a few years Japan became the largest exporter of guns in Asia. Sakai, Negoro and Omi were the major centers of gun production; since Saiga—mentioned above—is near to Sakai and Negoro, it is no wonder that they could provide mercenary arquebus companies. (The Japanese could not initially produce high quality gunpowder, however, and had to depend on imports for much of their needs.)

The introduction of *ashigaru* foot soldiers and massed hand-to-hand fighting had changed the whole aspect of traditional Japanese combat. There were no more battle-opening ceremonies with shouted introductions and whistling arrows; there was no more drawing aside in battle for warriors to engage in personal duels. Since the samurai were protected by strong armor, thrusting weapons such as

lances became more important and swords were to some extent relegated to weapons of last resort. The importance of the archer was unchanged, however. Bowmen were never superceded by arquebusiers, but fought side by side with the gun companies; their rate of fire was much greater and their effective range was comparable. Arquebusiers, archers and spearmen formed combined forces led by the samurai. It is false to assume that it was the introduction of the firearm which completely altered Japanese fighting methods: the gun was just one factor that contributed to a process which was already under way.

Oda Nobunaga

The Oda family were formerly subjects of the Shiba, a *shugo* family in Owari, but seized power in the province while the Shiba leaders were away in Kyoto during the Onin War. Oda Nobunaga's father belonged to a collateral branch of the Oda, but superceded the main family line and became a baron in Owari. Nobunaga inherited the barony in 1551 at the age of seventeen. In 1560 one of the most powerful local daimyos, Imagawa Yoshimoto, attacked Owari's border from his province of Mikawa with an army of 25,000 men. The young Nobunaga attacked him with just 3,000 soldiers in a gorge at Okehazama, took him by surprise, and killed him. It was after the death of Yoshimoto that a promising young samurai in his service was able to return to

Above: Arquebus mercenary from Saiga, Kyushu, identified by the distinctive helmet and by the flag of a three-legged crow. These Saiga-shu *provided one of the main military assets of the Ishiyama Honganji temple, which defied Oda Nobunaga for years.*

Above right: In 1568, Oda Nobunaga entered Kyoto and installed the shogun Ashikaga Yoshiaki as his puppet. Nobunaga (right) with one of his retainers, his brother-in-law Shibata Katsuie.

Opposite: At the age of 47, Shibata Katsuie was the most versatile warrior in Nobunaga's forces. The tall ornaments on his helmet are silver roof tiles or kawara; *the* maedate *at the front represents two flying birds. Katsuie was defeated by Hideyoshi after Nobunaga's death, and committed suicide.*

his home in Okazaki. This was Matsudaira Motoyasu—later known to history as Tokugawa Ieyasu.

In 1567, Nobunaga made an alliance with Matsudaira Yasunobu to secure his rear; he then attacked and destroyed Saito Tatsuoki in Mino (Nagoya)—the Saito were his wife's family, but they were torn by internal hatreds. Nobunaga moved to the Nohbi Plain, where rice production was abundant, and the main road from Sagami and Kanto to Kyoto passed by. While offering good access to the capital, this place was far enough away from Kyoto to keep him clear of the political turmoil of the court aristocracy. That turmoil provided him with a useful card however, when a desperate young man named Ashikaga Yoshiaki, brother of a puppet shogun, took refuge with him. In 1568 Nobunaga entered Kyoto with a force of 60,000 men and installed Yoshiaki as his own puppet. The Ashikaga shogunate was a 'lame duck', but Nobunaga intended to use his favored position in Kyoto to win control of the Kinki district.

In April 1570 he mounted a campaign against Asakura Yoshikage in Echigo. This encountered an unexpected difficulty, however; the rear of his march was harassed by Asai Nagamasa to such an extent that Nobunaga had to return to Kyoto. Nagamasa interfered because under one of the terms of their alliance, when Nobunaga wanted to move his army he first had to inform Asai, which he had not done. Asai Nagamasa's wife Oichi-no-kata was Nobunaga's sister,

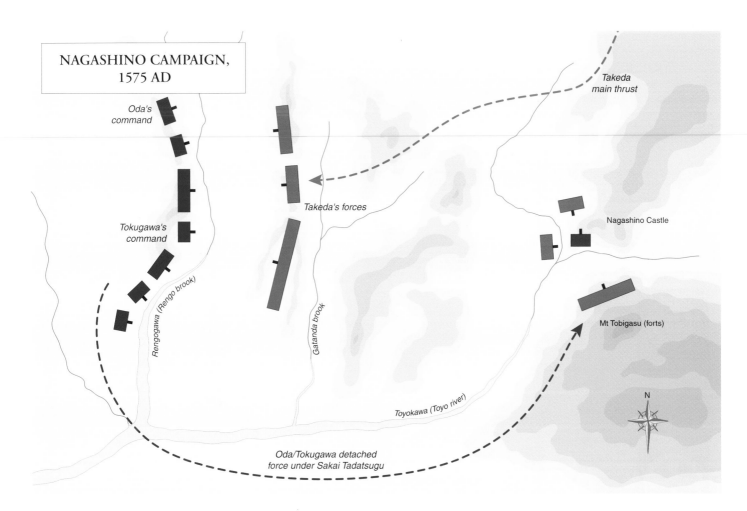

NAGASHINO CAMPAIGN,
1575 AD

Oda's
command

Takeda
main thrust

Takeda's forces

Nagashino Castle

Tokugawa's
command

Rengogawa (Rengo brook)

Gatanda brook

Mt Tobigasu (forts)

N

Toyokawa (Toyo river)

Oda/Tokugawa detached
force under Sakai Tadatsugu

and relations between the families had been intimate;
unfortunately, those between Asai and Asakura were as
good. In July 1570 Nobunaga defeated the allied forces of
the Asakura and Asai in the furious battle of Anegawa. A
move to pursue them to final annihilation was foiled by a
flank attack by the monkish army of the Enryakuji temple.
In September 1571 Nobunaga attacked Enryakuji, burning
it down and massacring men, women and children without
mercy.

In 1572, Takeda Shingen marched from Kai to the
Mikawa border (Matsudaira Motoyasu's domain) on his way
to Kyoto. Shingen defeated the heavily outnumbered
Motoyasu at the battle of Mikatagahara, but as Motoyasu
prepared a hopeless defense of his Hamamatsu Castle the
Takeda army withdrew due to wider strategic considerations.
(Takeda Shingen died of illness in April 1573.)

Oda Nobunaga came to believe that all moves against
him were orchestrated by the shogun Ashikaga Yoshiaki, so
in 1573 he expelled Yoshiaki from Kyoto, thus finally
bringing the Ashikaga bakufu to an end (though Yoshiaki
fled to Mori territory in Chugoku, and continued plotting
against Nobunaga). In this year Nobunaga finally destroyed
Asakura Yoshikage at Ichijogadani and Asai Nagamasa at
Otani Castle, but his sister Oichi-no-kata was rescued.

The great rival of Takeda Shingen of Kai was Uesugi
Kenshin of Echigo. They fought several battles at

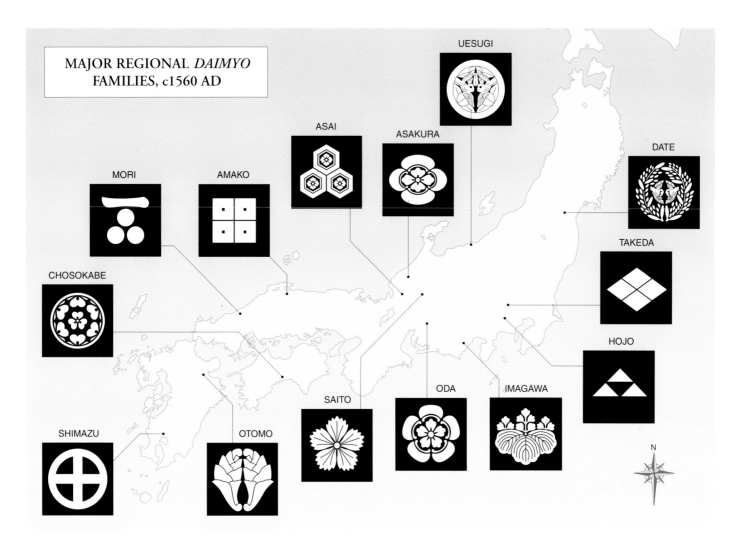

MAJOR REGIONAL *DAIMYO*
FAMILIES, c1560 AD

UESUGI

ASAI

ASAKURA

DATE

MORI

AMAKO

TAKEDA

CHOSOKABE

HOJO

SHIMAZU

OTOMO

SAITO

ODA

IMAGAWA

N

Kawanakajima, on the borders of their domains, but neither side was able to deliver a fatal blow (see pages 172–178). After the death of Shingen his son Katsuyori succeeded to his domain and proved a powerful daimyo. In June 1575 he responded to Ashikaga Yoshiaki's call for the destruction of Nobunaga, and moved his army up to the Mikawa border where Tokugawa Ieyasu (the former Matsudaira Motoyasu) held land for Nobunaga. Ieyasu sent asking Nobunaga for reinforcements; and the armies met at the historic battle of Nagashino.

The battle of Nagashino

At first, the Takeda army attacked Nagashino Castle, which was stubbornly held by one of Ieyasu's retainers. Takeda could not take the fortress by siege, and soon a combined Oda-Tokugawa army approached. The allied army, encamped at Shitaragahara, did not try to attack Takeda Katsuyori's forces immediately, but began constructing field fortifications. Afraid of being attacked from the rear, and ignoring his old retainers' advice to withdraw, the outnumbered Takeda Katsuyori abandoned his attack on Nagashino Castle and moved his army to confront the allied forces at Shitaragahara.

Why is this battle so famous in Japanese history? How did the allied forces destroy the 'invincible' Takeda cavalry?

Did it happen as it was depicted in Kurosawa's famous film '*Kagemusha*'? Was the employment of arquebusiers behind palisades a new tactic? Historians of the Edo period often exaggerated the importance of the Tokugawa contingent in this battle to flatter the reigning Tokugawa shogunate; for that reason we should approach their accounts with some caution. Careful study of the contemporary document written by Nobunaga's retainer Ota Guichi paints a slightly different picture.

At Shitaragahara, where the Rengogawa brook passes between steep hills, the 15,000-strong Takeda army met the Oda-Tokugawa army of 30,000 men. At the time Takeda's army was mistakenly thought to be the stronger; so in spite of their actual numerical supremacy the Oda-Tokugawa army believed that they needed to fight from a defensive position. This was thoroughly prepared, with ditches and palisades defended by archers, spearmen with long lances, and arquebusiers.

It has formerly been claimed that the allies used 3,000 gunners at this battle, but recent study has revealed that the actual figure was less than 1,500. Indeed, the original document states that there were 1,000[1], and there is proof that someone later changed the number to 3,000. In any case, it is clear that massive and innovative employment of

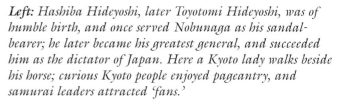

Left: Hashiba Hideyoshi, later Toyotomi Hideyoshi, was of humble birth, and once served Nobunaga as his sandal-bearer; he later became his greatest general, and succeeded him as the dictator of Japan. Here a Kyoto lady walks beside his horse; curious Kyoto people enjoyed pageantry, and samurai leaders attracted 'fans.'

Below left: Niwa Nagahide was aged thirty-four when he came to Kyoto. He wears a helmet imitating the shape of a Chinese Tang aristocrat's cap. The rich surcoat worn over armor was called a jinbaori.

Below: Oda Nobunaga's mon *or family emblem.*

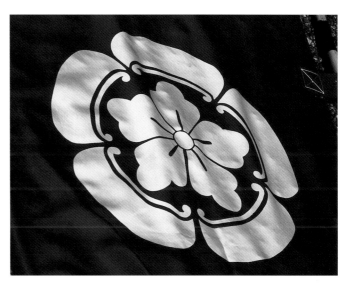

the arquebus was not the most important factor at Shitaragahara. Otomo Sorin in Kyushu had employed 2,000 guns in 1561; and Nobunaga himself, probably backed up by Saiga reinforcements, had 2,000 to 3,000 guns when he fought the Miyoshi clan in 1570. Of course, the Takeda army also possessed guns, but at Shitaragahara they were not used to give concentrated fire support.

Another myth is that the Takeda cavalry charged the allied position en masse, only to be shot to pieces and annihilated. In the late Heian and Kamakura periods mounted samurai with bows indeed formed the main body of armies; but the introduction of new fighting techniques had changed the way in which mounted soldiers deployed, precisely to avoid the guns. At the time of Shitaragahara the Japanese samurai dismounted to fight, supported by their retainers. The repeated cavalry charges as depicted in Kurosawa's 'Kagemusha' simply did not happen. At the very least we may be confident that after the first wave of the Takeda assault had failed, they would know that the muddy ground was unsuited for cavalry charges. Why, then, was the Takeda army defeated?

The topography of Shitaragahara is as follows: the brook passed north to south through a swampy basin. On each bank there was a narrow area of flat ground, with quite steep hills behind. On the west bank the allied forces had constructed

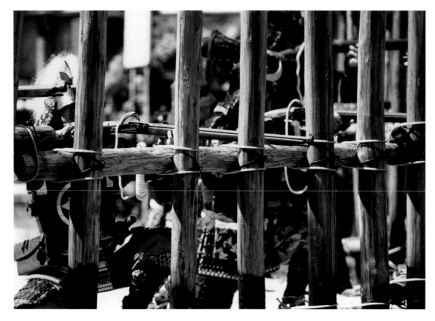

Left: Arquebus soldiers at the re-enactment of Shitaragahara. This kind of conventional palisade would not have stopped the attacks of the Takeda forces; it could be pulled down easily enough with ropes and grappling hooks.

Right: On a still day the blinding smoke of an arquebus salvo definitely hindered the next volley; before it cleared the enemy could have rushed the palisade. This is another reason to speculate that Shitaragahara was not a straightforward confrontation, with the Oda and Takeda armies lined up three deep and trading volleys. It is more likely that the Takeda assaults were rather sporadic, allowing the allied army to deal with them piecemeal. If Takeda had tried to overcome the defense line with one push by 10,000 men, it is unlikely that the allies could have won.

ODA NOBUNAGA'S CAMPAIGNS IN KINKI, 1570-80 AD

1573 Ichijogadani

1573 Otani Castle

1570 Amekawa

1576 Azuchi Castle

1571 Enryakuji Temple

Kyoto

Kiyosu

1571 Nagashima Ikki

(1575 Nagashino)

Advance to Kyoto 1568

1580 Ishiyama Honganji (Osaka)

1577 Sakai

N

three lines of field defenses—ditches, earthen walls thrown up from the soil, and timber palisades. The allied soldiers were strictly forbidden from coming out of this position to meet the Takeda troops. Excavation of this area has revealed that the allies had constructed their defenses on a fairly massive scale despite the short time available.

A composite force of allied soldiers armed with bows, matchlock guns and long spears awaited Takeda's charge. Takeda's first wave, consisting of men prepared to force paths through the defenses ('sappers'), was annihilated by salvos of arquebus fire while they were approaching the palisade over slippery, swampy ground. But the next wave reached the first palisade and managed to pull it down, only to be confronted with another ditch to cross. Attacks were made sporadically, probing forward piecemeal, perhaps using their own dead as fascines to bridge the ditch. Many more fell in attacks on the second palisade; and finally the exhausted survivors were called back and Takeda Katsuyori abandoned the assault. The myth of the invincible Takeda army was broken where they died in the ditches of Shitaragahara.

Why did Takeda Katsuyori order this charge into hell? Because the allied army threatened his rear and forced him to engage. Because Katsuyori was a young man, overconfident in his splendid army. Because the Takeda *ninja* scouts had all been killed by the allied troops before they could report the depth of the defensive position, and the mist of the rainy season obscured the view. Katsuyori should have avoided a frontal assault on such a well defended position. In that season he could have waited a

day or two for heavy rain, which would have neutralized the allies' firearms. Takeda's old vassals who had served his father Shingen all advised against accepting battle in such conditions, but Katsuyori would not listen to them. One general finally said, after the council of war, that he had no choice but to charge if so ordered.

What was the most important lesson of Nagashino? Nothing more revolutionary than that an outnumbered force cannot break into a well fortified and strongly defended position. Neither Oda Nobunaga, Toyotomi Hideyoshi, Tokugawa Ieyasu or Takeda Katsuyori ever mentioned any particularly effective use of arquebuses, because the deployment of concentrated firepower was nothing new in Japanese tactics.

The Ikko-ikki

Some historians refer to this battle as the turning point of Nobunaga's campaign of unification; but his real foe was soon revealed.

It is no exaggeration to claim that Nobunaga's most stubborn enemy was the Ikko-ikki. As mentioned above, this radical Buddhist religious sect was based at the Ishiyama Honganji, a strongly sited and fortified monastery-cum-castle at Osaka. Unlike other temples such as Enryakuji, Koyusan or Todaiji, Honganji had neither warrior monks of its own nor any special military organization. It depended on the fighting men among its many adherents, and when the sectarian leaders summoned them, samurai gathered from all over the provinces to protect the foundation.

The most famous painting of Shitaragahara (Nagashino): Tokugawa (Matsudaira) resists the Takeda attack with palisades and arquebusiers. The defenses shown here are, of course, greatly oversimplified; and the armor worn by the samurai is of the wrong period. (Osaka Castle Museum)

Nobunaga's confrontation with the Ikko-ikki was sparked by his challenge to their acquired right that no secular authority could intervene on their religious territory either economically or politically. In the course of his process of unification Nobunaga needed manpower to prosecute his wars, and that meant he needed the means to pay soldiers. Confiscating sect lands provided that means. The people who composed the Ikko-ikki movement included merchants and sea traders as well as local petty samurai, artisans and peasant farmers. The intelligence and ability of their leadership was impressive, otherwise they would have been unable to oppose the vastly superior military power of Nobunaga for ten years. Their main military asset was the group called Saiga-shu,[2] an arquebus force which could mobilize 2,000 gunners for battle. In 1563 these troops had obliged Tokugawa Ieyasu (Matsudaira) to retreat when he attacked the sect in Mikawa.

In 1576, when Nobunaga surrounded Ishiyama Honganji, his retainer Harada Naomasa was ambushed by Saiga arquebusiers and killed in the ensuing action. Finally, seeking to cut off the sect's most dangerous protectors at source, Nobunaga attacked the Saiga district in 1580. Even after two attempts with 60,000 soldiers he could not completely destroy this thorn in his flesh. After ten years' conflict and following mediation by the emperor, Ishiyama Honganji surrendered to Nobunaga and the sect withdrew to Saiga.

* * *

In 1576, Nobunaga started the construction of Azuchi Castle by Lake Biwa in Omi district, the largest lake in Japan, and gathered people to inhabit the surrounding town. He started resurveying land to calculate his taxes, since improvements in agricultural technology had increased the rice production upon which all such calculations were based. He abolished *Ichi* and *Za*, the exclusive rights to open markets, in order to weaken the economic base of the major temples and the aristocracy; he also abolished toll gates, and constructed new roads and bridges for convenience of transport and communication. His policies freed many petty samurai from their previous confinement on their farmland, and it became easier for him to mobilize men in the numbers he needed to sustain his large army.

Now that Nobunaga had secured his eastern flank, he started eliminating the possible threat from the Mori family in Chugoku. He entrusted this campaign to his general Hashiba (later Toyotomi) Hideyoshi, but it did not prosper, and Hideyoshi sent to request reinforcements. In 1582, Oda Nobunaga left Azuchi and marched into Kyoto on his way to join Hideyoshi's army. While he was staying at the Honnoji temple in Kyoto, one of his generals, Akechi Mitsuhide, conspired against him and killed him. Mitsuhide's reasons are obscure. Oda Nobunaga was a cold, merciless, calculating power-seeker; but he achieved extraordinary results in pursuit of his far-sighted vision, and in an age of treachery he attracted the lasting loyalty of two of the other most impressive leaders of his day—Toyotomi Hideyoshi and Tokugawa Ieyasu.

Trade and missionaries

A new wave from far away began to surge on Japan's coasts while the country's barons were struggling in their huge game of survival.

In 1517, during the Reformation in Europe, the Roman Catholic Church was looking not only to rebuild its influence in the Old World but also—in this age of great voyages of exploration—to extend it to the newly discovered lands far across the oceans. The Society of Jesus, founded in 1539, was very active in Asia, and ten years later its founder Francis Xavier was preaching in Japan. The Jesuits sent missionaries to Japan in Portuguese trading ships, and in time rival Spanish missionaries arrived from Manila. After the threat of piracy diminished, the Portuguese and Spanish established stronger trading contacts; the novelties that they brought into Kyushu were welcomed by the daimyos, who were soon competing to attract European ships into their ports. The most popular imports were gunpowder, silk, cotton, wool, glasswear and clocks; in return the Europeans bought Japanese silver and slaves. The latter trade was naturally something of a problem for the missionaries, but they were never so serious about stopping it that they would endanger their local rights to preach the gospel.

By 1555 the missionaries counted 1,500 Christian believers in Bungo, 500 at Hirato and 2,000 in Yamaguchi. Even some daimyos in Kyushu became converts, and not only for the sake of the precious gifts of the Portuguese. In the domain of Arima Harunobu there were some 60,000 believers, and soon they spread into Goto and Amakusa districts. Finally, missionaries were presented to Oda Nobunaga, and through Ohotomo in Chugoku they obtained permission to build a chapel in Azuchi Castle. Nobunaga's toleration of these contacts was entirely pragmatic, as a move in his strategic game against the Buddhist temples. Some Kyushu daimyos sent envoys to the Vatican; but by the time they returned from their long journeys they would find that the situation of Christians in Japan had changed. Hideyoshi was hostile to any foreign focus of loyalty, as later was Tokugawa, and under their regimes Japanese Christians enjoyed, at best, an uncertain and short-lived toleration.

The rise of Toyotomi Hideyoshi

Hideyoshi was born in the humblest circumstances in 1536, a son of Kinoshita Yaemon, an *ashigaru* gunner in the service of Oda Nobuhide, Nobunaga's father. The boy, whose name in youth was Tokichiro, ran away from home at an early age and lived as a drifter until the age of sixteen, when he became a servant of Oda Nobunaga. He did well, and rose in Nobunaga's service with astonishing speed. When Nobunaga destroyed Asai Nagamasa he gave the domain of Asai to his clever young retainer, who changed his name to Hashiba Chikuzen-no-kami Hideyoshi. As mentioned above, Nobunaga appointed him to command the force sent to suppress the Mori family in Chugoku; his request for reinforcement brought Nobunaga to Kyoto in 1582, where he was killed (or perhaps committed suicide when trapped in the burning temple).

As soon as Hideyoshi was informed of this incident, he concluded peace with the Mori without letting them know about Nobunaga's death, and returned to Kyoto to face Akechi Mitsuhide's army. Within two weeks he had defeated Mitsuhide at Yamazaki, and the latter was killed by a bandit

Takeda Katsuyori's forces attack Matsudaira's fortification. Although some of the Takeda troops were indeed mounted, their attack at Shitaragahara should not be misunderstood as resembling that of the French cavalry at Agincourt. (Osaka Castle Museum)

guerrilla during his retreat. Hideyoshi hosted Nobunaga's funeral rites, and ostensibly supported his infant grandson and heir, Samboshi. A senior general, Shibata Katsuie, opposed Hideyoshi and he supported Nobunaga's third son, Nobutaka. In 1583 their armies clashed at Shizugatake near Lake Biwa, and Katsuie was defeated. Katsuie fled to his own territory, where he committed suicide with his wife Oichi-no-kata, formerly the wife of Asai Nagamasa. After this battle all Nobunaga's other leading former generals became obedient to Hideyoshi—except Tokugawa Ieyasu.

Hideyoshi started constructing his own castle at the site of the former Ishiyama Honganji temple in Osaka. He invited merchants of Kyoto and Sakai to settle there, and created a great city. But Tokugawa Ieyasu in Gifu supported Nobunaga's second son, and started advancing on Kyoto. In 1584, Hideyoshi's army checked this movement at Nagakute. Initially the battle was favorable to Tokugawa, but its course soon reversed. Hideyoshi did not want to prolong this war, since he was eager to launch his planned invasion of Korea; and his policy was wherever possible to offer terms which bound former opponents to his cause rather than annihilating them. Ieyasu recognized that his long term advantage lay in allying himself with Hideyoshi's campaign of national unification. Peace terms were therefore concluded, and Tokugawa Ieyasu became Hideyoshi's subject.

The only great families still defying Hideyoshi in Honshu were the Hojo and Date; and beyond, the islands of Shikoku and Kyushu. In 1585, he united Shikoku and Kii after an easy operation; he was granted the ministerial title of *kanpaku* or 'regent' by the court, and took the name Toyotomi Hideyoshi (his humble birth made it impossible for him to be named shogun). A year later, in 1586, he became *daijodaijin*. Early in 1587 he successfully organized a campaign by some 250,000 troops against the Shimazu family in Kyushu—the largest military enterprise Japan had yet seen, which ended in a mass suicide when the Shimazu capital of Kagoshima fell to his army.

Next, in 1589, it was the turn of the Hojo of the Kanto Plain. They were completely outnumbered, and after a five-month siege of Odawara the Hojo leader Ujimasa committed suicide; his domain was given to Tokugawa Ieyasu. Either during or soon after the Odawara campaign the last independent daimyo, Date Masamune—the 'One-Eyed Dragon' in the far north from Tohoku—came in to render homage to Hideyoshi. By 1590 Toyotomi Hideyoshi had unified all of Japan under his sole authority.

(1) Fujimoto Masayuki

(2) 'Saiga people'

Top right: *Oda Nobunaga's camp; he is mounted on a white horse at far left. (Osaka Castle Museum)*

Right: Do maru *armor; originally it had a helmet,* sode *and* kote *but these have since been lost. Toyotomi Hideyoshi gave this armor to Wakizaka Yasuharu as a reward for his prowess in the battle of Shizugatake in 1583. Yasuharu later changed sides and joined Tokugawa Ieyasu during the battle of Sekigahara in 1600, helping to defeat the Toyotomi army.*

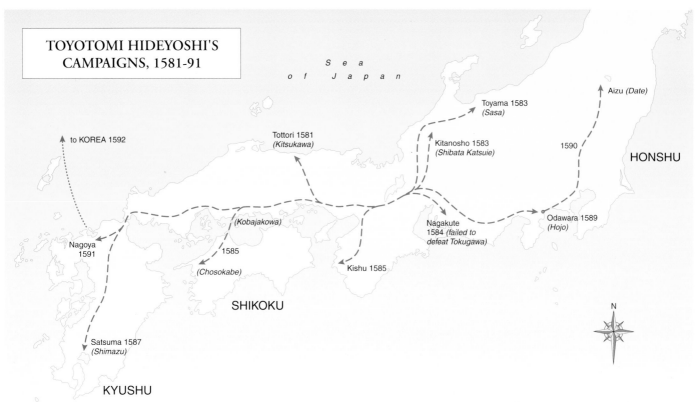

TOYOTOMI HIDEYOSHI'S
CAMPAIGNS, 1581-91

*Sea
of Japan*

to KOREA 1592

Tottori 1581
(Kitsukawa)

Toyama 1583
(Sasa)

Aizu *(Date)*

Kitanosho 1583
(Shibata Katsuie)

1590

HONSHU

(Kobajakowa)

Nagakute
1584 *(failed to
defeat Tokugawa)*

Odawara 1589
(Hojo)

Nagoya
1591

1585

(Chosokabe)

Kishu 1585

SHIKOKU

N

Satsuma 1587
(Shimazu)

KYUSHU

WEAPONS OF THE SAMURAI: THE SWORD

Elaborately decorated tsuba *sword guard. These are regarded as works of art and have become prized collectors' items. (Tokyo National Museum)*

Today the Japanese sword has become the symbol of the samurai spirit, and even during World War II Japanese officers preferred to carry it in battle. The *kamikaze* pilot carried his sword in the cockpit when he took off for his final mission. The graceful shape of the sword, and the extraordinarily sharp cutting edge, makes it a treasured collector's item over the world. There were many famous swordsmiths in Japan, who crafted blades of legendary quality and beauty; but the samurai of the age of battles was not excessively interested in the refinements of his sword. In battle it was considered to be a defensive weapon. Even a samurai wanted to kill his enemy while they were still as far apart as possible, using the bow or at least the lance.

Before the Heian period there were two types of sword: *tachi* and *tsurugi*. The former term probably came from the word *tatsu* or 'cut,' and the latter from *tsuranuku* or 'thrust.' The latter, influenced by the Chinese, had a straight, double-edged blade, while the *tachi* had a single edge. During the Heian period the *tachi* was given a slight curve from the root of the hilt for convenience on horseback. When samurai wearing *oyoroi* harness tried to use the sword from the saddle they could only cut at the enemy with diagonal blows; the *fukigaeshi* of the helmet hindered the use of the sword vertically. Even a man fighting on foot could only sweep the sword in transverse slashes. In either case, he could not normally either cut through his enemy's armor or deliver a fatal blow.

From the late Kamakura to the Muromachi period (14th century) the sword began to curve equally through the length of the blade. One reason was that samurai now began to grip it with both hands. A two-handed blow gave a stronger cut, and sometimes a skillful warrior managed to cut through his opponent's helmet. With the shift to a two-handed grip, and the change of armor style from *oyoroi* to

do maru, samurai began to use a large sword called the *nodachi* or 'field sword.' Introduced to the battlefield during the Nanbokucho period (1336-92), it was longer than the samurai's height. It gave the opportunity to deliver fatal blows in single combat, and was also effective when defending against a cavalry charge by sweeping at the legs of the horses. Such a long blade naturally could not be drawn from the scabbard by the samurai alone; a retainer carried it for him, and held the scabbard when his master wanted to draw it.

Meanwhile, Japanese swordsmiths had perfected a special method of forging blades which were sharp but not brittle. They enveloped the softer iron of the core with harder iron around the edge, and forged it together by heating, folding, hammering and quenching the blade many times. This process hardened the edge to a sharpness beyond that of modern steel, while preserving a certain elasticity in the blade as a whole so that it flexed under impact rather than shattering. The repeated folding could also produce complex and beautiful patterns in the surface of the polished blade.

Above: Early Kamakura
period sword. The tachi *was wielded with one hand, and while
the blade has a slight curve, that of the hilt is more noticeable.
The design was influenced by the sword of an earlier period
called a* warabite katana. *(Tokyo National Museum)*

Below: Another tachi *hilt,
covered with sharkskin, and attached to the tang of the blade by
a pin called the* menuki. *It is decorated with small birds. The
hangers of brazed wire are termed* Hyogo kusari, *after the
name of the official arsenal. (Tokyo National Museum)*

Above: *In the 14th century Nanbokucho period swords
became sturdier, because samurai began to fight mostly on
foot. This example is lacquered black from the hilt to the
scabbard, the latter with diagonal gold paint bands.
(Tokyo National Museum)*

Below: Tachi *with black lacquered scabbard, the hilt bound
with braid which extends over the upper part of the scabbard.
(Tokyo National Museum)*

Above: Uchigatana *with black lacquered scabbard. This was carried by thrusting it into the* obi *or sash, so unlike the* tachi *it was worn with the blade edge up and the point curving down.*

Below: *Another* tachi, *with a brown lacquered scabbard with gilt mounts. (Tokyo National Museum)*

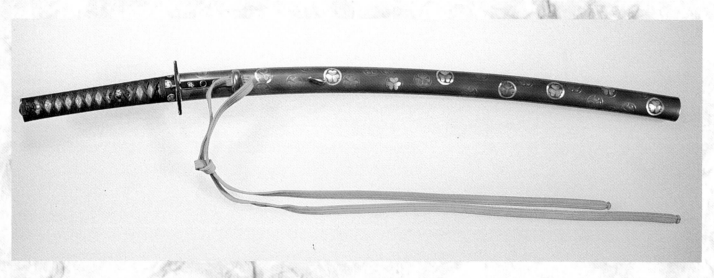

Above: Uchigatana, *its scabbard painted with* aoi— *Tokugawa emblems. (Tokyo National Museum)*

Below: *Dai-sho sonae or 'large and small equipment'—a long and short sword (*katana *and* wakizashi*) attributed to Toyotomi Hideyoshi, and certainly colorful enough for that general's flamboyant taste. (Tokyo National Museum)*

HANDLING THE ARQUEBUS

The reloading sequence for a short Japanese-made matchlock arquebus of the Sengoku period:

After firing, remove the smoldering slowmatch from the cock and keep it wrapped around the left hand, out of the way while handling powder. (The matchcord was made from cedar bark fibre, which contains natural oil and is not easily extinguished.)

1: Load the powder charge and ball into the muzzle.

2: Ram the powder and ball home with the ramrod.

3: Open the cover of the priming pan.

4: Pour priming powder into the pan.

*5: Close the pan cover, and blow excess powder off to prevent
accidental detonation when the glowing match is re-attached.*

6: Blow the end of the match to a lively glow.

7: *Attach the match between the sprung jaws of the cock, with its lighted end above the priming pan.*

8: *Take first aim. Note that this* ashigaru *has a short sword stuck under his sash, blade edge upwards. Unlike samurai gunners,* ashigaru *hardly ever carried full length swords; the former carried them blade edge down.*

9: *Open the pan cover.*

10: *The arquebus is now ready to shoot; pressure on the button trigger releases the cock to swing down and press the glowing end of the match into the priming powder.*

CHAPTER 10:
THE REIGN OF HIDEYOSHI

Toyotomi Hideyoshi. In 1585 he was given the aristocratic position of kanpaku *and could thus be admitted into the imperial ministry. By nerve and skill he had climbed from the* ashigaru *class to the highest level of Japanese society. (Osaka Castle Museum)*

Hideyoshi had started his great land survey—*kenchi*—the year after Nobunaga's death. He standardized the method of measurement, and registered the cultivated land according to the amount of rice it produced. Every daimyo was assessed in numbers of *koku* (equal to about five bushels of rice), and had to provide the appropriate numbers of soldiers when summoned for service. This was the basis of the mobilizations for the pacification of Kyushu in 1587 and the invasion of Korea in 1592.

While the basic purpose of the survey was to assess the farmers for taxation and to make it easy to collect their dues, the centralization did at least free them from the multiple demands of the temples, shrines and aristocracy which had plagued them during the Muromachi period. At the same time the new system bound farmers to their land. In 1588 Hideyoshi issued a law to disarm the urban and rural population and to fix their places of residence. This was not

the first time such a decree had been issued: Nobunaga had ordered the disarmament of the people of Echizen and Kii when he defeated the Ikko-ikki in those areas. Another law of 1590 prohibited movement by individuals between classes. Until then social mobility had been relatively free and unhindered by legal prohibitions; but henceforth samurai were forbidden from changing their profession. The enforcement of this policy was given point by Hideyoshi's planned invasion of Korea, for which huge enterprise he needed easy mobilization of manpower and logistical support. Though the invasion of Korea would prove fatal to Hideyoshi's prestige, it would strengthen the feudal system he installed in Japan.

At first Hideyoshi followed Nobunaga's foreign policy; but when he sent his army to Kyushu to conquer the Shimazu he learned that Nagasaki had been registered at the Vatican as a colony by Roman Catholic missionaries, and that many poor Japanese had been sold into Southeast

Right: A samurai leader of the Maeda family with his horse standard. Maeda Toshiie became a retainer of Nobunaga at the age of only 14, and won renown by his skill with the lance. He later became a vassal of Hideyoshi. After Hideyoshi's death he supported Hideyoshi's son Hideyori, but Hideyori's death and that of his infant son at Osaka in 1615 marked the final fall of the Toyotomi family.

Below right: During Hideyoshi's expedition to Korea, massed use of the arquebus brought early dominance over the Korean forces. However, the Koreans soon deployed ship-mounted artillery, and easily won naval supremacy on the Japanese supply routes across the sea.

Asia as slaves by European traders. Consequently he ordered the expulsion of missionaries from Japan; but he allowed trading with the Portuguese to continue. Hideyoshi did not interfere with the Japanese Christian converts, however, since many influential daimyos in Kyushu had accepted conversion to the new faith.

The Korean adventure

It is difficult to know at what point Hideyoshi conceived his dreams of conquest in China. It may be speculated that when he made his compromise agreement with Tokugawa Ieyasu after the battle of Nagakute, he was already anxious to prepare for this next ambitious campaign. For his day and his background, Hideyoshi's world view was a good deal more developed than that of his contemporaries, to whom 'the world' did not stretch far beyond their own provinces. When he was a retainer of Oda Nobunaga, Hideyoshi used to attend meetings between his master and European missionaries. Nobunaga was fond of listening to missionaries explaining the wider world, using a globe which they presented to him. It is possible to say that it was these missionaries who stimulated the young Hideyoshi's megalomaniac ambition.

Another factor which forced Hideyoshi into war overseas was simply the end of his wars in Japan. After more than a century of intermittent but basically continuous warfare, Japan, though now unified under his authority, had no living memory of anything other than a 'war society.' Huge numbers of samurai and *ashigaru* were waiting for the next campaign, on which they depended for subsistence. This great accumulation of bellicose energy had to find some outlet; not only Hideyoshi, but many other Japanese wanted another war, and for him that could only mean a war on foreign soil. Hideyoshi built many temples and castles, not only to gratify his own showy tastes but also for reasons of social control. Nevertheless, in the short term there was no hope of changing the whole structure and character of society. It was brutalized and explosive, and it depended on the acquisition of wealth through conquest or a conqueror's gift. It was inevitable that Hideyoshi should start another war.[1]

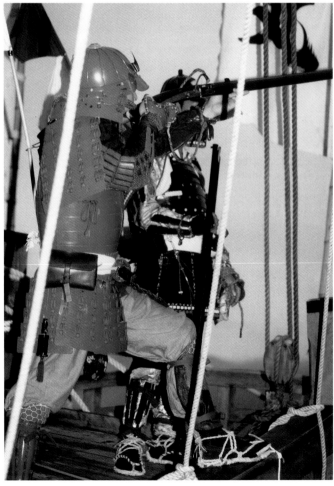

In 1587, Hideyoshi had ordered the So family in Tsushima to send messengers to Korea. Over the following years there were a number of exchanges, in which Hideyoshi made clear his intention of using Korea as his road to Ming China. The Koreans replied defiantly, giving him his pretext for an expeditionary force. The invasion of Korea was intended as a preliminary step which would bring him a secure base and a source of supplies on the Asian mainland. In accordance with this defective strategy, only five months' rations would accompany the expedition and the invasion force, and inadequate preparations were made for its longer term resupply by sea from Japan.

The expedition was launched in May 1592, and some 160,000 soldiers were landed at Pusan under the command of Konishi Yukinaga, Kato Kiyomasa, Kuroda Nagamasa, Kobayakawa Takakage and Mori Terumoto. There was no unified command, and each division operated independently (and in competition—particularly those of the Christian Konishi and the Buddhist Kato). The Korean forces were no match for samurai and foot soldiers practiced and hardened by a lifetime of Japanese internal wars. Seoul soon fell to Konishi Yukinaga's division, and in July they reached and took Pyongyang. Kato Kiyomasa's troops pushed north-eastward, taking Woosan and moving towards the Tumen River and the Manchurian border. Konishi Yukinaga stayed in the west, awaiting major reinforcements which would enable the

Above: A night battle at sea.

Below: This helmet of the Momoyama period, 1580s-1600, is associated with a surviving do maru. It is basically a zunari construction, a simplified bowl built up from only three plates. On top of this the shape of a samurai's eboshi cap has been created from paper coated with silver leaf. The shikoro is of iyo sane construction, i.e. using fewer and larger plates, and is covered with peacock feathers. In its day this would have been regarded as very modern indeed. (Itsukushima Shrine)

A very striking 'modern' armor attributed to Kato Kiyomasa, one of Hideyoshi's divisional commanders in the 1592 Korean campaign. The helmet is covered with bearskin, not only for ornament but also to protect it from direct sunlight and rain. The cuirass, whose overall outline is of European style, is made from a combination of laced sane and a muscle-embossed metal plate.

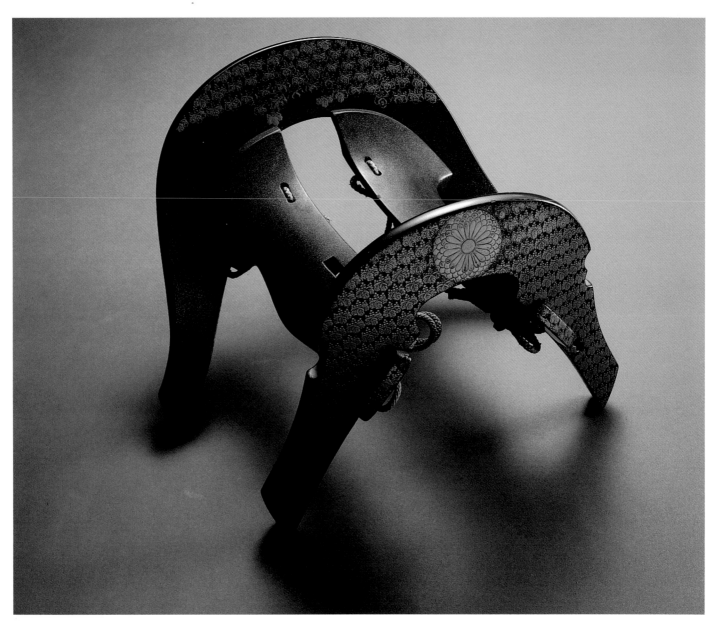

expedition to advance the last 80 miles to the Yalu River and into China.

Although the Korean army was inferior to the Japanese, their navy was far more advanced, both technically and tactically. Admiral Yi Sun Sin soon won control of the seas around Korea, and cut off the expeditionary force both from its expected reinforcements and from resupply. As autumn turned into the bitterly cold Korean winter the Japanese—unable to gather enough provisions locally, as they had intended—began to suffer seriously from hunger and sickness. Gradually, the Korean people organized themselves into a volunteer guerrilla army, and their growing resistance began to take a serious toll of the invaders. A modest Chinese attempt on Pyongyang failed, but they learned from their errors; and in February 1593 the city was recaptured by strong Ming forces. The Japanese fell back towards Seoul, and repulsed the pursuing Chinese at the battle of nearby Pyok-je-yek. A stalemate now set in; increasing Korean guerrilla activity led to an extremely

Above: Saddle with decoration of gold lacquer chrysanthemum and paulownia blossoms, attributed to Hideyoshi.(Osaka Castle Museum)

Below: Fan with the crest of a paulownia— the flower of the Chinese 'goddess tree'— attributed to Hideyoshi. (Osaka Castle Museum)

harsh Japanese response, but these massacres of civilians only provoked further Korean resistance.

It is interesting to note that during the war Japanese forces drafted huge numbers of porters and laborers from Japan to support the army in the field. At the same time, however, they took many Korean prisoners whom they sent back to Japan. These were skilled workers in ceramics, paper, silk and print manufacture, who were responsible for the later development of Japanese local craft industries.

Peace negotiations dragged on while the Japanese settled down in their camps and fortresses in south Korea. After three years of futile talk, the Ming sent Hideyoshi a letter which offered nothing better than recognizing him as 'king of Japan.' Outraged, in 1597 he shipped another 140,000 men to Korea, but despite a number of bloody battles they were no more successful than the first expedition. In September 1598 Hideyoshi died of illness at Fushimi Castle; and based on his dying wish, Japanese forces soon began to withdraw from Korea. The Satsuma force from Kyushu under Shimazu Yoshihiro defeated the pursuing enemy at Sach'ong, but a peace was soon concluded and the whole army withdrew to Japan by the end of the year (Admiral Yi Sun Sin was killed in one of the last sea fights).

The seven years of war left Korea devastated, and partly occupied by Ming garrisons; but it was also damaging to the legacy of Japan's ruler. During the course of the war many daimyos had—not surprisingly—found reason to quarrel with one another. This left ominous rifts among the Toyotomi vassals, at a time when Hideyoshi's inheritance passed perilously to a five-year-old son.

(1) Fujiki Hisashi: *Zouhyo tachi no senjo*

Above left & right: *This style, one of the more striking examples of the radical diversity of armor typical of the Momoyama period in the late 16th century, is variously know as* nioh do, *'devil's cuirass'; or* abara do, *'rib cuirass,' recalling the starving Buddha. Painted with red lacquer, it bears on the back plate a gold character meaning 'heart.' (Tokyo National Museum)*

WOMEN IN SAMURAI SOCIETY

*Shizuka-gozen, mistress of the legendary Minamoto Yoshitsune in the late 12th century. She was an entertainer—*shirabyoshi—*in Kyoto. When Yoshitsune escaped to Yoshino from his brother Yoritomo's pursuit, she followed him. She was captured there, sent to Kamakura, and taken before Yoritomo and many other samurai leaders. They demanded that she entertain them; unafraid, she sang and danced an impromptu celebration of her love for Yoshitsune.*

During the Heian period women played a key role in the relationships between aristocratic families. A daughter owed undiminished respect to her parents even after marriage, and through a married daughter her family could often exert influence with her husband's family. In this society a widow could inherit her husband's estates and wealth. During the Kamakura period (12th-14th centuries) a woman of the samurai class could go to court to claim or protect her rights of inheritance. Such rights extended to include the widows of *gokenin* vassals of the regime. Under the Kamakura bakufu there was an office which judged disputes over such matters (*monchujo*). During the course of the Hojo regency (1210-1333) the government strengthened its control over the *gokenin*, and women's rights were relatively weakened. Even so, many women visited Kamakura from all over the country to pursue lawsuits; they were attended on such dangerous journeys by escorts of retainers and servants. Some women were very active in the defense of their inherited estates, standing at the head of bodies of armed retainers.

Some religious shrines had women priestesses especially in northern Kyushu. In ancient times, when supernatural beliefs were strong, the people worshiped many goddesses, as in the classical Greek world; consequently, female high priestesses presided over their rites. Such figures could still be found as late as the Muromachi period of the 14th-16th centuries. For this reason some researchers assume that throughout history the northern region of Japan was characterized by a patriarchal society while the south was matriarchal. It is of interest to note that southern Japan developed first into an agricultural society through rice production, while the northern part long remained a hunting society. It was when the 'agricultural south' gradually extended its authority over the 'hunting north'

Momoyama period, c.1600; handmaidens of Yodogimi, Oda Nobunaga's niece and Toyotomi Hideyori's mother. They wear the kosode *or narrow-sleeved* kimono.

that the confrontations between the Kyoto government and the *emishi* occurred.

It is not surprising that a multi-layered society in a process of change threw up examples of strong and determined women obtaining and wielding power. After the death of Minamoto Yoritomo, his widow Masako established a power base within the bakufu with the help of her father Hojo Tokimasa. Her power in fact far exceeded that of her father because of her position as widow of the shogun and mother of his son. In the Muromachi period the neglectful shogun Ashikaga Yoshimasa's wife Hino Tomiko became the richest and most influential woman in Japan.

Apart from the women of the aristocratic classes, those at humbler levels of society—farmers, artisans, newly emerging merchants and moneylenders—were far from powerless. However, in the war-torn Sengoku period of the late 15th to mid-16th centuries, when military strength alone decided the fate of provinces, women gradually lost their power as rulers. The last powerful woman was Yodogimi, the Toyotomi matriarch, who committed suicide when Osaka Castle fell to Tokugawa Ieyasu in 1615.

During the long peace of the Edo period, women's position in samurai society was held in low regard in accordance with the teachings of Confucianism. However intelligent and wise in the ways of society, they could never be acknowledged as anything but the subservient sex. Confucian beliefs ensured that women's position remained inferior after the 19th century Meiji imperial restoration. It has taken a long time to restore women's position in Japanese society, and the basically feudal ideas of the distant past were only overturned as part of the drastic changes introduced by America after World War II. Today women's rights are championed by an active movement for reform.

CHAPTER 11:

SEKIGAHARA —
A DECISIVE BATTLE ?

Right: *Shimazu cavalry at the battle of Sekigahara. Shimazu Yoshihiro's grudge against Ishida Mitsunari made him an unwilling ally. His last charge into the Tokugawa centre in wedge formation, which only he and a handful of his men survived to return to Kyushu, made him famous; but to the Mitsunari army, Shimazu's defensive inactivity up to that late point was little better than treachery.*

Below: *As a battle started the first samurai who attacked the enemy line was praised as* ichiban yari *or 'first lance.' However, the samurai who brought up the rear to hold back a pursuing enemy, or stayed back to help a wounded comrade, were even more highly regarded. In a hard-pressed retreat the wounded were often abandoned—or killed, to avoid their hindering their companions' flight, by those who pretended to be trying to save them. In such an environment those who genuinely risked themselves for their injured friends were greatly admired. (SY)*

When Toyotomi Hideyoshi unified Japan in 1590 he appointed five magistrates to govern the country: Ishida Mitsunari, Mashita Nagamori, Asano Nagamasa, Maeda Gen-i, and Nagatsuka Masaie. Later he appointed five regents from among the most powerful daimyos to secure the future of his heir; these were Tokugawa Ieyasu, Maeda Toshiie, Ukita Hideie, Mori Terumoto and Uesugi Kagekatsu. This policy was based on a fragile balance of power, however, and it was impossible to expect that it would achieve long term stability.

In practice, two factions were apparent among the Toyotomi vassals. One consisted of generals who had distinguished themselves in Hideyoshi's service during his long wars; the others were essentially military bureaucrats who had supported Hideyoshi's regime as administrators. The leader of the latter group—and the foremost among his vassals while Hideyoshi lived—was Ishida Mitsunari. Originally born of a petty daimyo family, he had risen to become Hideyoshi's most powerful official through his brilliant administrative talents.

After Hideyoshi's death a simmering hostility came to the surface, between Ishida Mitsunari on the one hand and military vassals such as Kato Kiyomasa, Fukushima Masanori and Asano Yukinaga on the other. These soldiers detested Ishida Mitsunari because he protected his son-in-law Fukuhara Nagataka, who had been a military inspector during the war in Korea. Nagataka had assessed as cowardly the behavior of Kato Kiyomasa and Asano Yukinaga after an action at Chinju, on the grounds that they did not pursue the Korean troops immediately after the victory. As a result of Nagataka's report to Hideyoshi many military vassals were reprimanded and some lost their domains.

and shut himself up there to brood over his future plans.

The quarrel between Hideyoshi's widow Kita-no-mandokoro and his mistress Yodogimi also became open after the dictator's death. Yodogimi was a daughter of Oichi-no-kata, Oda Nobunaga's sister, and was the mother of Hideyoshi's infant son Hideyori. Yodogimi flaunted her pride in being the niece of Nobunaga, and was used to being indulged. By contrast the widow Kita-no-mandokoro was born of petty samurai stock, and had shared the life of the equally low born Hideyoshi in his hard early years, taking care of the young man's first retainers. It was no wonder that many of his military vassals supported his widow after Hideyoshi's death, while the bureaucratic group, feeling no such loyalty, gathered around the mother of the child heir Hideyori.

These tensions provided sufficient opportunities for Tokugawa Ieyasu to destroy the unity of Hideyoshi's vassals. After Hideyoshi's death Ieyasu was regarded as the senior regent, but was still only one among a number of powerful vassals. The ambitious and intelligent Ieyasu worked vigorously to divide these vassals into two factions, with the initial aim of getting rid of his versatile opponent Ishida Mitsunari.

After Hideyoshi's death one of the regents, Uesugi Kagekatsu, returned from Osaka to his domain at Aizu and prepared for what he saw as the inevitable struggle between the supporters of the Toyotomi heir and Tokugawa Ieyasu's family. Without the permission of Ieyasu, the senior regent, he recruited masterless samurai (*ronin*), collected weapons,

In 1599 this bitter resentment prompted Kato Kiyomasa, Fukushima Masanori and Asano Yukinaga to attack Ishida Mitsunari at Osaka Castle. But Mitsunari escaped and took refuge in a house at Fushimi Castle, in which Tokugawa Ieyasu lived. This was Ieyasu's chance to destroy Ishida, who had been consistently hostile to him; but—ever patient—he did not take it. By Ieyasu's intervention Mitsunari was able to return to his own castle at Sawayama,

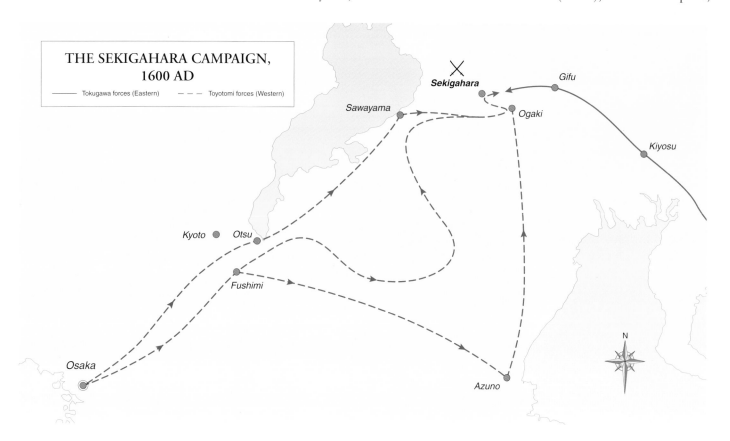

THE SEKIGAHARA CAMPAIGN,
1600 AD

—— Tokugawa forces (Eastern)   — — — Toyotomi forces (Western)

Opposite: The place where Tokugawa Ieyasu viewed the severed enemy heads after the battle of Sekigahara; and an artist's impression of the scene.

Right: Armor of Sanada Yukimura. He defended Ueda Castle when Tokugawa Hidetada was trying to march his force to Sekigahara, and by his skillful delaying action prevented Hidetada from joining his father Ieyasu in time to take part in the battle. The ladder design on his cuirass signifies a step up the ladder of promotion. He would be prominent at Osaka in 1614-15, but would not survive the final battle there. (SY)

assembled food and supplies, and strengthened his fortress. His domain lay north of Edo, Tokugawa's capital, and if Uesugi Kagekatsu revolted against Tokugawa the latter would have to fight on several fronts. Ieyasu was so threatened by Kagekatsu's moves that he ordered all the daimyos to send troops against him, on the grounds that he had disobeyed the authority of the senior regent. Ieyasu's orders had the same weight as Hideyoshi's, and even Hideyoshi's vassals responded to his call and tried to join him. Ieyasu was skilled at commanding men's loyalty, and was popular among the other daimyos. It is not certain whether Uesugi Kagekatsu was acting in support of Ishida Mitsunari or simply wanted to enlarge his domain during the coming struggle. Whatever his motives, a punitive force departed Osaka on June 16, 1600.

It was obvious to everyone that if Ieyasu left Osaka, Mitsunari would rise up against him. But Ieyasu wanted to draw any conspiracy against him out into the open where he could identify his enemies and destroy them. Furthermore, he hoped that many of the daimyos serving with the punitive force—even Hideyoshi family loyalists sympathetic to the heir's party—might follow him once he was confronted openly by Mitsunari.

Ishida Mitsunari's conspiracy

As Ieyasu anticipated, from Sawayama Castle Mitsunari called on many pro-Toyotomi daimyos to revolt against Ieyasu. Mitsunari's plan was to elect Mori Terumoto as the chief commander, and invite him to install himself at Osaka Castle; to send a letter of support to Uesugi Kagekatsu; and to invite Otani Yoshitsugu to join their cause. The father of Otani Yoshitsugu, born in Kyushu, had served the daimyo

Otomo Sorin; but after Sorin's defeat by the Shimazu he became a *ronin*, wandering through many provinces with his family. When Yoshitsugu was sixteen he became acquainted with Ishida Mitsunari, and entered the service of Hideyoshi. Yoshitsugu was leading a force to join Ieyasu's punitive expedition against Uesugi Kagakatsu; as he passed through Sawayama, Mitsunari invited him to his castle and asked him to join the anti-Tokugawa group. At first Yoshitsugu tried to persuade Mitsunari to abandon his revolt against Ieyasu; but when this proved fruitless he finally agreed to join him.

Yoshitsugu and Mitsunari were close friends, and this bond had been cemented by one bizarre incident in particular. Yoshitsugu had long been afflicted by leprosy; and once, when he was taking part in the tea ceremony in Hideyoshi's presence during an aggravated episode of this disease, discharge had fallen from his nose into the teacup. Guests at the tea ceremony drank from the same cup, passing it one to another but turning it to avoid contact with the same part of the rim; and Yoshitsugu was so paralyzed with embarrassment that he could not pass the fouled cup to his neighbor. Seeing his plight, Mitsunari approached Yoshitsugu and took the cup, saying that though it was not his turn he could not resist drinking because he was very thirsty. Yoshitsugu never forgot this gesture; and now he made up his mind that it was time for him to fight to the death for the sake of old friendship.

In fact, if the daimyos who agreed to support him had acted according to his plan then Mitsunari's attempt was not a desperate risk. Before the two sides met in battle Mitsunari and Ieyasu both sent letters and messengers to many commanders, trying to enlist their aid or identify their intentions; but neither could be sure who would support or betray them.

The advancing Tokugawa forces divided in two. The main army, led by Ieyasu's son Hidetada, marched on the Nakasendo road to reach Osaka, but was obstructed by the Sanada family at Ueda (Nagano). The skillful defensive tactics of Sanada Yukimura considerably delayed this force, preventing it from taking part in the forthcoming battle at Sekigahara. Ieyasu's other force took the Tokaido road— the southern route; this army was strengthened by many ex-Toyotomi daimyos who had declared against Mitsunari,

Ishida Mitsunari in his camp, at the 400th anniversary festival of Sekigahara in the year 2000.

Ii Naomasa, Tokugawa Ieyasu's great retainer who was seriously wounded at the battle of Sekigahara.

such as Fukushima Masanori, Todo Takatora and Ikeda Terumasa. Ieyasu's fear of treachery among his coalition kept him in his base at Edo which he was unwilling to leave. The vanguard daimyo, assembled at Kiyosu Castle, were mainly former Hideyoshi commanders; and they became unsettled at Ieyasu's delayed departure. Finally, they received a message from him saying that he would not leave before they had proved their commitment in battle. They immediately hurried to the Toyotomi-held Gifu Castle, and defeated Oda Hidenobu. As soon as Ieyasu learned of this he started his own advance towards Osaka on 1 September 1600.

The main body of Tokugawa forces was still blocked at Ueda, however, and initially Ieyasu hesitated to march straight for Osaka to attack Mitsunari's army before his son could join him. Nevertheless, at a council of war he allowed himself to be persuaded to advance by his vassal Ii Naomasa as soon as possible.

On 9 September, Mitsunari left Ogaki Castle for Sekigahara to block Ieyasu's direct advance on Sawayama

Castle. Sekigahara is surrounded by mountains: Mts. Momokubari and Nangu to the east, Mt. Matsuo to the south and Mt. Tengu to the west. The Nakasendo road passes through it from east to west beside the Fuji River, from Ise towards Kyoto and Osaka. Mitsunari's force encamped west of Sekigahara to block the road to Osaka. His ally Kobayakawa Hideaki's troops camped on the top of Mt. Matsuo, situated south of the road; and the troops of Mori Hidemoto, Ankokuji Eiki, Nagatsuka Masaie, Kikkawa Hiroie and Chosokabe Morichika stretched eastwards from there along the high ground south of the road. Ieyasu's forces arrived from the east, passing the Kobayakawa and Mori positions on their left and confronting Mitsunari's main force, drawn up west of the town, face to face. The soldiers of both sides were wet and tired from marching in bad weather. If the Kobayakawa and Mori troops played their part for Mitsunari, however, then Ieyasu's maneuver should be doomed; he had apparently thrust his head through a door which the enemy could slam shut at any moment.

The battle of Sekigahara

Unlike Hideyoshi, Ieyasu was a good field general and did not like siege warfare. That was the reason why he decided to bypass Ogaki Castle and lure out Mitsunari's forces by showing them his direct advance on Osaka.

In Japan, the first samurai who charged the enemy in battle was honored. This honor at Sekigahara went to Ieyasu's fourth son Matsudaira Tadayoshi, age twenty-one. Ieyasu wanted the ex-Toyotomi generals on his side to acknowledge that this was a war between the Toyotomi and the Tokugawa.

It had rained the previous day, and the fields were muddy. In the thick early morning mist of 15 September 1600, some 30 mounted soldiers led by Matsudaira Tadayoshi and Ii Naomasa passed forward through the position of their ally Fukushima Masanori, which formed the left wing of the Tokugawa (Eastern) army. Tadayoshi made a diversion to the left and made contact with Ukita Hideie's force of the Toyotomi (Western) army. Accordingly, 800 arquebusiers of Fukushima Masanori's force began to advance on Ukita Hideie, and opened fire.

The left wing of the Eastern army, made up of Todo, Kyogoku and Terasawa troops, clashed with the Otani forces who defended the right wing of the Western army. Matsudaira's and Ii's troops changed direction and attacked the Shimazu forces in the Western center. In the thick mist it was difficult to distinguish the course of events from Ieyasu's camp, and he had to send his messengers to each of the Eastern units. Mitsunari's own division of the Western army, on the left, were attacked by Kuroda, Takenaka and Hosokawa troops. His vanguard was by-passed and attacked from the flank by arquebusiers and one of his generals, Shima Katsutake (Sakon), was wounded; but his unit was equipped with several cannons, and managed to repel this attack. On Ieyasu's left Fukushima Masanori's force was counterattacked by Akashi Teruzumi and driven back; the enraged Masanori charged Akashi, but was again repulsed.

During the morning the battle seemed to favor Ieyasu's Eastern army; but the Westerners stood firm, and it settled into a bloody stalemate. At about mid-day Mitsunari believed that his moment had come to launch the Western army in an all-out assault. He signalled Kobayakawa, on the high ground above the Tokugawa left flank, and Mori, in the rear of Tokugawa, to close the trap. But they never moved from their positions.

Kobayakawa Hideaki was a nephew of Hideyoshi's widow Kita-no-mandokoro; at one time he was raised as a son to Hideyoshi, since Hideyoshi then had no son of his own. Although Kobayakawa was neither intelligent nor brave, Hideyoshi still cared for him like a real son. Once Hideyoshi's son Hideyori was born, however, Hideaki was adopted by the Kobayakawa family. After his father-in-law's death Hideaki succeeded to his domain. During the Korean campaign he was accused of leading his troops badly and expelled to Fukui. But Tokugawa Ieyasu saved him after Hideyoshi's death, and restored Hideaki to his former *(continued on page 110)*

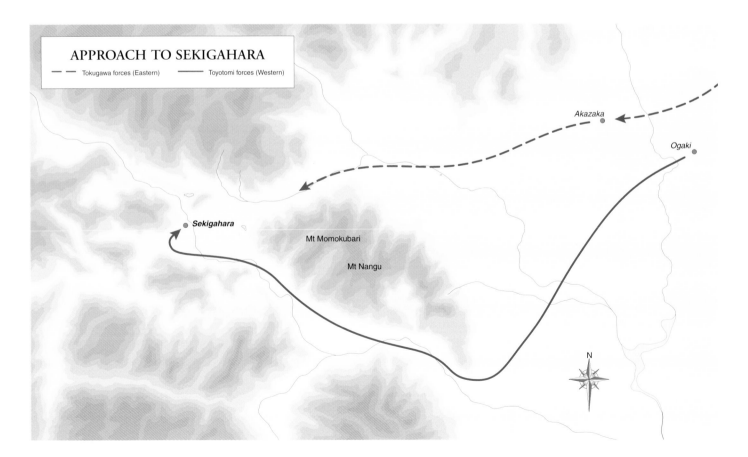

APPROACH TO SEKIGAHARA

– – – Tokugawa forces (Eastern) ——— Toyotomi forces (Western)

Akazaka

Ogaki

Sekigahara

Mt Momokubari

Mt Nangu

N

FLAGS OF FAMILY CONTINGENTS IN THE SEKIGAHARA CAMPAIGN

A: *Ukita Hideie, in front of his flag; West*

B: *Oda Nagamasu (Yuraku); East*

C: *Maeda Toshiie; East, but not present at Sekigahara*

D: *Yoshida Katsushige; East*

E: *Nambu Toshinao; East, but not present at Sekigahara*

F: *Yamanouchi Kazutoyo; East*

G: *Arima Toyouji; East*

A

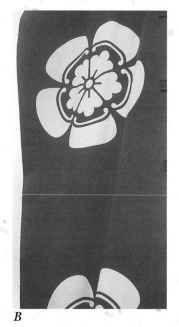

B

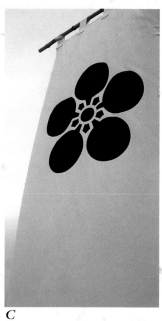

C

D

E

F

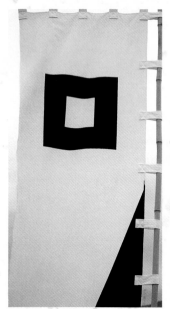

G

H: *Asano Yukinaga; East*

I: *Honda Tadakatsu; East*

J: *Asano Yukinaga; East*

K: *Tanaka Yoshimasa; East*

L: *Ikoma Kazumasa; East*

M: *Terasawa Hirotaka; East*

N: *Kyogoku Takatomo; East*

H

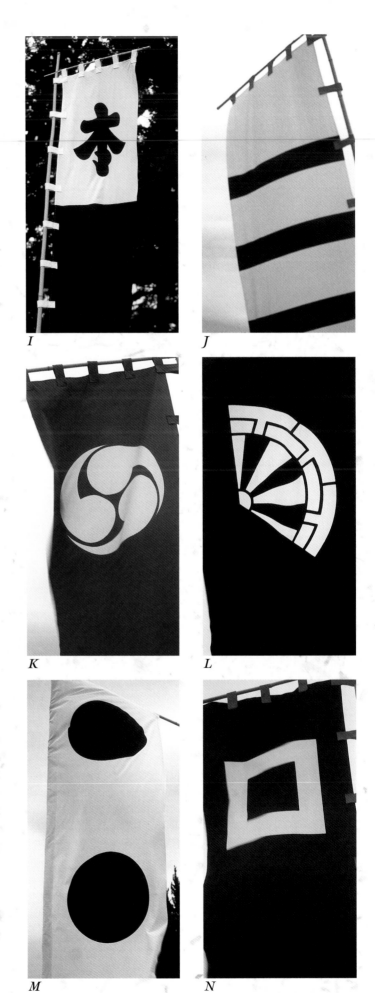

O: Akazawa Kazuyasu; West, changed to East

P: Wakizaka Yasuharu; West, changed to East

Q: Kuchiki Mototsuna; West, changed to East

R: Ishida Mitsunari; West

S: Ogawa Hirotada; West, changed to East

T: Kobayakawa Hideaki; West, changed to East

U: Shimazu Yoshihiro; West

V: *Hiratsuka Tamehiro; West*

W: *Ikeda Terumasa; East*

X: *Tokugawa Ieyasu's message riders*

Υ: *Ukita Hideie; West*

W

V

X

Υ

Left: Yoshida Shigekatsu.

Opposite: Shimazu Toyohisa.

Mitsunari's own division on the Western left wing. Finally, the Western army broke up and began to flee the field. Mitsunari's friend, the leper Otani Yoshitsugu, had fought faithfully; now he committed suicide. He ordered his retainers to bury his disfigured head on the battlefield so that it could not be taken as a trophy.

Before the campaign the sixty-six-year-old Shimazu Yoshihiro had at first tried to join the Tokugawa side, sending a message to that effect to Torii Mototada, a samurai of Ieyasu's old guard, when Mototada was holding Fushimi Castle. Mototada had shot Yoshihiro's rider and rejected his offer, however, so he was obliged to join the Mitsunari side (neutrality was not a realistic option on these occasions). At Sekigahara he had—to his shame—only some 1,500 men; his brother in Kagoshima had refused to send more. A plan which he had suggested, to cut across the Eastern army's rear when Ieyasu marched to Sekigahara, had been rejected by Shima Sakon, a general of Ishida Mitsunari's staff.

In spite of the relatively small size of his division these Kyushu warriors had fought fiercely—though only in defense. Shimazu Yoshihiro's command post was situated in front of Ishida Mitsunari's forces, in the center. On his right, Konishi Yukinaga's division had clashed with Honda Tadakatsu's and Togawa Michiyasu's troops. Yoshihiro ordered his men not to attack the enemy but to stand their ground, killing any who tried to assault his post. After the defeat of Konishi's men, and of Ukita Hideie's troops beyond them at the hands of Fukushima Masanori and Terasawa Hirotaka, the Shimazu unit—now only some 500 strong—was left protruding into the Eastern army's front. Yoshihiro wanted to make a direct attack on Ieyasu's command post if the situation seemed desperate. However, his staff begged him to escape from the battlefield by thrusting straight forward through Ieyasu's front line, since the bulk of the Tokugawa forces were concentrating on pursuing fleeing Western units.

The Shimazu troops rushed forward in a wedge formation, passing in front of Ieyasu's command post and trying to leave the field. Fukushima Masanori did not attack him, but Ii Naomasa tried to stop the move. A retainer of Yoshihiro's loaded two bullets in his arquebus and shot Naomasa himself; hit in the arm, Naomasa fell from his horse. The fall of their leader caused momentary confusion among Naomasa's red-armored soldiers, and the Shimazu wedge pushed on hard. Honda Tadakatsu tried to attack Yoshihiro from the rear, but was blocked by the old daimyo's determined retainers. In the end Yoshihiro managed to lead only 50 or 60 men from the field, escaping

estates. Before the Sekigahara campaign both sides had tried to persuade him to join their forces.

Hideaki had agreed to Ieyasu's request that he change sides from the Western to the Eastern army during the battle; nevertheless, he still hesitated to commit himself until he was actually threatened by Ieyasu's army. Both Mitsunari and Ieyasu were waiting for him to engage his troops, and both sent messengers to his command post on Mt. Matsuo. Furious at his delay, Ieyasu ordered his arquebusiers to open fire on Kobayakawa's camp; and an officer sent by Kuroda Nagamasa also pressed him in the strongest terms to send his men into action on the Tokugawa side. Shaken, Kobayakawa finally made up his mind to commit himself, and his whole force rushed down the slopes to attack Mitsunari's right wing.

Prepared for Kobayakawa's betrayal, Otani's troops on this flank counterattacked and pushed the Kobayakawa force back to Mt. Matsuo. However, at the example of Kobayakawa's treachery other Western units, which had been placed in order to counter just this possibility, were now encouraged to change sides in their turn, and started to attack other Mitsunari forces. Now sheer weight of numbers began to tell against the Western army. First Konishi Yukinaga's troops in the center started to disengage from the battle. Ieyasu ordered his guards unit to attack

Opposite top: *Reconstruction of the palisade at Mitsunari's camp on Mt. Sasao. It is unlikely that Mitsunari could have constructed such palisades in one night after his march from Ogaki Castle. He is supposed to have come this way a month beforehand and had it built in advance.*

Opposite below: Ashigaru *carrying the flags of Konishi Yukinaga at the Sekigahara 400th anniversary festival.*

Right: *This armor is called 'Ichinotani,' and a similar harness was worn at Sekigahara by Kuroda Nagamasa. The cuirass is constructed of horizontal plates and decorated with etched effects and large gilded rivet heads. Ichinotani was the battle in 1184 where the hero Minamoto Yoshitsune attacked the Heishi's flank by leading his horsemen down a precipitously steep hillside; the shape of this helmet symbolically recalls that cliff.*

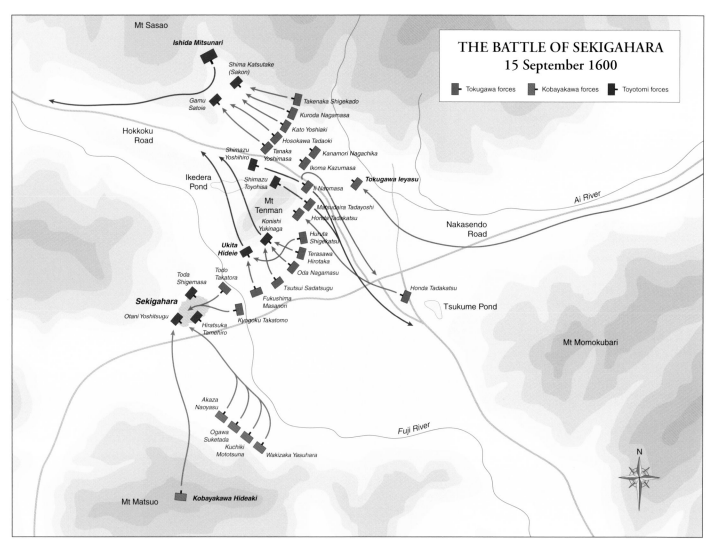

THE BATTLE OF SEKIGAHARA
15 September 1600

Tokugawa forces   Kobayakawa forces   Toyotomi forces

via Ise to the port of Sakai near Osaka. He went aboard ship and returned to Kagoshima on Kyushu, with relatives who had been kept as hostages at Osaka Castle. Yoshihiro's brother Yoshihisa, who had stayed at Kagoshima, asked Ieyasu's mercy for Yoshihiro (they were prepared for another war if their request was rejected); and two years later Ieyasu pardoned Yoshihiro.

Ukita Hideie, age twenty-nine, was—like Kobayakawa Hideaki—an adoptive son of Toyotomi Hideyoshi. He had been eager to attack Ieyasu's forces immediately when they arrived at Sekigahara; but Mitsunari decided to wait at Ogaki Castle, because he knew Ieyasu was not skilled in siege warfare. In any event Ieyasu by-passed the castle, obliging Mitsunari to change his plan and try to block the Eastern army at Sekigahara. Now the contrary Ukita Hideie argued for staying at Ogaki Castle until reinforcements arrived from the siege of Otsu Castle; but Mitsunari overruled his opinion, and accepted battle at Sekigahara.

Ukita's division in the right centre had 1,500 cavalry, 15,000 foot soldiers, and a supply unit 500 strong; it was the most important contingent in the Western main battle line. During the morning of the battle his troops had almost silenced Fukushima Masanori's force after four hours of recurrent fighting. But the treachery of Kobayakawa and other ex-Toyotomi troops crushed Otani's and Konishi's forces on Ukita's right and left respectively, exposing him to attacks from the flanks and rear under which his force eventually crumbled. Ukita Hideie also took ship from Osaka and sought refuge with the Shimazu in Kagoshima. After Hideie had been in hiding for three years Ieyasu learned of his survival, but after that length of time he was inclined to be generous. Hideie's punishment was exile with his retainers to Hachijojima Island, where he spent the rest of his long life.

After Sekigahara, Kobayakawa Hideaki, whose treachery had turned the course of the battle, attacked Mistunari's castle. He was granted a large domain by Ieyasu in reward, but did not enjoy it for long—he died mad two years later.

Ishida Mitsunari, Konishi Yukinaga and Ankokuji Ekei were captured. On 1 October, Tokugawa Ieyasu had them all executed on the riverside at Rokujo in Kyoto (Konishi staying firm in his Christian faith to the end).

But winning the battle of Sekigahara did not of itself secure the 'Pax Tokugawa.' Hideyoshi's son Toyotomi Hideyori was still alive in Osaka Castle, and it was there that the final reckoning was destined to take place.

CHAPTER 12:
THE OSAKA CAMPAIGN

Right: The aftermath of battle. After the fall of Osaka Castle, ladies and ashigaru *try to escape from the inferno, abandoning all heavy belongings as well as weapons and armor. The victors try to capture men and women as trophies of war, to sell them as slaves. Local samurai or bandits attacked, robbed and killed fleeing samurai without mercy. (SY)*

Below: Kinkozane kurenaiitodoshi nakajiro haramaki—*the full description of this armor means that is is made of golden sane and laced with red braid, with white braid in the middle section. In the Azuchi-Momoyama period* tosei gusoku *or 'modern' armor was in common use, but senior commanders also used* haramaki *and* do maru *as traditional status symbols. It has been said that this* haramaki *was worn by Toyotomi Hideyori. (Tokyo National Museum)*

Although, after the battle of Sekigahara, the status of the Toyotomi fell, Toyotomi Hideyori was still regarded as a potential future ruler of Japan, and the family remained extremely rich. In the opinion of most of the daimyos, Tokugawa Ieyasu should support Hideyori. The main forces of the Eastern army which had actually fought at Sekigahara were those of ex-Toyotomi daimyos; it was their specific hatred for Ishida Mitsunari that destroyed him. But their loyalty to Toyotomi Hideyoshi's memory and his surviving family was still genuine. After Sekigahara ex-Toyotomi generals had been rewarded for their important contribution to the victory with larger domains, and their influence became stronger.

In 1603, Tokugawa Ieyasu was named as shogun, and thus the legitimate head of the samurai class, who were obliged to obey his orders. Even so, in order to mollify the Toyotomi family and pro-Toyotomi daimyos he married his granddaughter to Hideyori. In 1605, however, Ieyasu's son Tokugawa Hidetada was named as his heir to the shogunate, thus showing the world that the office was hereditary. Ieyasu ordered the daimyos to come and celebrate this announcement, and Toyotomi Hideyori was not excepted. This was an insult to the Toyotomi family; the outraged Yodogimi, Hideyori's mother, refused the invitation and protested to Ieyasu. Although Ieyasu cancelled the order, he later continued to provoke the Toyotomi with insulting behavior. In 1611, Ieyasu met Hideyori at Fushimi Castle, and found that he had grown up to become a man capable of seeking the mastery of Japan. It has been speculated that this meeting was the direct cause of Ieyasu's decision to destroy Hideyori.

Tokugawa Ieyasu. In 1603, three years after Sekigahara, he was appointed shogun. He finally destroyed the Toyotomi family at Osaka in 1615; he broke every promise he had made to Hideyoshi when he was alive, and after the dictator's death he worked tirelessly to destroy Hideyoshi's son Hideyori. But his merciless destruction of the Toyotomi family assured some 250 years of peace in Japan. (Osaka Castle Museum)

In 1613, Ieyasu complained that an inscription engraved on a temple bell which Hideyori had had cast included a curse on him; this was another provocation aimed at Yodogimi, and Hideyori was innocent of the claimed intention. The Osaka party sent Katagiri Katsumoto as a negotiator, but he was refused an audience with Ieyasu, who forced him to accept very harsh conditions on the Toyotomi family. Another delegate sent by Yodogimi privately was allowed to meet Ieyasu, and received a friendly word. After returning to Osaka, Katagiri was abused for bringing such unacceptable conditions. Nevertheless, he still persisted in his attempts to ensure peace; but, being isolated, he had no choice but to leave Osaka Castle. As soon as Katagiri returned to his domain, Ieyasu persuaded him to become his vassal. Thus Ieyasu's plot to destroy the unity of Toyotomi's vassals prospered; on the other hand, a scheme of the Osaka party's to attract ex-Toyotomi vassals to Osaka was mostly unsuccessful, they were not short of men.

By 1614 many *ronin* who had lost their masters or their employment after Sekigahara were gathering at Osaka, sensing war in the offing. Sanada Yukimura and his son, who had fought at Ueda Castle to delay Tokugawa Hidetada's march to Sekigahara, came down from the Kudozan Mountains and entered Osaka castle. Other important samurai such as Chosokabe Morichika, Mori Katsunaga, and a son of Otani Yoshitsugu came to Osaka Castle, where it is said that some 90,000 soldiers were now gathered.

Tokugawa Ieyasu followed an anti-Christian policy, and many Christian samurai rallied to the Osaka party. Akashi Teruzumi was one; a minister of Ukita Hideie, he had been a general in the Toyotomi army at Sekigahara. After fighting stubbornly in appalling conditions, he was unable to commit *harakiri* in response to the Western army's defeat since he was a Christian. He sought honorable death by charging the enemy on foot, but they could not stand against him and got out of his way. When he encountered his relative Kuroda Nagamasa, a general in the Eastern army, Kuroda begged him to flee the battlefield and save his life. After 14 years in hiding he decided to take up arms again in protest of Ieyasu's treatment of Christians. Leaving his refuge in Kyushu with a small number of retainers, he was joined by many other Christians along the road to Osaka; when he entered the castle it was at the head of some 5,000 samurai marching under six great flags bearing the Christian cross. (It should be emphasized that his motive for joining the Osaka army was quite unusual; most of the other samurai who gathered there were seeking the usual prizes of war.)

The winter campaign

Tokugawa Ieyasu prepared for war with his usual thoroughness, and eventually, in winter 1614, he assembled at Osaka an army whose strength is variously reported at between 180,000 and 300,000 men. They made their main camp at the relatively more vulnerable south of the castle. In fact Osaka was the strongest castle in Japan, its high stone walls defended by a river mouth, canals, moats and outworks. These had recently been strengthened, and the siege expert Sanada Yukimura had constructed a protruding barbican on the south side which was occupied by some 5,000 soldiers. The castle was also fully provisioned to withstand a long siege.

The actual battle began on 2 December. The Tokugawa forces bombarded Osaka Castle day and night, and the sound of cannon fire could be heard from Kyoto. Several attempts to assault the castle failed, however, due to Sanada Yokimura's skillful counterattacks. After some weeks of costly stalemate in freezing weather, and the failure of attempts to bribe his way in, Ieyasu offered peace terms—

Left: The Osaka summer campaign of 1615—Tokugawa Ieyasu's headquarters. A crowd of samurai guard the shogun; and note in the inner circle surrounding him several carrying gold fans marked with the Chinese character '5'. The significance of the number five derives from belief in Acalanatha. (Osaka Castle Museum)

Below: The Osaka summer campaign, 1615. Although they were famous for it, red armor was not unique to the Ii forces, but was also worn by Sanada Yukimura's opposing troops. His final charge towards Ieyasu's HQ caused a panic and the shogun's troops were pushed back, but the Sanada were finally overcome by weight of numbers. (Osaka Castle Museum)

ostensibly in order to halt the drain of casualties, but in fact to improve his long term position. Hideyori's mother Yodogimi, frightened by the cannon fire, pressed her son to accept, and he agreed against the advice of his commanders. Yodogimi could not know that she had sealed the doom of the Toyotomi. Peace was signed on 23 December and Ieyasu returned to Kyoto in triumph. Part of his army departed; but no sooner had he left his camp than the rest of his men started to batter down the external wall so it fell into the outer moat—and then proceeded to fill in the internal moat as well, in violation of (deliberately ambiguous) terms regarding the partial slighting of the castle's defenses. The Toyotomi commanders protested, but by the time the delayed replies were received most of Osaka Castle's outworks had been destroyed.

The summer campaign

In April 1615 the Tokugawa army marched out of Kyoto once more to finally crush the Toyotomi. The pretext was that the defenses of Osaka had been partially rebuilt (this was an exaggeration), and that *ronin* had been gathering there again (this was true—the Osaka army was soon stronger than it had been in December). Various expeditions were mounted into surrounding provinces by the Toyotomi forces, hoping to defeat the Tokugawa contingents before they could assemble. This time Ieyasu estimated that it would only take three days to destroy his foe; the Toyotomi could no longer rely on the strength of their defenses to sit out a siege, and Ieyasu planned to fight his favorite sort of open field battle. The Tokugawa forces, totalling about 150,000 soldiers, approached Osaka from three directions. Determined to fight to the death, some 55,000 defenders came out and met them on the field of Tenno-ji south of the castle. It was said that Chausuyama Hill turned red when Sanada Yukimura's red-armored soldiers encamped there.

In the center, Mori Katsunaga's men charged through the Tokugawa vanguard led by Honda Tadatomo, and pushed them back against the main body. The Tokugawa troops were shaken when reinforcements coming up behind their left wing were misidentified as enemies. In hand-to-hand fighting the lines swayed this way and that in murderous confusion. Ieyasu had left the field command to his son Hidetada, and from the enemy reserve Ono Harunaga led a furious attempt to reach him, but was foiled by Ii Naotaka and Maeda Toshitsune from the Tokugawa right flank. A message to Hideyori to bring reinforcements forward from the castle went astray. Eventually the numerical superiority of the Tokugawa army overwhelmed the Toyotomi troops, who lost heart at the news that Sanada Yukimura had been killed while, exhausted, he was taking a break from the fighting.

By dusk Ieyasu's troops were swarming through the blazing Osaka Castle. In the keep Hideyori and his mother Yodogimi committed suicide; and Hideyori's little son was ruthlessly executed, to put a final end to Hideyoshi's line. Kita-no-mandokoro, Hideyoshi's widow, survived the war and became a nun. At the age of seventy-four, after fighting and plotting since he was a teenage boy, Tokugawa Ieyasu was now the unquestioned ruler of the whole of Japan. The following spring he died in his bed, to be succeeded by his son Hidetada.

Opposite: The penalty of defeat: Toyotomi followers trying to escape from the fall of Osaka Castle. (Osaka Castle Museum)

Below: A set of tosei gusoku *attributed to the Sanada family, because it has six coin crests on the arm guard. The tub-shaped cuirass is clearly influenced by European models but it was made in Japan in the 17th century. (Osaka Castle Museum)*

CHAPTER 13:

THE CHRISTIAN REBELLION IN SHIMABARA

The full description of this helmet in Japanese is tentsukiwakidate-tsuki-kuronurizunari-kabuto . . . *which means 'a black lacquered* zunari *helmet with* tentsuki *side ornaments.' Tentsuki ('sky-thrusting') was a rather popular design in the Sengoku period; it symbolized a variation of the crescent moon, and the round golden* maedate *at the base naturally represents the sun. (Osaka Castle Museum)*

The Christian converts in Kyushu had previously been protected by the provincial daimyo of the Arima family; but after the extinction of the Toyotomi in 1615, the Tokugawa bakufu ordered all daimyos to suppress them. This process of persecution was gradual and uneven. Matsukura Shigemasa, who had distinguished himself in the Osaka campaign, was at first well disposed towards the Christians; but after being rebuked for this lack of zeal by the third Tokugawa shogun Iemitsu he begun to persecute the Christians in earnest, and was supposedly responsible for the deaths of some 10,000 people.

Arima Harunobu's son Naozumi was transferred from Shimabara to Hyuga, but many of his retainers remained there and returned to farming. After the capture and execution at Ieyasu's orders (following Sekigahara) of the Christian daimyo Konishi Yukinaga, his retainers—seeking an opportunity for revenge on the Tokugawa—also took refuge around Shimabara.

In his anxiety to demonstrate his loyalty to the Tokugawa, Matsukura proposed the extraordinarily ambitious plan of attacking Luzon in the Philippines, which was the base of Spanish missionaries to Japan. Having received the informal agreement of the bakufu he borrowed money from the merchants of Sakai, Hirato and Nagasaki and purchased many weapons. But the bakufu soon decided that the time was not ripe for this bold attempt to root out the overseas supporters of the Christian community, since the internal situation was highly fluid. After the sudden death of Matsukura Shigemasa his son Katsuie was oppressed by debt. He therefore imposed very heavy taxes, which he set about collecting ruthlessly; farmers who could not pay their dues died at the hands of his torturers. The situation in Shimabara became extremely tense, and rumors begun to spread that one day an apostle would appear there and would save the farmers.

Masuda Jinbei, one of the retainers of Konishi Yukinaga, was himself a devout Christian; he and other followers of Konishi and Arima Harunobu held meetings to plan a revolt against the cruelties of the Matsukura family. In 1637 the spring weather was appalling and the harvest threatened to be so poor that famine loomed. Desperate, the farmers anticipated the appearance of a savior—and we may speculate that this kind of rumor was encouraged by would-be rebels. In North Arima and South Arima, 16 farmers were arrested on charges of praying to Jesus. All were executed and this proved to be the spark for rebellion. A furious crowd of farmers attacked the officiating magistrate and killed him, and soon others were rising against the government and attacking temples. They killed Buddhist priests, and carried their heads mounted on poles when they marched to Shimabara Castle.

Nanbando gusoku *or European armor, attributed
to Sakakibara Yasumasa. Only the helmet is in fact
foreign-made; the cuirass,* kusazuri *and* kote *are
thought to be of local manufacture.*
(Tokyo National Museum)

On Amakusa Island another uprising broke out, and the rebels succeeded in defeating the troops of Miake Tojuro who were sent to suppress it.

Now Masuda Jinbei put forward his son Shiro Tokisada—whose Christian name was Geronimo—as the savior whom the Christians had longed for. Despite mounting a long siege the rebels were unable to take Shimabara Castle; so, in preparation for the punitive force which would inevitably be sent by Tokugawa Iemitsu, they repaired the deserted Hara Castle. On 3 December 1637, Shiro Tokisada entered the castle; and soon about 35,000 people gathered there. The samurai leading this rebel army were only 40 strong, and 12,000 to 13,000 of this total were women and children. Others were peasants, who in earlier years—ironically—had been trained to use guns by their persecutor's father Matsukura Shigemasa in anticipation of his planned attack on Luzon.

A bakufu army some 30,000 strong attacked Hara Castle in vain and suffered heavy losses from the marksmanship of the defenders, and its commander was killed in action. The government now realized that the situation was serious: history has taught that an example of successful defiance could be fatal. Mustering the forces of daimyos in Kyushu, especially former Christians who had renounced the faith, the bakufu besieged Hara Castle with 120,000 soldiers equipped with arquebuses and cannon. The defense remained stubborn and effective, however, and still the Tokugawa army could not destroy the castle. Next the bakufu sent a Dutch ship from Hirato with orders to bombard the castle with its modern ordnance. The rebels got wind of this, and sent a letter accusing the bakufu of cowardice in hiring a band of foreigners to fight their battles. Interestingly, this charge—or the fear of others' reactions to its slur against their honor—persuaded the bakufu to recall the Dutch ship. The Tokugawa government also sent *ninja* spies to infiltrate the castle; some of these were captured, trembling with fear in the moat, and others, inside the castle since they could neither speak the Shimabara dialect nor understand Christian words.

After three months, by mid-February 1638, the defenders of Hara Castle had come to the end of their ammunition and food. Some foragers were killed when they attacked the bakufu camp. The commander Matsudaira Nobutsuna ordered that they should be autopsied to find out what kind of food they were eating—and only grass and leaves were found in their stomachs. He therefore decided to launch a full-scale attack on 29 February; but the Nabeshima contingent began the attack the day before, so the actual battle started on the 28th. After two days' continuous fighting Hara Castle finally fell; Shiro Tokisada was killed during this action, and all the people in the castle were then massacred, including the women and children.

In April 1638 the bakufu confiscated the Matsukura domain, and tyrant Katsuie was executed.

Left: This 32-ken suji kabuto, of akoda or melon shape, is constructed of 32 radial plates; the joining edges of each plate are gilded. The shikami goblin crest is suspected of having been attached at a later period. Note the menpo face guard.
(Osaka Castle Museum)

Opposite: Sengoku period armor, attributed to Akechi Samanosuke. The helmet ornament is a pair of horse's ears and a moon. The cuirass, of European type but made in Japan, is embossed with a small skull and the Chinese character ten or 'sky.'
(Tokyo National Museum)

CHAPTER 14:
THE TOKUGAWA BAKUFU

The most important problem facing the Tokugawa bakufu in the longer term was how to control the daimyos. Unless an effective solution could be found the bakufu would always be threatened by the energy and ambition of the most powerful barons; and Toyotomi Hideyoshi had already proved that the short term distraction of a foreign war was an expensive and chancy option. The Tokugawa regime therefore introduced a steady stream of innovations with the cumulative aim of weakening the daimyos.

Power in the provinces around Edo was given to the longest-standing retainers of the Tokugawa, the *fudai* ('inner lords'). The bakufu transferred many ex-Toyotomi loyalists—*tozama* ('outer lords'), whose loyalty was always suspect—to remote parts of the country, disconnecting them from their ancestral lands and retainers (though some were left in their ancestral fiefs). Many were simply destroyed and their domains confiscated; before long the shogunate owned approximately a quarter of the rice production of the entire country. To oblige them to spend money, the shogun ordered the daimyos to build Edo Castle, repair the moat, and reclaim Tokyo Bay. In the longer term, each daimyo was ordered to travel to attend the shogun at Edo once every two years. At first these assemblies was performed as a military drill, to test their loyalty and readiness; but over the course of time this procession to Edo became an extravagant opportunity for the daimyos to display their wealth, which enhanced the economic development of the towns along the main road. At Edo the bakufu effectively held the daimyos' wives and children as hostages; although these visits were at first voluntary, and the baronial families were always ostensibly treated as honored guests, in time they became compulsory, and the guests were watched carefully to see that they could not escape.

Nevertheless, the basic policy of the bakufu was to let daimyos take care of their own domains and manage their *han*—this might be translated as 'dukedoms.' The bakufu did not as a rule intervene in a daimyo's domestic problems unless the regime wished to terminate his rule over a *han*. Under the *han* system the daimyo was the summit of the hierarchy in his domain, and in peacetime samurai carrying this responsibility needed some bureaucratic ability.

The townspeople of Edo and Osaka now flourished, and with them Japan's culture. By the restriction of free trade Japan was maintained as an inward-looking society, and developed to a high degree her own distinctive cultural expressions such as *kabuki*, *haiku*, *ukiyoe*, *sumo*, etc. The population of Edo City would rise to 1,100,000, making it larger than any contemporary European city; but the comparison is meaningless, because Japan's ever more refined urban culture developed in complete isolation. From 1636 the third shogun prohibited trade with the Portuguese because of their strong connection with Christianity. Only Holland, China and Korea were licensed to continue sending a limited number of merchants to Japan, Dutch contact being strictly controlled through a single trading station on Dejima Island at Nagasaki (which would become the gateway to modern Japan in the late Tokugawa period). For 260 years under the Tokugawa shogunate Japan slumbered in peace, sealed off from the rest of the world. In consequence, the Industrial Revolution and every kind of scientific, technological and political movement of this supremely energetic period in Western history simply passed Japan by. Among the factors to be completely neglected were Japan's defenses against any potential foreign threat.

During this long, conservative peace the bakufu encouraged the study of Confucianism, which was

Above: *A descendant of the Nakamura family at the Soma festival, wearing the* horo; *by the Sengoku period this was mainly worn by message riders. Inside the cloth a light whalebone frame holds it open.*

Opposite: *The Edo period: a samurai of the 500-*koku *class arrives in camp during his progress to the capital. Although paid twice as much as his Hojo forebear illustrated on page 179, he has no more combatant attendants—during the long peace under the Tokugawa bakufu his entourage has no military purpose, and the aim is simply to display his wealth and dignity.* (SY)

supportive of the regime's ideology. Education, during more than two centuries of isolation, according to Confucian principles of deference, hierarchy, and respect for the past affected the spiritual structure of the Japanese people. It was during this Edo period that the code of *bushido* was developed, to give meaning and identity to a samurai class which was no longer needed for any practical service in peacetime.

The fall of the bakufu and the restoration of imperial rule

At various times from the late 18th century Russian, British and American ships occasionally called at Japanese ports. The Americans, in particular, urged the bakufu to open their ports to US shipping, since they needed supply facilities for their Pacific whaling fleet.

In 1853 the US Navy's Commodore Perry anchored his four 'black ships' in Tokyo Bay and presented letters from his government addressed to the emperor—ignorance of Japan was so great that the central role of the shogunate and the purely ceremonial character of the imperial family was not understood. The reevaluation of Japan's comparative military weakness—by a factor of some two and a half centuries—came as a severe shock, and the bakufu showed indecision which drew bitter criticism. In 1854 Perry returned, and the bakufu concluded the Treaty of Kanagawa: the ports of Shimoda and Hakodate were opened to American ships, and in due course a US consul would be accepted. Treaties with Britain, France, Holland and Russia soon followed; meanwhile the bakufu sought rapid rearmament, largely through trade with the Dutch.

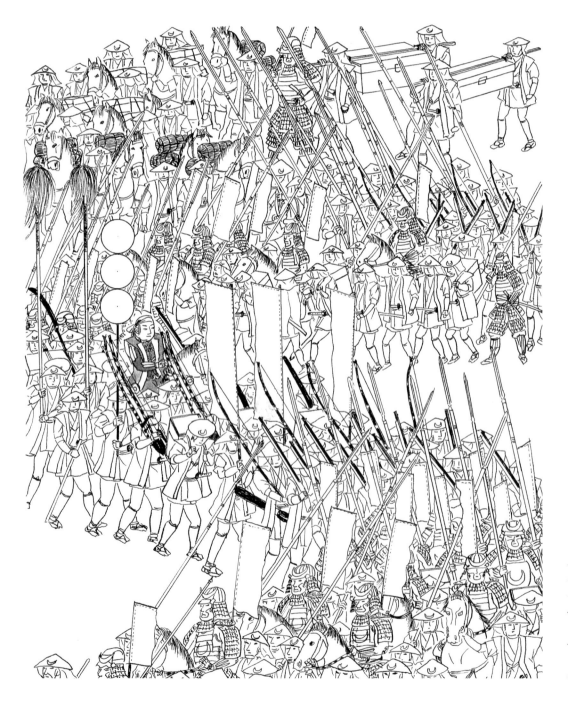

Left: The Edo period: the arrival of a 10,000-koku daimyo. Ten mounted samurai, 16 foot samurai, ten horse-holders, foot soldiers—a total of 235 men, of which only half are combatants. (SY)

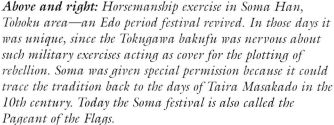

Above and right: Horsemanship exercise in Soma Han, Tohoku area—an Edo period festival revived. In those days it was unique, since the Tokugawa bakufu was nervous about such military exercises acting as cover for the plotting of rebellion. Soma was given special permission because it could trace the tradition back to the days of Taira Masakado in the 10th century. Today the Soma festival is also called the Pageant of the Flags.

For more than a decade already a heated debate had raged among the ruling class as to the desirability of increasing outside contacts. Some ultra-nationalists were rigidly opposed to opening up Japan to the outside world, starting from the position that the country was uniquely sacred and that even the presence of foreign barbarians on her soil was sacrilegeous pollution. Others saw such contacts as inevitable, and best managed by gradual compromise. The signing of the treaties brought the debate to a new level of violence, and the strongest minister of the shogun's council, Ii Naosuke, was assassinated in 1860. In 1863, under the influence of these ideologues, Choshu Han fired upon foreign ships, but the province was punished by a combined British, American, French and Dutch fleet. Satsuma in Kyushu was another region strongly under nationalistic influence; here a British merchant, Charles Richardson, had been killed at Namamugi in 1862 for

failing to pay proper respect when he met on the road the procession of the Shimazu daimyo. The indemnity demanded from the bakufu was finally paid only under the guns of a Royal Navy squadron, and the stubborn refusal of the lord of Satsuma to pay his part led to a heavy naval bombardment of Kagoshima.

Having decided to open the country, the bakufu oppressed those who spoke out against it, thus forcing into each other's arms the nationalist extremists and all other enemies of the shogunate. These combined into an anti-bakufu league called the Joi, which encouraged acts of terrorism by samurai against leaders of the bakufu, and provoked retaliation in kind. In time the impossibility of winning any confrontation with the strong foreign fleets was accepted. Although the surviving leaders of the Joi grudgingly acknowledged that the only path to eventual revenge was through learning the foreigners' technical skills, nevertheless their hostility towards the bakufu whose weakness and incompetence had exposed them to this bitter choice did not abate. The most active elements in this movement came from the lower class of samurai in Satsuma (Kagoshima), Choshu (Yamaguchi) and Tosa (Shikoku); and their rallying point was a plan to overthrow the shogunate and restore the dignity of the emperors.

The daimyos influenced by the Joi organized an army and advanced upon Kyoto. The last shogun, Tokugawa

Karutakane gusoku *or armor of 'card'-shaped plates, linked together with wire rings and sewn on to a fabric base. Very flexible, cheap, and easy to carry, this style was used by the poorer soldiers from the late Sengoku until well into the Edo period. (Osaka Castle Museum)*

Yoshinobu (Hitotsubashi Keiki) was not a good military leader; indeed, he had already resigned the shogunate when he tried to stop the advance of these forces at Toba-Fushimi in 1868. The 'outer lords' had enthusiastically embraced the weapons of the barbarians, however; their forces consisted of samurai, townspeople and farmers equipped with modern guns and cannon, and on this occasion supported by the threat of a British naval squadron. The shogun's army, defeated by these modernized forces, fled back to Edo. In March, Edo Castle was surrendered unconditionally and without a battle to the 'imperial' army, led by the forces from Satsuma, Choshu and Tosa in the name of the Meiji Emperor.

After the overthrow of the bakufu, some daimyos loyal to it led stubborn resistance in the Tohoku area, particularly in Aizu family territory. They built up an army consisting not only of samurai but also of old men, women and young boys, and many of these fought to the death. After the defeat of the Aizu considerable numbers of samurai escaped to Hokkaido. A force led by Enomoto Takeaki attacked imperial troops sent to establish the new government in Matsumae on Hokkaido. Enomoto's troops were equipped with efficient modern rifles and were trained according to French doctrine. Despite this, the outnumbered Enomoto army was finally obliged to surrender to the imperial forces at Goryokaku fortress after using up all its ammunition. After surrendering Enomoto was imprisoned in Edo (Tokyo); he was later pardoned, and thereafter worked for the development of Hokkaido.

In 1871 the new Meiji imperial government announced the abolition of the *han* system; from now on all land was taken under the direct authority of the national government. The four rigidly separate classes of the Edo period—the samurai, the farmer, the artisan and the merchant—were abolished, and all became equal except the aristocrats. Conservative samurai naturally clung to the old ideas, and their discontent with this policy prompted several attempted revolts against the new government; but the new imperial army, formed by an amalgamation of the classes, quelled them all. In 1877 the pacification of the last revolt against the new government, led by Saigo Takamori in Satsuma, brought internal insurgence to an end.

The samurai class had dominated Japanese history for seven centuries, since Minamoto Yoritomo established his bakufu in Kamakura in 1192. Their resilience had been extraordinary; but complete victory in 1615 had proved fatal to their energy. The outside world, so long shut out, had finally touched them; and within 20 years the institution they had built to preserve their power had collapsed from within.

THE SAMURAI CODE

From the earliest times the principal victims of war have been the women and children, the old, the poor and the defenseless, and the samurai world was no exception. It was mainly lower class samurai who engaged in this kind of pillaging. Commanders sometimes forbade it, but such orders were usually disregarded: most samurai went to war in order to seize its prizes. (SY)

Today we consider that the samurai's system of moral values was crystallized in the so-called code of *bushido*. The famous Hagakure text explains *bushido* as the idealization of dying; perhaps it might be more suitable to replace the final word with 'killing'. The extreme essence of *bushido* in the Edo period was supported by the absolute power of the bakufu. We know, however, that there was a wide gulf between ideals and reality. For example, if we study how members of the Minamoto family actually died, we understand that they were simply killers. If we study the lives of the non-samurai classes in the samurai period we hear their heartfelt protests against the consequences of this code. It is inexplicable to the author that there are still those today who think that the core values of *bushido* are relevant to daily life. If we appreciate the historical background which gave rise to the code, we must see this as an illusion—comparable, in European terms, to approaching modern life from the viewpoint of a Celtic warrior. No doubt some of its more positive elements are still applicable in modern society; but these are not peculiar to the samurai code—they are in fact universal human virtues, such as loyalty, trustworthiness and fortitude. We should not confuse the romantic illusion with reality; the medieval samurai was superstitious, irrational, and held human life cheap.

The samurai code was also abused from the Meiji period up to the end of World War II. After the Meiji restoration the samurai class was integrated into the common population; but the government advocated the ideological aspects of the samurai code. In this hierarchical society, in which the emperor held absolute power, the code of *bushido* was an ideal tool for controlling the people.

In the 1930s education in the extreme tenets of *bushido*, combined with the wielding of absolute power and domination of all media by a militarist regime, drove young soldiers to fanatical resistance during World War II, epitomized by the so-called *banzai* charge and the *kamikaze* suicide attack. This ideology was a complete distortion of its supposed inspiration: in the past the samurai did not regard surrender to an enemy, or even changing sides, as an unforgivable deed. If samurai lost a battle they would flee from the field and prepare for the next. A close reading of the historical sources proves that for samurai to choose to fight to the death was a rather unusual event; they may have aspired to the unbending code of *bushido*, but in reality they often failed to live up to it.

In the last part of this book the author has referred to the negative side of the samurai code. The very harsh historical conditions which gave birth to that code molded and affected the Japanese psyche in some ways; but it is as inappropriate to judge the nature of the Japanese people only in this light as it would be to judge any whole nation solely by the darkest aspect of its history.

CHAPTER 15:

DRAGON HORSE, A PIONEER OF MODERN JAPAN

Kondo Isami, who led the Shinsengumi police in Kyoto for the Tokugawa bakufu in the late Edo period, was born in Chofu in Tokyo. One of the last brave swordsmen of the samurai government, he surrendered to imperial forces and was executed at Itabashi in Tokyo.

Prologue

If, as Shakespeare says, all the world's a stage, then when the time comes for one act to end and another to begin, history is made by a limited number of very important players. Their roles may be harsh and unmerciful, so that it seems that none can survive until the end of the drama. But by brilliant achievements their parts, however brief upon the stage, shine in history forever. One such player appeared at the turning point of Japanese history, when the country began to evolve into the modern age from the long absolutism of the Edo period. Although he was neither a famous warrior nor a powerful daimyo, his thoughts were respected by many Japanese and have inspired younger generations after him. When bloody terrorism gripped the ruling class he wanted to guide Japan towards peaceful change, rather than following the example of Tokugawa Ieyasu when he had established the last bakufu. His story may be presented as the successive acts of a drama—though as in many plays, some acts necessarily reveal what was happening simultaneously in different places.

Act I: Sakamoto Ryoma and the black ships

Sakamoto Ryoma was born on November 15, 1835, the second son of Sakamoto Heihachi. The Sakamoto family was descended from petty samurai in Tosa, and moved into the city of Kochi from the countryside. There the family opened a pawnshop, and in time they acquired considerable wealth. With this money the family bought once more the position of *goshi* or minor samurai. Ryoma's grandfather succeeded to the position and left the shop.

Back in 1600, when the Toyotomi forces lost the battle of Sekigahara, the domain of their followers the Chosokabe in Tosa (now Kochi) was given by Tokugawa Ieyasu to Yamanouchi Kazutoyo. The Yamanouchi family established the *han* or dukedom of Tosa, but the petty samurai who had served the Chosokabe resisted them. After severe oppression of the old Chosokabe retainers, the Yamanouchi secured their power in the region; but ever since that time the samurai of Tosa were divided into two classes. Yamanouchi retainers were called *joshi* or superior samurai; the others were the *goshi* or 'provincial men.' The *goshi* had suffered humiliating discrimination at the hands of their arrogant rulers—this even extended to sumptuary laws governing what sort of shoes they were allowed to wear, the wooden *geta* being forbidden to them. It is reasonable to assume that such treatment at the hands of the Yamanouchi—which they suffered for more than 200 years, throughout the 'Pax Tokugawa'—fostered a rebellious streak in the *goshi* class.

Ryoma's father was not only skilled in martial arts, but also a good poet and calligrapher. As his mother died young, Ryoma became very close to his sister, three years older than

An Edo period samurai's house. At the entrance the lady of the house greets a guest. (Aizu wakamatsu samurai house)

he, who was as good as a man at archery, horse-riding and fencing. He also often visited the house of his uncle, who was a successful merchant; and there he learned something of the world of trade. This broad education in an environment of free enquiry strongly affected his way of thinking.

In 1853, Commodore Perry's four warships appeared in Tokyo Bay demanding that the emperor grant US ships access to Japanese harbors. The incompetent Edo bakufu, unable to persist with the policy it had pronounced a few years earlier of ejecting any foreign fleet from Japan, decided to open the country and accepted the US government's demand. This had not come as a complete surprise to everyone. Some years beforehand the Dutch—the only country whose ships were permitted to harbor in Hirato—had informed the bakufu about the result of the Opium War of 1839–42: that is, the utter humiliation of China at the hands of a Western nation. The bakufu's counselors had thus been aware that Japan's situation in Asia was fragile and her isolation untenable. Even though the bakufu made the right decision in accepting the inevitability of foreign contacts, it caused a strong reaction among the faction which believed Japan to be a sacred land.

It was in 1854, the year of the treaty, that Ryoma came to Edo to attend the famous fencing school. The samurai of the capital were seething and the air was full of the talk of war. When Tosa Han ordered its retainers in Edo to guard

the Shinagawa coast, Ryoma joined up for guard duty. He was nineteen years old; and he felt that the world was changing.

In 1856, in accordance with the treaty, the US government sent Consul-General Townsend Harris to Japan. He persisted in pressing for the conclusion of a US/Japanese commercial treaty; the bakufu counselors came to the conclusion that it was impossible to refuse this demand, and sent a letter to the imperial court at Kyoto asking permission to open up the country. However, the Komei Emperor's court still clung to their old view of the world, and failed to respond to this request. The situation was aggravated by an internal conflict over the shogun's succession which tore the Tokugawa family in two.

In 1858, Ii Naosuke from Hikone Han—the shogun's strongman—was appointed chief counselor of the bakufu. He quickly concluded the commercial treaty without the consent of the court at Kyoto, and proceeded to persecute the opposing faction. This dictatorial behavior provoked the conservative samurai, who eventually assassinated Ii at the gates of Edo Castle early in 1860. In that same year, young Sakamoto Ryoma finished his swordsmanship training and returned to Tosa, but he was already beginning to dream

Edo period: the bansho *was the guardroom where retainers kept watch. (Aizu wakamatsu samurai house)*

that Japan would one day establish diplomatic and trading contact with the rest of the world.

In Tosa Han, the faction which corresponded to the rejectionist, 'sacred land' movement in other dukedoms formed the Tosakinnoto party, which did not hesitate to murder those who were active in opposing it. Despite his internationalist leanings Ryoma joined this ultra-nationalist factions. Troubled, he left the Tosa Han and returned to Edo, where he entered the Chiba fencing school. In 1862, Ryoma and a friend visited Matsudaira Shungaku, the daimyo in Echizen (Fukui), asking for a letter of introduction so that he could meet either Katsu Rintaro Kaishu or Yokoi Shonan, both leading advocates of the opening of the country. As a member of the ultra-nationalist party his intentions were highly suspect, but Kaishu agreed to meet him. When Ryoma was guided to the guest room Kaishu said, 'You have come to kill me; let us discuss the state of the world first—then, do as you like.' Both were skilled swordsmen, but they never drew their weapons.

Act II: Seapower and terrorism
Katsu Kaishu was born in 1823, a son of Katsu Kokichi, a direct retainer of the Tokugawa in Edo. Although he was employed by the bakufu he was very poor, so to supplement his income he opened a Dutch language school. When he was twenty-five years old he was commissioned into the naval defense section of the bakufu. By learning something of Dutch culture he had attained a wider knowledge of what was happening in Asia. Many young people gathered to learn from him, not only bakufu retainers but also people from the provinces who were avid to learn more about the

world. In 1860, Katsu crossed the Pacific on the Japanese ship *Kanrin Maru* to the United States, and was a signatory of the commercial treaty. By 1862, when he met Sakamoto Ryoma, he had been appointed as a magistrate of naval forces of the bakufu.

After the debate between the two men, Ryoma decided to become a student of Katsu's. Katsu wrote in his dairy: 'Sakamoto visited my house with his friend Chiba Shutaro, a swordmaster. From early evening until midnight I preached about the reasons that we need a new view towards the world, and the necessity of building new naval forces to defend Japan from colonialists. He (Ryoma) said to me that he had intended to kill me, but after my lecture he felt ashamed of his ignorance about Japan's situation in Asia, and he declared that he would become my student. After this he would concentrate his mind on building our naval forces . . . After his visit Ryoma also told his friend that he had come to chop me. I laughed at this; but actually he has some kind of dignity, and in the end he showed himself to be a good man.'

The meeting with Kaishu persuaded Ryoma that Japan had to adopt a realistic program of modernization. In the same year he sailed with Kaishu to Osaka on the bakufu ship *Jundo Maru*. The next year he invited many samurai from his home province of Tosa into Kaishu's school. By now Ryoma was working for Kaishu as his secretary.

Up to this date the bakufu's maritime training school at Tsukiji had been open only to the retainers of the regime; but Kaishu wanted to create a new school for naval officers at Kobe for able volunteers from the provinces. Kaishu argued the necessity of founding such a training school with bakufu counselors, influential daimyos and court aristocrats.

Edo period: the lord's audience chamber. (Aizu wakamatsu samurai house)

Agreement was not easy to obtain, since any such project tended to become yet another bone of contention between the factions supporting and rejecting the opening up of the country. When Kaishu was staying in Kyoto a samurai attacked him, but he was saved by a bodyguard. As part of his campaign for the new naval school, Kaishu invited the shogun himself, Tokugawa Iemochi, on board his new steam-powered vessel; and on this very ship he was granted permission to create the maritime training school at Kobe.

Naturally, Sakamoto Ryoma was among those who entered the new school. Kaishu recalled that this was beneficial, as Ryoma raised the morale of the students. The degree of financial support from the bakufu was not sufficient to operate the school; and Ryoma again visited Matsudaira Shungaku, the daimyo of Echizen, asking him to invest money in it. Ryoma busied himself in many ways as a leader of Kaisho's students.

When foreign naval forces threatened to punish the stubborn nationalists of Choshu Han who had bombarded US, French and Dutch vessels in 1863 at Shimonoseki, the bakufu's advisor Hitotsubashi Keiki (later the shogun Tokugawa Yoshinobu) ordered Katsu Kaishu to negotiate a settlement with representatives of the foreign powers. With Ryoma and other students from the school, Katsu visited Nagasaki and held discussions to find a solution to the incident that Choshu had created; but the negotiations did not reach any agreement beyond the postponement of hostilities for two months. When Kaishu returned to Edo, Ryoma did not accompany him but visited another mentor of his, Yokoi Shonan, in Kumamoto.

Shonan had been born of petty samurai stock in Kumamoto. His plans for economic improvement had been approved by Matsudaira Shungaku of Echizen Han; invited there to put them into action, he tried to pursue a program of reforms. However, his ideas seem to have been premature; he was accused of an 'un-samurai attitude', and had to return to Kumamoto. When Ryoma visited Shonan there he complained of the bakufu's abandoning of Choshu to its fate at the hands of the foreign fleet; but Shonan advised patience and caution rather than rebellion. (Later, during the Meiji period, Yokoi Shonan would be assassinated because of his pacifist and Christian beliefs.)

During the early 1860s inter-faction violence between the pro-bakufu, pro-contact party and the Joi rejectionists became chronic. The 'exclusionists', led by Takechi Zuisan and Kusaka Genzui in Tosa and Choshu respectively, conducted a campaign of terror against the bakufu's supporters in Kyoto. They assassinated pro-bakufu figures one after another; the regime's police hit back at them; and in a short time Kyoto was running with blood. In reaction the exclusionist Joi faction in Tosa was severely punished by Yamanouchi Yozan, the lord of Tosa Han.

The previous year Shimazu Hisamitsu of Satsuma Han, an obedient bakufu vassal, had been hostile to the anti-bakufu movement in Choshu. He wanted, nevertheless, to reform the organization of the bakufu, which had become rotten, and was a supporter of Hitotsubashi Keiki, who recommended him as an adviser to the shogun. Even though some of his reforms were reluctantly accepted by the bakufu, Hisamitsu was badly treated by the opposing faction in the regime. The bakufu refused Hisamitsu's request to use a government ship when he returned to

Satsuma; he had to travel home by land, and it was while he was on his way back that his retainer killed the Englishman, Charles Richardson, at Namamugi for failing to show respect and to clear the road for Hisamitsu's procession.

This incident, as we have seen, brought a fierce protest from the British. A British squadron appeared in Satsuma Bay, demanding compensation and the extradition of the samurai responsible. The lord of Satsuma refused, but soon regretted it after a severe bombardment of his city of Kagoshima by the British warships. Satsuma Han agreed to British demands during the subsequent negotiation. After this incident relations between the British and the Shimazu became quite friendly. This was not surprising in the context of Japanese history, which had seen countless daimyos allying themselves to former enemies who had proved stronger. The lord of Satsuma recognized strength when he saw it; and secured British help in the modernization of the Satsuma forces. (The British motive was to counter French influence over the bakufu.)

In July 1863 the Choshu extremists were attacked by the Shinsengumi, the bakufu's police force led by Kondo Isami, while they were staying at the Ikedaya inn in Kyoto. Kondo and four swordsmen forced their way into the room where Choshu and Tosa exclusionists were holding a meeting and killed five, while other members of the bakufu 'hit squad' waiting outside killed 11 more—only a handful escaped. This incident at the Ikedaya inn only provoked the Joi faction in Choshu to new heights of fury; the exclusionists organized an armed force and, early in 1864, they marched on the imperial residence in Kyoto to seize the court. Men from Aizu Han, with the co-operation of Satsuma soldiers, crushed this attempt at the Kinmon Gate (Hamaguri Gomon) of the emperor's residence. After this episode the bakufu became afraid of the influence of the Tosa and Satsuma Hans over the Komei Emperor. The shogun Iemochi pursued an opportunist policy, for which he would soon have to pay a price; his main method seems to have been to play off the powerful daimyos of Choshu and Satsuma against one another to prevent them allying themselves against him.

In August 1863 a British naval squadron bombarded Kagoshima, the Satsuma capital, when the deadline for payment of indemnity for the killing of the British merchant ran out. The Komei Emperor ordered the punishment of the Choshu Han; of more immediate consequence, the ships of four navies took direct action in the Kanmon Strait, bombarding Choshu batteries on the hills of the Shimonoseki coast. Western warships silenced the batteries one by one with overwhelming firepower, and their landing parties destroyed the guns or took them as trophies.

The bakufu's punitive force, led by Tokugawa

Original wooden cannon of the late Edo period, preserved in Aizu, scene of one of the last risings against the Meiji imperial restoration. Obviously such weapons did not have the strength or compression to fire close-fitting roundshot to batter walls; but they could fire a load of metal balls, like grapeshot, at infantry targets.

Yoshikatsu, left Osaka for Choshu in September. Shortly before this, in August, Katsu Kaishu had ordered Sakamoto Ryoma to visit one of the staff officers of the punitive force from Satsuma Han.

Act III: Ryoma and Takamori

The officer of the Satsuma punitive force against Choshu whom Sakamoto Ryoma was instructed to visit in August 1863 was Saigo Takamori. Takamori had been born into a family of the second lowest class of samurai retainer in Satsuma Han. When he was young he injured his right elbow; obliged to give up his intention to serve the dukedom as a soldier, he applied himself to administration. His policy to reform the Han's agricultural economy attracted approving attention, and soon he was permitted to meet his lord, Shimazu Nariakira, quite freely. It was a remarkable rise for a man from the poorest position to be promoted to the status of one who could talk to his lord without seeking permission from senior retainers. But Nariakira was perhaps the most brilliant of his contemporaries, and far-sighted in his plans to reform the Satsuma economy by introducing modern industry. He developed a factory district where he constructed a blast furnace, a glass plant, a spinning mill and a porcelain factory.

Politically, Nariakira intervened in the succession issue after the death in 1858 of the 13th Tokugawa shogun, Iesada. He actively supported Hitotsubashi Keiki, whom he regarded as the most suitable man to handle the difficult situation which faced Japan. But, disappointingly, both Tokugawa Yoshitomi and Iemochi were supported by Ii Naosuke, the supreme counselor, and this secured the succession for Iemochi. After the death of Shimazu Nariakira his nephew Hisamitsu succeeded to the Shimazu Han. Saigo Takamori's loyalty to Nariakira and Keiki attracted the dislike of his new lord; he was dismissed from the central government and sent to Amamioshima Island. After the assassination of Ii Naosuke he was summoned back from his rural exile by Shimazu Hisamitsu; his lord wanted to make use of Takamori's political experience in Edo for which he had been trained by Nariakira.

Takamori was rather skeptical about his new lord's capability as a politician. Hisamitsu, like his uncle, wanted to become an important man by intervening in the reform of the bakufu, but Takamori tried to persuade him not to go to Edo—advice which was received with displeasure. When Takamori was ordered to go to Shimonoseki as a forerunner of Hisamitsu's contingent in the bakufu's punitive campaign against the Choshu exclusionists, he did not obey his instructions to stay there and wait for his master's arrival. Instead Takamori departed for Kyoto on his own judgement, intending to stop a reckless attempt at a coup by the Joi faction in Satsuma.

Both Nariakira and Hisamitsu supported the opening of Japan; moreover, it was suicidal to attempt a coup at this time. Being informed of the threat, Hisamitsu led his own army from Satsuma and marched for Edo. The Joi faction misunderstood Hisamitsu's move as a declaration of war on the bakufu; but Hisamitsu only wanted to demonstrate his power to the bakufu, and had no intention of destroying it. On Hisamitsu's orders, some of his retainers attacked members of the Joi faction who were staying at the Teradaya inn in Kyoto and killed some of them. Takamori's disobedience to Hisamitsu brought him another period of island exile, but, like the phoenix, he revived.

On the advice of Okubo Toshimichi, Hisamitsu reluctantly consented to Takamori's recall to his council, since he was the only man who had connections in both the emperor's court and the bakufu. He was responsible for crushing the Choshu rebellion at Hamaguri Gomon in 1863, which led to the sending of the bakufu's punitive force to Choshu. At first the leaders of Satsuma were positive about this move, and recommended Keiki as the general commander; but once again Takamori's (and the late Nariakira's) wish to make the brilliant Hitotsubashi Keiki a leader of the bakufu was disappointed. Tokugawa Yoshikatsu was named as general of the punitive army, with the strong support of the Kii Han; the enmity between the Kii and Hitotsubashi families now stood in the path of the Satsuma project to reform the bakufu.

Saigo Takamori still believed that the bakufu fundamentally supported the idea of reform; but in fact the regime's constant internal conflicts made this impossible. When he met Sakamoto Ryoma in Osaka on the eve of the Choshu expedition, the message sent by Katsu Kaishu astonished him: 'The bakufu is like an old tree, rotten in the trunk and helpless. A new government must be built by the powerful *hans*. Pacification of Choshu is meaningless in these critical days; this is not the time for the *hans* to fight one another.' Ryoma later told Kaishu that Takamori's reaction had been like a bell: struck gently, it makes a small sound, but if struck hard it makes a great sound. Kaishu nodded his agreement, no doubt remembering the evening which he had spent talking Ryoma out of killing him.

During the first government expedition to punish Choshu Han, Ryoma followed Katsu Kaishu. After suffering bombardment by the powerful foreign warships Choshu's leaders concluded that they could not resist the bakufu's attack, and surrendered to the regime with apologies. After this episode the bakufu recovered its confidence. Kaishu's maritime training school at Kobe became a target for the conservative faction within the regime, on the grounds that it trained samurai other than those serving the bakufu. Katsu Kaishu was dismissed from the school and summoned to Edo in October 1864; Ryoma and colleagues from the other *hans* lost their jobs, and the school closed in 1865. They were protected by Satsuma Han, however—partly because Kaishu asked Takamori to do so; and partly because they could be useful to a project to reorganize the Satsuma naval force after the defeat by the British.

Act IV: Ryoma's alliance

In May 1865, Saigo Takamori arrived in Satsuma and informed Ryoma that the bakufu were planning a second punitive war against Choshu. Furthermore he asked him to attempt a reconciliation between Satsuma and Choshu. On the face of it this was a daunting task, as these two *hans* belonged to basically opposed factions. The Satsuma wanted moderate reform of the bakufu, while Choshu had always been more radical, even extreme. Neither Shimazu Yoshihisa in Satsuma nor Yamanouchi Yodo in Tosa wanted to change the Japanese political structure which assured them of high position; they had never dreamed of true revolution. On the other hand, in Choshu the radical faction had connections with some ambitious aristocrats in

Right & opposite: In the Edo period, daimyo from the provinces were ordered to come to Edo to attend on the shogun. They travelled with their retainers, in processions designed to show off their status. When they arrived at way stations along the way, the head of the procession put on a performance of marching; but since passers-by were all supposed to sit and bow to pay respect, in theory no one saw it. These yakko *were the performers; the daimyo was carried in a* kago, *a kind of sedan chair, curtained from the gaze of the vulgar.*

Kyoto who eagerly pursued the idea of a restoration of imperial rule. Reconciliation of the two provinces behind a single plan did not at first seem realistically possible. In Choshu the daimyo, Mori, was in fact a puppet, and the true leader of opinion was Katsura Kogoro, the son of a wealthy doctor. (In the movement for restoration of imperial rule most of the activists came from the poor samurai class, beside whom Kogoro and Ryoma were both of wealthy background.) The Satsuma had been instrumental in destroying the Choshu Joi faction in the Hamaguri Gomon rebellion, and Katsura and his group distrusted Saigo Takamori. However, Ryoma visited Katsura to persuade him to become reconciled with Satsuma. Nakaoka Shintaro, another Tosa Han retainer and keen member of the Joi, visited Saigo Takamori and arranged a meeting at Shimonoseki; but Takamori did not appear there, because he went directly to Kyoto. Ryoma and Shintaro followed him there in some haste, and rebuked him for not attending the arranged meeting.

At the end of the year Kuroda Ryosuke, a Satsuma retainer, visited Katsura Kogoro and asked him to meet Takamori in Kyoto. Kogoro was naturally unwilling. To melt these Choshu suspicions of Satsuma required some material steps. Ryoma established a trading company in Nagasaki called Kameyamashachu, later renamed as Kaientai. (Trade with countries all over the world was Ryoma's ultimate dream; indeed, it might even be true to say that it was in pursuit of this dream that he became involved in the reformation of Japan.) After the bakufu's first punitive war against Choshu, foreign countries were strictly prohibited from trading in weapons with the dukedom. Ryoma's company purchased small arms from the British merchant Thomas Glover and sold them on to Choshu. Consequently the pro-alliance party in Choshu became stronger, and finally Katsura Kogoro consented to visit Takamori. In January 1866, Kogoro entered the gate of the Satsuma residence in Kyoto.

The meeting was not conducted with Western bluntness. The conversation between Takamori and Kogoro did not address immediate political concerns; the question of face was important, and perhaps Takamori did not at once suggest alliance because he wanted Kogoro to beg his help

for Choshu Han. Kogoro took the position that Takamori had invited him to Kyoto, and if Takamori did not start talking about the alliance then there was no use in staying any longer. This stalemate went on for ten fruitless days, until Kogoro was actually having his clothes packed to leave. Sakamoto Ryoma visited him and criticized this stupid over-concern with personal honor. Kogoro replied that Choshu Han was facing destruction at the hands of a vindictive bakufu and of four foreign navies. They needed helping hands to save them; but they did not care about their own destruction, if only Satsuma would definitely commit itself to destroy the bakufu. Ryoma fully understood Kogoro's concerns, and persuaded Takamori to sit down with him and conclude an alliance. With Ryoma's participation it was not long before Satsuma and Choshu reached agreement. The six articles of their secret alliance, concluded in January 1866, declared their goal to be the destruction of the Tokugawa bakufu.

The next evening, while Ryoma was staying at the Teradaya inn, the Fushimi police department sent men to attack him. For the past several months he had been tailed by agents of the bakufu's conservative faction, and he had been warned by a friendly bakufu retainer that he should be more careful. Ryoma and his friend Miyoshi Shinzo were discussing his great achievement in brokering the Choshu/Satsuma alliance in a room on the second floor of the inn. Suddenly Oryu, the adopted daughter of the innkeeper, burst into their room naked to warn them of the imminent raid: she had been taking a bath downstairs when through the window she saw the police approaching with

lanterns and spears. No sooner had Ryoma thrown a kimono to her and drawn his revolver than the police came through the door. He shot one of the attackers, and he and Shinzo made good their escape to the rear courtyard, from which they battered their way through the lightly built walls and partitions of neighboring houses until they reached the street. A party of Satsuma retainers soon rushed up to rescue them, and the injured Ryoma took sanctuary in the Satsuma residence in Kyoto. After this incident he and Oryu were married, and departed to Kyushu (this is supposed to have been the first 'honeymoon' in Japan).

Act V: The shogun's dilemma

While these retainers of the daimyos were vigorously pursuing their plans to terminate the bakufu, the regime had been facing a major dilemma.

The bakufu had concluded a commercial treaty with the US, but they needed to manipulate the Komei Emperor's dislike of foreigners. When the pro-bakufu faction crushed the coup by the Choshu Joi exclusionists at Hamaguri Gomon in 1864, it would have been a good opportunity to persuade the imperial court to agree to the opening of Japan. However, afraid of losing the emperor's support, the bakufu pretended to be somewhat sympathetic to the Joi faction.

In 1864 four powerful and influential daimyos assembled in Kyoto to discuss Japan's future policy; however, no real agreement was reached and they dispersed with nothing settled. Above all the bakufu had feared that the meeting would conclude with the opening of Japan, thus robbing the bakufu of the initiative with the court and the power to shape events—the domestic power struggle was of more concern to the bakufu than foreign relations. The shogunate had made concessions to the daimyos which allowed the latter to be far more independent, and many maintained private armed groups in or around Kyoto. Meanwhile it was in the interests of both the court and the bakufu that they should co-operate; and it was this wish for unity which gave rise to the campaign to punish the most zealous Joi of Choshu.

The results of the first punitive expedition to Choshu were not fully satisfactory to the bakufu, since Saigo Takamori of Satsuma had advised the commanding general Tokugawa Yoshikatsu not to be too harsh. The shogun Iemochi and the bakufu's counselors felt that Choshu deserved another lesson; and in 1865, Iemochi entered Osaka Castle to prepare for this greater punishment.

However, it was in 1865 that foreign frustration over the non-fulfillment of the commercial treaty brought US, Dutch, French and British ships to Osaka Bay. The foreign envoys brought the message that if the bakufu would not act to open the country to trade, they would negotiate with the emperor directly. The shogun Iemochi now attended on the emperor at court—for the first time in some 250 years, in an apparent admission of weakness. Komei dismissed two of the bakufu counselors who came to Kyoto with the shogun for intending to open Kobe harbor without imperial permission. In protest at this violation of his prerogatives Iemochi resigned his position; but after reconciliation by Hitotsubashi Keiki he withdrew his resignation. Keiki also

Samurai costume of the end of the Edo period.

and Goto Shojiro created the fundamental policy of the future government, which consisted of eight articles embracing the modernization of Japan. Although it was clearly stated that the emperor should have supreme authority, Ryoma wanted a peaceful transition from the *baku-han* system to an imperial restoration. His next move was to try to persuade the bakufu to return sovereignty to the emperor—a process known as Taiseihokan. At first Ryoma sought the help—as often before—of Matsudaira Shungaku; but the Echigen daimyo was unresponsive. Then Ryoma enlisted the aid of Yamanouchi Yodo, the daimyo of Tosa Han. Yodo was a rather conservative personality, who wanted a major role in the revolution as a great vassal of the bakufu.

On 13 October Tosa Han submitted to the bakufu a petition concerning the return of sovereignty to the emperor; and the shogun Tokugawa Keiki ordered the counselors to assess it. Naturally, Satsuma approved the submission. On 14 October the bakufu presented to the emperor a document for the execution of Taiseihokan, and this was approved by the imperial court.

The previous alliance between Satsuma and Choshu had envisaged the destruction of the bakufu by force; but Ryoma believed that in the critical situation confronting Japan a smooth and peaceful transition was essential. If the bakufu returned sovereignty to the imperial court, then Satsuma and Choshu would lose their reason to destroy the bakufu; and anyway, Satsuma's lord Shimazu Hisamitsu had never truly sought this end. The hand-over of sovereignty released the shogun Keiki from a complex situation involving simultaneous pressures from the Joi faction and the foreign powers, but still left him in the position of the greatest daimyo in Japan. Ryoma was deeply impressed with Keiki's decision, which vindicated his view that Tokugawa Keiki was the most suitable man to lead Japan into the future under imperial sovereignty.

Act VII: Ryoma's birthday visitors

At around 9 o'clock on the cold evening of November 15, 1867, Nagaoka Shintaro, a Tosa Han retainer who belonged to the faction favoring the destruction of the bakufu by force, arrived at the Omiya inn with three companions. One of the samurai asked the inn servant if there was a man called Saiya staying there—'Saiya' was Ryoma's codename. The servant, unsuspecting, confirmed it, and began to lead the way up the staircase. One of the samurai drew a blade and struck him in the back; then the four swordsmen climbed the staircase and advanced along the dark corridor. One of them said, 'Master Saiya, I have longed to meet you,' as he opened the sliding door of Ryoma's room.

As Ryoma looked up the assassin swept his sword in a

threatened the Joi faction at court and forced them to allow the execution of the commercial treaty. The Komei Emperor changed his mind in accordance with Keiki's advice, to favor opening the country. This solved the bakufu's dilemma by releasing them from the need to appear to support two opposed policies at once. The Joi faction at court now faced a difficult situation.

The second punitive expedition to Choshu was duly launched in summer 1866, and was a complete failure. The government troops compared badly with those of the Choshu Han in both morale and modern weapons; and the British naval squadron blocked the shogun's ships from operating off Shimonoseki on the arrogant pretext that this would endanger international shipping. After the failure of this second expedition to Choshu, Tokugawa Iemochi died at Osaka; and Hitotsubashi Keiki was elected as the 15th Tokugawa shogun, taking the name Yoshinobu.

Act VI: The surrender of the bakufu

In January 1867, Goto Shojiro, a Tosa counselor who had formerly belonged to the bakufu faction, visited Sakamoto Ryoma in Nagasaki. He offered to purchase the Kameyamashachyu Company on behalf of the Tosa Han, and to reorganize it in order to assist the dukedom's economy. In April it was renamed Kaientai or 'maritime aid company,' and Ryoma was appointed as the director. Members of the Kaientai were paid equally, and it became an economically independent company.

In 1867, while sailing from Nagasaki to Kyoto, Ryoma

Ornate Edo period armor. The 'turban shell' helmet is coated with gold leaf and has wakidate *side ornaments in the shape of waves. The cuirass is of European type, with armored sleeves and thigh protectors of scale construction. (Tokyo National Museum)*

sideways cut at his skull. Trying to seize the sword, Ryoma received another wound in the back. A third cut was blocked by Ryoma's scabbard, but he suffered a further head injury. In the confusion of the cramped struggle Nagaoka Shintaro was cut by another of the assassins; he tried to escape into the corridor but received a second wound. The assassins left the inn in haste, without delivering the *coup de grace* to their victim. Ryoma examined his face in his mirror-bright sword, and murmured 'A head wound—I am finished' as his consciousness faded. Nagaoka Shintaro, found lying unconscious himself by the innkeeper, lingered for two days before dying—long enough to give this testimony of what happened that evening. Sakamoto Ryoma had died on his thirty-second birthday.

Who was responsible for the killing of Ryoma? Under the Kyoto *shugo* there were two police organizations, the Shinsengumi and Mimawarigumi. When Matsudaira Katamori, the lord of Aizu, was appointed as *shugo* his soldiers were based at the Komyoji Temple. The Mimawarigumi stayed at a branch temple of the Komyoji

and executed their duties around the temples of the city. Ryoma was regarded as a criminal because he had killed one of the police raiders with his revolver during the attack on him at the Teradaya inn; so it would not be strange if he was a police target. According to the memoir of Teshirogi Suguemon, an inspector of the Shinsengumi who served under Matsudaira Katamori, it was Katamori who ordered Ryoma's assassination, and Suguemon is a credible source. But if Ryoma was a criminal why did the Mimawarigumi resort to assassination? Legitimate police activity did not have to be kept secret.

If it was not a simple matter of police revenge, then who profited most from Ryoma's death? The answer must be, that the men who wanted to unleash military violence against the bakufu broke from the spell of the most influential voice speaking against civil war.

The name Ryoma stands for 'dragon horse' in Japanese. He appeared in the last days of the samurai class, and ran like a dragon across the sky. His attractive character, which united those who wanted to change Japan from a stagnant feudal society into an active modern country, was lost to his people at a tragically early age. His dream of making Japan a free country open to worldwide trade would not be fully accomplished until the end of the Second World War.

Epilogue

Conveniently enough for the radicals of Choshu, in December 1867 the Komei Emperor—who disliked the violent Choshu samurai and young, ambitious aristocrats—died of smallpox. Because his death was too timely for Choshu rumors spread in Kyoto that he had been assassinated by extremist aristocrats. His heir Mutsuhito, the Meiji Emperor, was only fourteen years old and was helpless in this confused situation; the faction who gained control of him would obtain the cover of the imperial flag for any attempt to destroy their enemies. With Ryoma gone there was no longer any brake on Choshu's and Satsuma's ambition to tear down the Tokugawas. Yamanouchi Yodo of Tosa Han strongly resisted the extremist party, proposing a settlement which was acceptable to the shogun: the office would be abolished, but he would keep his lands and the position of prime minister, working with a council of the powerful daimyos. The settlement did not satisfy Choshu and Satsuma, however. During a meeting at the imperial court the radicals used threats on Yodo's life to bulldoze through their plot against Keiki. Ryoma's dreams of peaceful transition had died with him.

In January 1868 the young Meiji Emperor, in the hands of the radicals, proclaimed that he was assuming all powers. Outmaneuvered into a position where he had to choose between disobeying the emperor and losing his lands, the last shogun advanced on Kyoto from Osaka Castle with some

15,000 men. Soon the Tokugawa army met in battle at Toba-Fushimi the 'imperial' army of Choshu, Satsuma and Tosa, led by Saigo Takamori—only about a third of its size, but much better armed and trained. Defeated, Keiki fell back to Edo; and there, two months later, he surrendered.

Thus imperial government was restored by the hands of Choshu and Satsuma—long ago, the losers at Sekigahara. In 1869 the Meiji government abolished the rigid class hierarchies of the Tokugawa period; from now on all Japanese would be either nobles, gentry, or commoners, and the latter were granted freedom of occupation and residence—though this did not mean that the Japanese people were yet emancipated from the residue of feudalism. Nevertheless, in 1871 the position of daimyo was abolished, and their *hans* were replaced by prefectures administered by the centralized government. Their castles and private armies disappeared forever; thereafter the army would be a national conscript force drawn from all classes. After 700 years of history, the samurai's status and occupation

After the Meiji restoration there were a few last episodes of desperate resistance to the imperial forces. The Aizu wakamatsu of 1868, under Matsudaira Katamori, saw young boys and even girls sent into action, suffering great losses. In Nihonmatsu Han boys as young as twelve were given rifles and sent into battle against the royalists.

were gone; and in 1876 the wearing of swords was forbidden to all but members of the armed forces.

Katsura Kogoro died in 1877. So did Saigo Takamori, at the hands of a faithful retainer after he fell wounded in the last battle of the failed Satsuma rebellion which he led in Kyushu that year. In 1899, Katsu Kaishu died of apoplexy in his house. Men from Satsuma, Choshu and Tosa exclusively formed the governments of the Meiji Emperor; and this sectionalism, against which Sakatomo Ryoma had striven, would eventually lead Japan into devastating world war.

PART 2:
THE AGE OF
THE COUNTRY AT WAR
REPRESENTATIVE CAMPAIGNS AND FAMILIES

THE BATTLE OF OKEHAZAMA, 1560

In May 1560, Imagawa Yoshimoto, the daimyo of Suruga province, set off to the borders of Mikawa and Owari at the head of 25,000 men. His immediate purpose was to secure his grip over castles which had recently changed sides to Imagawa from Oda Nobunaga of Owari. Kutsukake, Odaka and Narumi castles in Mikawa had previously been allied to the Oda family, but they were basically in the domain of Yoshimoto's then vassal Matsudaira Motoyasu (the future Tokugawa Ieyasu).

In the past it has been supposed that the true aim of Yoshimoto's march to the Owari border was to enter Kyoto and demonstrate his power to the other daimyos in the provinces. In the Sengoku period the warlord who secured Kyoto, where the emperor resided, was acknowledged to be the strongest daimyo and was able to exert authority over others. In the early Sengoku period, at the end of the 15th century, daimyos struggled with one another simply to secure or expand their provincial domains. Gradually, however, they had become conscious of the possibility of unifying Japan under a central authority. According to such a point of view, Yoshimoto's march to Owari has been interpreted as a sign of his intention to enter Kyoto and establish his hegemony. However, there are arguments against this theory.

Generally, when a daimyo planned to attack his neighbor, he first negotiated vigorously with other regional warlords in order to secure his rear or silence any rivals around him while his forces were committed to this new campaign. In this case, however, Yoshimoto had taken no such precautions before his march. East of his domain there was another strong family, the Hojo of Sagami; without a preemptive alliance with the Hojo it is unlikely that Imagawa would have risked provoking them by such a major step as an attempt on Kyoto. Today it seems most probable that the goal of his march to the Mikawa-Owari border was indeed simply to secure the three castles which had recently become friendly to his cause.

On 18 May 1560, Yoshimoto entered Kutsukake Castle and held a council of war. His vassal Matsudaira Motoyasu sent troops and supplies to the other two castles, and then began to attack the Oda fortress at Marune. At the same time Yoshimoto's other vassals initiated an attack on the fortress at Washizu.

On the morning of 19 May, Oda Nobunaga departed Kiyosu Castle with just six horsemen and 2,000 *ashigaru*. He marched first to the fortress of Tange, and then to those at Zenshoji and Nakajima. These movements appeared to be intended to isolate Narumi Castle, which had by now fallen into Imagawa Yoshimoto's hands. For their part, Yoshimoto's main force moved to Okehazama with the intention of supporting Narumi Castle.

The famous account of the battle of Okehazama runs as follows. Seeing that the troops in the Imagawa camp were drunk and dancing in premature celebration of victory, Oda Nobunaga by-passed the enemy front line and moved through the hills to attack the camp from the rear, defeating the enemy and killing Imagawa Yoshimoto. However, a newly discovered memoir written by Ota Guichi, a Nobunaga retainer, paints a different picture.

Nobunaga's force of 2,000 samurai arrived at Nakajima fortress in the mid-afternoon of 19 May. Nobunaga announced his intention to attack the Imagawa main forces, although his retainers tried to persuade him against it. Nobunaga argued that the Imagawa forces were exhausted after attacking the two fortresses of Washizu and Imane, and weakened by having had to garrison Narumi Castle, whereas his soldiers were rested and morale was high—they should not let this chance go by! In this, however, he was

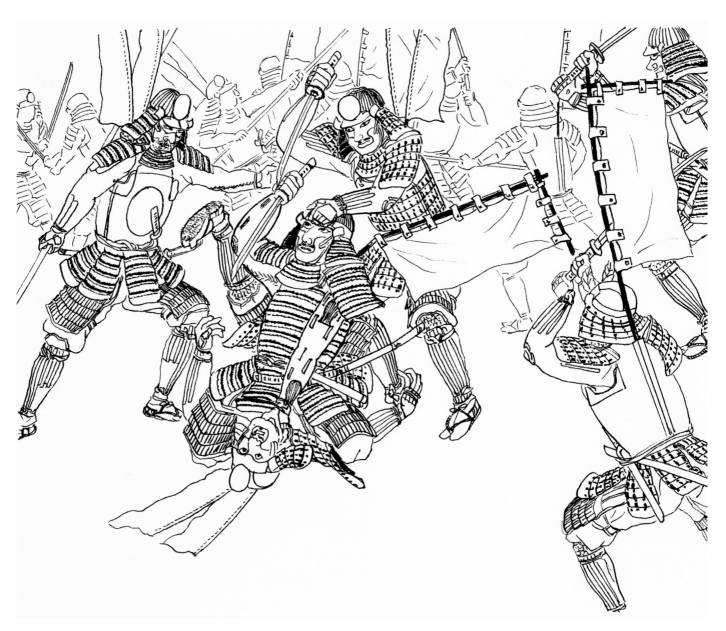

In late Heian and Kamakura period battles, when a samurai was challenged to personal combat by an enemy he had to accept, on pain of being considered a coward; and his retainers usually did not interfere with these personal duels. But by the Sengoku period the face of warfare had changed. In the confusion of battle, to seek to take a fallen opponent's head as a trophy was a dangerous hazard. His followers might easily intervene, and the victor could quickly become the vanquished.

mistaken: the troops which had attacked the friendly fortresses were not the Imagawa main corps—they were the forces of Imagawa's allies Matsudaira and Ii. Such errors sometimes lead to good results, however.

Oda Nobunaga's troops marched across low-lying ground toward the Imagawa front line; probably he aimed to attack the enemy by hit-and-run tactics, falling back after achieving limited gains. A direct attack on an overwhelmingly stronger enemy was suicidal; the samurai of this period were practical soldiers, and the calculating Nobunaga was certainly not stupid enough to commit his troops to a hopeless attack. One or two minor victories over Yoshimoto would be enough to stop his advance on Owari; it would be very risky for the enemy to advance deep into Nobunaga's domain without having secured their rear. But the unfolding of events changed the anticipated outcome.

When Nobunaga's forces reached the foot of Okehazama Mountain a furious storm broke out behind them, strong enough to bow down big trees. The Imagawa vanguard

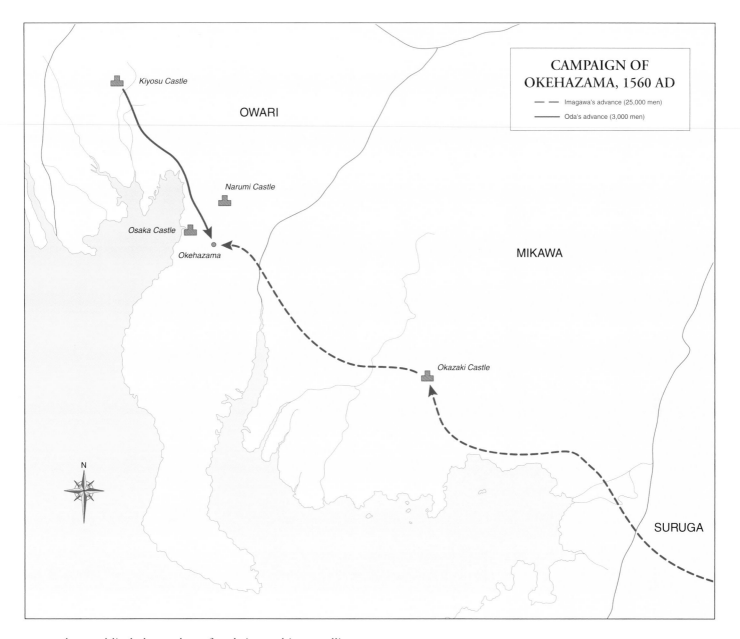

were almost blinded as they faced into this appalling weather, and Nobunaga's attack reduced them to confusion. Nobunaga's cautious orders had been to advance if the enemy retreated, but to fall back if the enemy pushed forward. In any event the Imagawa first line disintegrated like dust in the wind; Nobunaga's forces charged forward; and as they pushed into the enemy position he recognized Yoshimoto's flag, and ordered his men to rush towards it. The enemy commander was defended by 300 guards; after several charges these were reduced to 50 men. Nobunaga and his own bodyguard crashed into them; finally, Yoshimoto was killed by Hattori Koheita and Mori Shinsuke, and his head was taken as a prize in the usual way.

In the course of a battle both sides will make errors, and victory is only granted by the hand of Lady Luck. Historians often explain the results in terms of the victor making the right decisions and the vanquished the wrong ones. Okehazama is a useful reminder that on the battlefield there is always room for chance to play a part.

FORTIFICATIONS AND CASTLES

Right & opposite top: Reconstructed medieval fortifications of Sakasai Castle in Ibaragi prefecture.

Opposite below: The largest gate of Himeji Castle, built in the Azuchi-Momoyama style.

In the 8th century AD, when the Kyoto government tried to extend their rule toward Tohoku, they often clashed with a people they called *emishi*. In the course of their campaigns against these barbarians, as they were called, Kyoto forces constructed fortifications—*saku*—to prevent infiltration by the *emishi* into pacified areas. For hundreds of years the manner of constructing such fortifications never varied. Even in the famous battle of Shitaragahara (1575), fought by the allied armies of Oda and Tokugawa against Takeda, the basic construction of the field defenses was unchanged since those of the 7th/8th centuries AD.

The basic elements of such defenses were a ditch, a rampart and a palisade. In most cases the defenders also cut down trees and made an abatis by setting them with their untrimmed branches toward the enemy. Usually the defenders chose a hilltop position from which they could shoot down at the approaching enemy with bows. A range of booby traps was also added to further slow the enemy advance; and observation towers were sometimes built if time permitted. Before the introduction of firearms both defenders and attackers would use portable shields or mantlets, perhaps 4.5 x 1.5ft (roughly 1.4 x 0.45m) in size. These shields were connected together in the lines of fortification; in open field battles they were carried by retainers or peasants who advanced with the samurai who were armed with missile weapons, covering them while they shot and reloaded. Given the habitual tactics of early samurai warfare, the primary object of fortifications was to prevent the mounted enemy charging home.

At Atsukashi in Fukushima prefecture there are 1.86 miles (3km) of double ditches which are attributed to operations by Minamoto Yoritomo's forces during the war of 1189. Constructing these ditches supposedly took 5,000 workers a month's labor; this estimate excludes the manpower needed for other tasks such as building ramparts, palisades and tower. Such massive defenses had also probably been constructed during the preceding Genpei War of 1180-85; at Ichinotani in 1184, Heishi forces constructed major fortifications which Minamoto no Noriyori's army overcame only with great difficulty.

Such temporary field fortifications were constructed to block the main route of an enemy advance. On the other hand, during the Heian period a samurai's residence was defended by a moat and palisades. Such defended residences were also constructed in the field, but in such cases the tactical characteristics of the location had secondary importance. In the late Kamakura period (13th century) such field residences were more heavily protected by constructions on the spot, but the basic defensive elements were unchanged: ditch and rampart, fence and tower.

When the Mongols invaded Japan for the second time in 1281, the Kamakura bakufu ordered the building of stone walls at Hakata Bay. These walls are 12.4 miles (20km) long, 6.5ft (2m) high, and have a width at the top of 3.9ft (1.2m); on the inside of the walls are ditches. The purpose of the walls was obviously to prevent the landing and deployment of Mongol cavalry. Recent research has led to

Above: *The massive moat of Osaka Castle. After its fall in 1615 the castle was completely destroyed by Tokugawa Ieyasu. The second Tokugawa shogun, Hidetada, ordered its rebuilding on the same site, but instructed Todo Takatora, who was in charge of the project, to make the moat wall twice as high as before.*

Left: *Himeji Castle: a yahazama or arrow slit, giving onto a down-slanting tunnel through the wall.*

Opposite: *Hikone Castle: access bridge to main building over the ditch. Sengoku and early Edo period castles were thoroughly protected in various ways, and it was unusual for one to be taken by storm. Attackers normally encircled them and tried to starve the garrison out—or bribe their way in through treachery—so as to avoid the inevitably heavy casualties of an assault.*

the advance of a theory that this system of defenses was also used as a base for the abortive 16th century invasion of Korea, but it is reasonable to speculate that the walls were built for defensive purposes—it would not be efficient to raise such a long perimeter for a fort. Stone walls were still unusual in the 13th century, and it would be another hundred years or so, in the Muromachi period, before stone-built castles appeared.

In the Muromachi period the development of commerce and of urban economies under the *shugo-daimyo* led to a concentration of wealth. *Shugo* indicates a provincial executive appointed by the Muromachi bakufu, and *daimyo*, a landowner on a baronial scale. (It should be pointed out that some writers have translated *daimyo* as 'big name'; but *myo* refers to the kind of registered estate, not the name.) Such magnates usually raised fortresses on hilltops, and their retainers lived on the flats below. In peacetime the warlord lived in his house at the foot of the hill; but when enemies attacked he withdrew to his hilltop stronghold and waited for rescuers to arrive. The numbers are astonishing:

it is speculated that in the early Sengoku period some 30,000 to 40,000 mountain fortresses existed in Japan.

It has been believed that the first castle constructed with massive stone walls and a high tower was Azuchi, built by order of Oda Nobunaga beside Lake Biwa. Azuchi was the most suitable place to control the approaches to Kyoto from the east and north. Since Biwa is the largest lake in Japan, water-borne trade proliferated. Nobunaga raised a sizeable town in the shelter of the castle and ordered retainers and soldiers to take up residence there. The castle had thus started to fulfill several functions: residence, fortification, checkpoint, commercial center, and symbol of the ruler's power. Various buildings such as a temple, church and tower were added to the castle, and profusely decorated.

After Nobunaga's death in 1582 Toyotomi Hideyoshi took over the hegemony of Japan, and decided to raise an even larger stronghold than Azuchi. The following year he ordered work started on Osaka Castle on the location where the former Ishiyama Honganji temple had stood. During Nobunaga's siege of the temple it had proved its virtual

impregnability; not only was it tactically formidable, but its location on the Yodo River ensured Hideyoshi's communications to Kyoto and Lake Biwa, and sea trade via Setonaikai or the Inland Sea brought tremendous wealth from China. Osaka was the first large castle to be built on flat ground. After this example, daimyo began to construct their own castles in places geographically favorable for commerce. Among these, Himeji Castle near Kobe has the most beautiful proportions. Ikeda Tarumasa ordered its construction in 1601, and it was completed in 1616 by Honda Tadamasa. With its original wooden interior structure basically intact, Himeji boasts not only a beautiful appearance, but also elaborate defensive works.

Most Japanese castles suffered destruction not in war but by earthquake and accidental fire. The final blow was the order of the 19th century Meiji government by which all but three of the keeps were destroyed. Himeji, Hikone and Matsumoto Castles alone still lend their beauty and grace to their home cities.

Top left & left: *Himeji Castle: racked arquebuses with gunpowder bags and match cord, and spears. These are not very long, so as to be easier to handle indoors.*

Below: *Himeji Castle.*

THE BEARS OF KYUSHU
FROM THE 8TH TO THE 16TH CENTURIES AD

Completely equipped typical Muromachi period samurai leader. The details show the left armpit area without sode *or gyoyo; and armored shoes, of iron plates attached together with narrow strips of ring mail. (SY)*

In ancient times the peoples of Kyushu were called Kumaso or Hayahito. They did not acknowledge the Yamato government in Kyoto, which had sent forces to subjugate them. Even today we do not know exactly what kind of people they were. We do know that Kyushu was the 'front door' of Japan, and civilization mainly arrived on the islands from across the sea and by way of Korea; so Kyushu had undoubtedly been hotly contended in all periods. Around AD 700, when the Yamato government established an empire stretching from Kyushu to Tohoku, it founded Dazaifu, near Hakata. Dazaifu was the seat of a semi-independent government and was sometimes called the 'distant court'. It was not only a capital of Kyushu, but also a defensive center for Japan as a whole, and a center of commerce with the Asian mainland and particularly Korea.

Today archaeological evidence proves that in northern Kyushu there were many settlements whose people engaged in rice culture. Obviously they were descended from immigrants from the continent, partly through the Korean peninsula. Mythological analysis also suggests that a very influential kingdom—possibly that of the Japanese emperor's ancestors—moved east from Kyushu to Yamato; however, the exact relationship between the imperial dynasty and that of Kyushu is not clearly understood.

When a Japanese expeditionary force sent to help the Korean Paekche dynasty was defeated by the allied forces of Silla and Tang, the Yamato government decided to withdraw from Korea; and fearing an imminent invasion by these allied peoples, they reinforced the defenses of Dazaifu and concentrated a guard force there. These guard troops—*sakimori*—were drafted from the Kanto area, and their service was hard; when they were called to serve they had to travel the long distance

Kamakura to Nanbokucho periods. **Top:** *Samurai leader wearing the* do maru, *the chest covered with a decorative printed leather panel. His helmet has long antlers or* kuwagata *and a dragon* maedate *or frontal ornament. He wears a cape, to entangle arrows from behind him; this later evolved into the* horo *or balloon-shaped back-flag.* **Bottom:** *Poorer samurai wearing* haramaki *and, at left, the* menpo *face guard over the cap rather than a helmet. (SY)*

Unfortunately for the Go-Daigo Emperor, Ashikaga Takauji rebelled against him in 1335; and when Takauji had been defeated by the imperial forces, he escaped to Kyushu subjugating Shoni Yorihisa. In spite of Yorihisa's obedience, Takauji appointed Ishiki Noriuji as chief *tandai*. Displeased with this, Yorihisa began to support the imperial forces. Such short-sighted behavior on the part of Takauji prolonged the conflict in Kyushu between the southern and northern courts. By 1354 the Ishiki family had been expelled from Kyushu by Shoni Yorihisa, and for ten years a faction friendly to the southern court was dominant on the island.

The shogun Ashikaga Yoshimitsu sent Imagawa Ryoshun to Kyushu to suppress the southern court's partisans. Ryoshun's pacification almost succeeded after two years of turmoil; he finally surrounded the Kikuchi family, major supporters of the southern court, in their castle. At the final stage, he invited three powerful *shugo*—Shimazu Ujihisa, Otomo Chikayo, and Shoni Fuyusuke (Yorihisa's son)—to discuss the post-war dispositions on Kyushu. As Fuyusuke did not respond to Ryoshun's invitation, Ryoshun asked Shimazu Ujihisa to mediate. Unable to refuse, Fuyusuke presented himself at Mizushima; but during the banquet Imagawa Ryoshun's brother Nakaaki stabbed Fuyusuke to death. Shimazu Ujihisa naturally lost face, and he returned to Satsuma in anger. This incident set back Ryoshun's efforts disastrously, and it was 20 years before he finally managed to restore peace in Kyushu. Shortly thereafter, Ryoshun was dismissed as *tandai* by the shogun Yoshimitsu and recalled to Kyoto. Naturally, his dismissal pleased the three *shugo* families in Kyushu.

Unlike his predecessor, the next *tandai*, Shibukawa Yorimitsu, was not a potent governor, and only managed to retain his position with the help of the Ouchi family of Nagato. In 1423 the powerful Shoni Mitsusaza drove him out of Hakata. The Ashikaga (Muromachi) bakufu naturally reacted against this rebellion and made Hakata its direct domain, appointing Ouchi Moriharu as the regime's magistrate there; this began the intervention of the Ouchi family in Kyushu. The Otomo family in Bungo were displeased by the bakufu's intervention and allied themselves with the Shoni; this alliance attacked the Ouchi and killed Moriharu, but an Ouchi counterattack destroyed Shoni Mitsusada in 1433. The conflict was aggravated by the chaotic situation in Kyoto during the Onin War, 1467-77;

to Kyushu at their own expense. However, peace in Korea brought prosperity to Dazaifu, which functioned as a trading station between Japan and the continent. The price was that it often became a target for rebels in Kyushu.

The Shoni and the Ouchi

In the Kamakura period, when the Mongols invaded Japan in 1274 and 1281, Dazaifu became a defensive headquarters; fortunately the Mongols did not penetrate far enough to reach it and it consequently escaped destruction. After the invasion, the Kamakura bakufu founded the office of *chinzei tandai* at Hakata—the holder of military, executive and legal power. The bakufu also appointed three *shugo* or governors to police Kyushu, granting this office to the Shoni, Otomo and Shimazu families. After the establishment of the *tandai*, Hakata became the front gate of Japan. During the invasions most of the active Japanese forces were provided by the samurai of Kyushu, who showed remarkable prowess under the leadership of their three *shugo*. Despite this, after the war the Hojo family descended from Kamakura to rule them. It was thus not surprising that when the Go-Daigo Emperor attempted a coup in 1333, Kyushu responded to his call and worked to destroy the Kamakura bakufu.

but by 1533, Ouchi Masahiro had destroyed both the Shoni and Shibukawa families and acquired northern Kyushu.

A Christian ruler: Otomo Sorin

The Otomo family were originally Kanto samurai. With the establishment of the Kamakura bakufu in the 1190s, Otomo Yoshinao was given a position as *jito* in Bungo, Higo and Chikugo by the first Kamakura shogun Yoritomo. Three generations later, Otomo Yoriyasu succeeded to the position of *shugo*. Although the family was favored by the bakufu, they rebelled against the Hojo regency and joined the imperial party following the Mongol invasions. After the destruction of the Kamakura bakufu in the 1330s, Ashikaga Takauji established the Muromachi bakufu and appointed another governor or *tandai* over Kyushu. Unlike the Shoni family, the Otomo did not react openly against this appointment; but, like the Shimazu, they did not welcome it.

During the Nanbokucho period of the rival northern and southern courts, 1336–92, domestic conflict hindered the development of the Otomo family. The Ouchi and the shogun in Kyoto intervened in the Otomo succession crisis. During the Onin War of 1467–77 the Otomo faced destruction. In 1498 the family feud was aggravated by the widespread dispute over the succession to the shogunate; Otomo Masachika killed his son Yoshisuke, and was himself driven to suicide by the Ouchi. But the Otomo somehow managed to survive this critical moment, and began to re-establish themselves.

In 1515, Otomo Yoshiharu succeeded to the leadership. During his rule he destroyed rebellious families such as the Kuchiki, Ohgami and Saeki, and established an unshakable position in Bungo. He approached the shogun and secured for himself the position of *shugo* in Higo. He governed his domain for 35 years, but in spring 1550 he met a tragic end.

The eldest son of Otomo Yoshiharu was Yoshishige. In 1550, Yoshiharu tried for unknown reasons to disinherit Yoshishige, and named as his heir Shioichimaru, his son by a favorite mistress. Yoshiharu sent Yoshishige away to Beppu, and summoned his four counselors to announce his intentions; but they objected strongly, and told him that such a decision would cause damaging conflict. Displeased by their resistance, he dismissed them; but after a few days he invited these four retainers to his house once more. Only two of them accepted his invitation, and were killed by their master. The other two excused themselves, feigning illness; and when they heard what had befallen their colleagues they decided that the only way to save their own lives was to kill their master. They assaulted Yoshiharu, wounding him severely and killing his mistress and Shioichimaru before they themselves were struck down by their master's guards. Yoshishige returned from Beppu, and Yoshiharu accepted his son's succession. Otomo Yoshishige's position after his

succession was unstable, and a few years later three retainers attempted his assassination. (These episodes are a reminder that in the Sengoku period the retainers of a baronial family still had considerable power, and their wishes had great influence on a prudent daimyo's decisions.)

* * *

The historical estimation of Otomo Yoshishige (Sorin) differs depending on the commentator. Edo period historians treated him as a villain, because Yoshishige was a patron of Christians, while Christian missionaries reported him to be an ideal monarch. It is not easy even to depict his real image; missionary reports to the Vatican are regarded as highly credible when they describe appearances, but in this case they contradict those of Edo period historians who reported that Sorin was physically weak. Of course, if this were true it would not bias a Christian against him. The facts seem to be that rather than being a warrior, Sorin had an aristocratic taste for such pastimes as the tea ceremony, ball games, painting and calligraphy.

The Otomo had been an old family since the Kamakura period and persisted in the traditional culture; they had revolutionary ideas neither on the management of domestic policy nor the abolishing of tradition. A daimyo or warlord who superceded the former master in his domain generally had to have progressive ideas in order to break through the rigid establishments of the Kamakura and Muromachi periods, when samurai society was organized in a hierarchical pyramid. The retainers of the Otomo family consisted of three kinds: related retainers, retainers who had followed them since the Kamakura period, and new followers. Since the master of the family was not powerful enough to control his retainers, he was often troubled by rebellion.

In 1551, Sorin invited the Portuguese missionary Francisco Xavier to Funai Castle where he lived. This invitation was at first prompted simply by curiosity and the wish for rare trade goods; but as time passed he was converted to Catholicism. When the mission was first given permission to preach in Funai only the poor and sick became believers; but soon it counted 1,500 converts. The daimyo himself had become a Buddhist priest of the Zen sect in 1562, and his wife was a Shinto high priest's daughter. She was naturally displeased when he showed an inclination towards Christianity, which inevitably provoked conflict between the Buddhists and Christians in his domain. Retainers who were attached to the Buddhist sect began to leave Sorin's service. Yet despite the dispute troubling his earthly kingdom, in 1567 he formally divorced his wife and married a woman who understood his beliefs.

His domain was located in the eastern part of Kyushu. Northern Kyushu had belonged to the Shoni and the eastern region to the Kikuchi family, but various conflicts had brought these areas into Otomo territory. The Ouchi had destroyed the Shoni, but in 1557 Ouchi Yoshitaka was slain by his retainer Sue Takafusa. Inevitably, the Otomo acquired the northern part of Kyushu, Chikuzen and Hozen. Since Sorin had destroyed the Kikuchi family of Higo in 1553, he now became the strongest daimyo in Kyushu. At this time the Shimazu family were spending all their efforts in domestic conflict and were not powerful enough to challenge the Otomo.

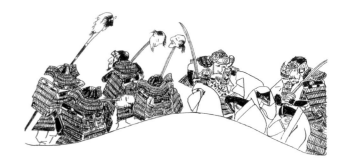

The struggle for Moji Castle

After the destruction of Sue Harukata by the Mori at the battle of Itsukushima Island, the victors claimed the former Ouchi domain in Kyushu from Otomo Sorin, who occupied it. Moji Castle, located facing the Kanmon Strait and dominating the entrance to the Inland Sea, was strategically important; for the Mori, Moji was the jumping-off place to Kyushu. In 1558, Mori Motonari took the castle from the Otomo and appointed Niho Uemon as its constable at the head of 3,000 soldiers. Otomo Sorin sent two generals, who drove Niho and the Mori garrison out. As soon as Mori Motonari learned of the recapture of the castle he ordered his son Takamoto and third son Kobayakawa Takakage to attack the Otomo forces.

In September 1558, Takakage's general Nomi Munekatsu crossed the channel and landed on the beach between Moji and Kokura. He assaulted Moji Castle from the rear, and wiped out the Otomo defenders. Furthermore, Munekatsu put Mori troops astride the Otomo supply route and forced their army to retreat. Although Moji Castle had been lost to him again, Sorin did not give up. In August 1561 he ordered his general Yoshihiro Kabei to attack it once more at the head of 15,000 Otomo troops. He also asked the captain of a Portuguese warship, which was anchored at the time in Funai Bay, to assist his attack on the Mori garrison. The warship, which is presumed to have had a broadside of 17 guns a side, duly bombarded Moji Castle; but despite their exposure to a devastating firepower which must have been entirely new to them, the Mori samurai held the castle. The crisis passed with the sudden retirement of the Portuguese ship; and the Otomo forces settled down to lay siege to Moji Castle.

On 21 August 1561 a Mori rescue force, led again by Mori Takamoto and Kobayakawa Takakage, set out for Hofu on the mainland side of the channel. The Mori had taken control of the sea with the help of the Murakami and Enouchi navies, so their crossing of the channel went unhindered by the Otomo. Troops from the Horitate and Sugi families crossed the Kanmon Strait and entered the castle, breaking the Otomo encirclement. But Otomo's forces, too, were strengthened by reinforcements. In spite of the Mori pincer tactics, of landing parties to cut the Otomo supply route, the siege was maintained. A general assault on the castle began on 10 October, but was foiled

After a defeat, the heads of the vanquished samurai were taken as trophies; and their people were taken as slaves, to be sold at market or put to hard labor on the victors' domains. History tends to disregard these wretched and nameless victims. (SY)

when Kobayakawa Takakage crossed the channel and entered the castle. Finally, Mori landing parties succeeded in cutting Otomo's rear lines; and on 5 November the Otomo army withdrew to avoid further losses.

In 1563 the two families negotiated a peace, reconciled by shogun Ashikaga Yoshiteru; the Mori agreed because they were nervous of being attacked simultaneously by the Amako family in Izumo. However, this temporary lull in northern Kyushu naturally ended after the destruction of the Amako by Mori Motonari. In 1567 many barons in northern Kyushu rebelled against the Otomo and asked for Mori support, drawing some 40,000 Mori soldiers into the region. Otomo Sorin sent 35,000 men in his turn, and for half a year the armies confronted one another at the River Tatara. While doing so, Sorin gave troops to some Ouchi relatives and let them attack to recover their former domain; harassed in the rear, the Mori forces withdrew to face the new enemy. By the time they returned to Kyushu after destroying Ouchi Teruhiro's forces in Yamaguchi, the

Otomo had crushed the rebels. It seems that half of the island was now in Otomo hands.

Kamakura period samurai in oyoroi *armor.*

The Ryuzoji

In the Kamakura period, Sato Suekiyo was appointed *jito* by the bakufu and moved to Ryuzoji village in Hizen; thereafter his family took the name Ryuzoji. In the late Muromachi period Ryuzoji Iekane served the Shoni as *shugo* in Hizen. In 1530, when the Ouchi in Chikugo sent forces to pacify Hizen, Ryuzoji Iekane followed Shoni Sukemoto, and defeated Ouchi forces with the help of Nabeshima Kiyohisa. A brave charge by Ryuzoji Iekane impressed the Nabeshima family, and he married off his granddaughter to Nabeshima Kiyuhisa's son Kiyofusa. In 1533, Shoni Sukemoto attacked Iwaya Castle and defeated the deputy *shugo* in Chikuzen, who had been appointed by the Ouchi. To recover the lost territory the Ouchi sent their powerful retainer Sue Yoshihiro to Chikuzen, and he duly smashed the Shoni forces at Tatarahama Beach, recovering

Dazaifu. Yoshihiro advanced into Hizen, surrounding the Shoni home castle and also the Ryuzoji base, Mizugae Castle. Ryuzoji Iekane directed a daring night raid on the Sue camp and dispersed the attackers, obliging them to retreat to Chikuzen. But the Ouchi onslaught brought down the Shoni family nevertheless: Shoni Sukemoto committed suicide at Senshoji Temple, and his son Fuyuhisa took refugee in Hasuike Castle.

Ryuzoji Iekane continued to support Fuyuhisa; but old retainers of the Shoni became resentful of Iekane's growing influence over their master. Baba Yorikane slandered Iekane to Fuyuhisa time after time; and in 1544, Fuyuhisa finally consented to destroy Iekane. A plot to wear down his forces took Iekane's army away to pacify a rebellion in west Hizen; when the weary and unsuccessful expedition withdrew from west Hizen, Shoni forces suddenly encircled Mizugae Castle. Baba Yorikane visited Iekane, pretending friendship,

During the Sengoku period the goshi *were the class which fell between the true samurai and the* ashigaru. *They were farmers in peacetime, but when an emergency arose they put on their armor—which was always kept ready in the fields—and marched straight off to battle. The summons was very unwelcome if it came in the rice-planting season. (SY)*

and advised him that if he would abandon the castle and retire to Chikugo, Baba would mediate for him with Fuyuhisa. Iekane left the castle to go to Chikugo; and Baba promptly attacked Iekane's sons and grandsons. His retainers killed them all, and their severed heads were presented to Fuyuhisa. Iekane, 90 years old, was left alone with his anger and grief in Chikugo.

Nabeshima Kiyohisa, father-in-law of Ryuzoji Iekane's daughter, collected his soldiers to exact revenge on the Baba family alongside his aged master. As soon as the news spread in his former territory that Iekane had returned, hidden retainers got together to help his cause. After retaking Mizugae Castle without difficulty, they advanced to Gionyama Castle which the Baba family were defending. All the people of the country, down to peasants, flocked to join the Ryuzoji forces. Baba Yorichika and his son escaped from the castle, but were caught by pursuing samurai and

beheaded. Iekane made his great-grandson Engetsubo return from his religious life to play his part in the leadership of the Ryuzoji (he was later called Takanobu).

Ryuzoji Tanemitsu, Iekane's great-nephew and next in line for the leadership, had escaped to Chikuzen, where he enlisted the help of the Ouchi in seeking revenge on the Shoni family. Tanemitsu and Takanobu co-operated to destroy the Shoni, with the support of the Ouchi deputy *shugo* Sugi Takamitsu. In 1548, Tanemitsu died of illness and the 20-year-old Takanobu succeeded to leadership of the main family of Ryuzoji by request of their old retainers.

In reality, the Ryuzoji relied most upon the solid support of the Ouchi. In spite of young Takanobu's confidence, the solidarity of his retainers was fragile. As soon as the Sue destroyed the Ouchi, Ryuzoji's retainers allied themselves to Otomo Sorin and attempted a coup against their master. Saga Castle was besieged by Takanobu's former retainers in 1551; he took refuge in Chikugo with his family, and it was five years before he could recover Saga Castle. In 1558, Shoni Fuyuhisa tried to attack Takanobu with the support of the Egami family, but the Egami later became reconciled with Takanobu. Wishing to avoid further conflict with the Ryuzoji, the Egami suggested that Shoni Fuyuhisa should commit suicide; in 1560 he did, and with him died the Shoni family, famous since the Kamakura.

After the destruction of the Ouchi family in Chugoku in 1557, Mori Motonari overcame the Sue at Itsukushima Island. As already related, the Mori claimed the former Ouchi domain in Kyushu; and simultaneously the powerful daimyo Otomo Sorin began to intervene in Hizen. For Sorin, Ryuzoji Takanobu with his 5,000 followers were merely a minor nuisance, and he set off at the head of 60,000 men to Hizen. Luckily for Ryuzoji, Mori forces began to invade Chikuzen and Sorin had to cancel his attack on Hizen. In 1560, on account of the Mori army's retirement to Chugoku, Otomo Sorin was again able to send a large army to Hizen to subjugate the Ryuzoji, led by his son Sadachika. After five months of maneuvering around the Saga plain, Sorin's forces prepared for a general attack on 20 August. Informed of this by their *ninja* scouts, the Ryuzoji war council was divided: should they resist, or talk peace? It was obvious that only 5,000 samurai could not defeat the overwhelming numbers of the enemy. While the council wrestled with their ugly choices, spies brought the news that the Otomo army was going to hold a banquet on the evening before the day of their attack. Ryuzoji's most brilliant retainer, Nabeshima Nobunari, argued for a night raid on the Otomo camp; but in view of the great risks of such a daring operation, most of the other retainers did not agree. At this, Ryuzoji Takanobu's mother told them: 'You all look like mice in front of a cat. If you are real samurai, make the night raid—gamble your lives, for death or victory!'

During the night a Ryuzoji force led by Nobunari passed silently through a gap in the encircling enemy army and waited behind Otomo Sadachika's camp on the lower slope of Ima Mountain. As the mountain was not very steep, Nobunari's force made their way above it without difficulty. The samurai waited until dawn, when the enemy were asleep after the banquet. At 6 o'clock Nobunari gave the order for his arquebusiers to open fire, and his 800 samurai charged through the smoke and down into Sadachika's camp. Taken off guard, Otomo's samurai could not organize a proper resistance, and the camp was soon splashed with their blood. It was a sheer massacre; some 2,000 of the 3,000 Otomo troops in the camp were wiped out, and in the confusion a Ryuzoji retainer, Narimatsu Nobukatsu, killed Otomo Sadachika. While Nobunari was leading his dawn raid, Ryuzoji's other retainers attacked the residual Otomo force which had surrounded Saga Castle, and broke the siege. Although the main Otomo army was still intact, Sorin withdrew it to his domain.

Within a few years of the battle of Ima Mountain, Ryuzoji Takanobu had subjugated the warlords throughout Hizen, Chikugo and Chikuzen. Although they became his subjects, however, he never attracted their loyalty. Some warlords were noted for their charismatic leadership, but it seems that Takanobu was a cruel and unattractive personality. Even the missionaries, whose comments were naturally biased in favor of a Christian leader, compared him to Julius Caesar. It is significant that when he lost the battle of Okita Nawate in 1584 the Ryuzoji 'kingdom' quickly disintegrated. But in any case, the Kyushu triumvirate of the Otomo, Ryuzoji and Shimazu was soon to be swallowed up by the unifying hunger of Toyotomi Hideyoshi.

The Shimazu

It is no exaggeration to say that the Shimazu family was one of the most formidable war-machines of the Sengoku period. The southernmost region of Kyushu consisted of two provinces, Satsuma and Osumi. Since the Kamakura period, the Shimazu family, who were appointed *shugo* by the bakufu, had exercised power over the local warlords. Sudden changes occurred in Japan in the terminal stage of the Muromachi period from the mid-16th century onward. The Ashikaga bakufu lost authority, and a centrifugal tendency emerged among the daimyos—not only in Honshu, but also in the Shimazu domain in Kyushu. *Kokujin* (small land-holders among the provincial samurai), and even collateral branches of the clan began to resist the *shugo* and—more significantly—to go unpunished for it. Twenty-four years of internal feuding among the Shimazu were brought to an end by Shimazu Tadahisa and his son Takahisa. As soon as they had settled the domestic conflict they began to recover their old domains, now occupied by powerful *kokujin* or *kunishu*.

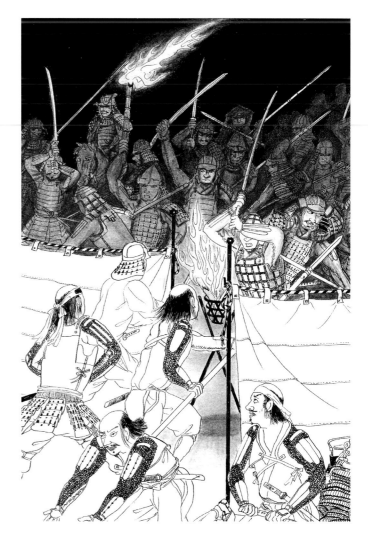

A night raid or an attack without warning were both good offensive tactics in samurai warfare, like that carried out by the Ryuzoji force under Nabeshima Nobunari on the Otomo camp in August 1560. In war, every ruse was considered fair as long as it brought victory. (SY)

In 1554, Takahisa advanced into Osumi to subjugate the Gamo family, driving them out after three years of resistance. Further north, the Shimazu attacked the Hishigari, who sought support from their neighboring warlords, the Sagara and Ito families. This help enabled the Hishigari to resist the Shimazu for two years. Next target was the Kimotsuki family, who had been resisting Shimazu hegemony for 80 years. In 1561, Shimazu Takahisa sent his brother Tadahisa and son Yoshihisa to recapture Osumi-Meguri Castle, which had fallen to Kimotsuki Kanesuke; but it was 16 years before Kimotsuki surrendered to the Shimazu. By 1574 the Shimazu had recovered their former territories in Osumi.

By integrating Satsuma and Osumi the Shimazu became powerful 'Sengoku daimyos'. The desire to expand their domain was far from satisfied, however, and the Shimazu now sent their tentacles to the north-east. In their view the Ito family of southern Hyuga, who had once supported the Kimotsuki, deserved destruction. When Ito forces attacked

Kakuto Castle, Shimazu Yoshihiro ambushed them while they were withdrawing from an abortive attack and killed the commander with many of his retainers. In 1577 the weakened Ito family moved to northern Hyuga and sought the protection of the Otomo. By extending their territory throughout the southern part of Kyushu the Shimazu family now began to come into contact with their two powerful counterparts in the north of the island.

In 1578, Otomo forces advanced into Hyuga, 35,000 strong, to support the Ito, and destroyed the Tsuchimochi family, who had changed sides to join the Shimazu. In the course of this campaign the Otomo army grew to some 50,000 men; but its unity was unstable, because it bore the banners of the Christian cross into Hyuga. The Otomo soldiers were ordered to destroy Buddhist temples and shrines, which provoked superstitious fear among those retainers who still held traditional Japanese beliefs. Some of them expressed their anxiety at the prospect of attacking the fierce Shimazu forces.

From Funai, the Otomo army advanced southward to capture the Shimazu stronghold at Takajo. This mountain fortress was protected on one side by the Takajo River and on the other by the Obaru, and was defended by the Shimazu retainer Yamada Arinobu with a small garrison of some 500 soldiers. For his part, Otomo Sorin stayed in Agata Castle and never came to the front, leaving the campaign to his generals. The Shimazu field forces were divided into three parts.

When the Otomo army laid siege to the castle of Takajo they cut off its water supply, and although the garrison were defending it stoutly it seemed doubtful that they could hold out for long. Shimazu Iehisa, with 1,000 men, broke through the encirclement and entered the castle; and Shimazu Yoshihisa's main force occupied the hills on the other bank of the Takajo River. In this worsening situation the Otomo generals' war council was divided in its opinions. Saeki Korenori suggested an indirect and masked operation, and at first this was agreed; but Takita Shigekane insisted that they should act to forestall any enemy initiative, and began attacking with his own troops. Expecting the enemy attack, Shimazu Yoshihisa had moved his army down to the riverbank on the previous day.

The Otomo troops crossed the river and charged the centre of the Shimazu force, led by Takita's division with Saeki's in support. The Shimazu pretended to be pushed back, and then maneuvered to surround the Otomo vanguard. A Shimazu detachment on the other bank ambushed the rear of the Otomo forces; and the defenders of the castle poured out and hurled themselves into the battle. Encircled by the enemy, the Otomo army collapsed; the fleeing soldiers jumped into the river to escape but, not knowing the fords, many were drowned in the cold November waters. The pursuing

Above & opposite: *Do-maru and associated helmet of the Muromachi period, from front and rear. The skirt armor has seven sections, in accordance with the trend for greater ease of movement in foot fighting. The helmet is the* suji kabuto *style, without visible rivet heads. The broad, parasol-like* shikoro *was common in this period; so was the three-horned helmet ornament or* mitsu kuwagata.

Shimazu defeated another Otomo force at Minikawa, and completely expelled the Otomo from Hyuga.

One of the secrets of Shimazu strength was their early introduction of arquebus companies in their army; they acquired large numbers of these firearms through trade with the Spanish and Portuguese. The massed, and therefore effective, use of arquebus fire preceded the charges of Shimazu samurai. Co-ordination of command and control between the four Shimazu brothers also functioned well on all occasions. Yoshihisa, the eldest, commanded the army, and his three brothers executed the battle plans on the ground. They usually reconnoitered the terrain thoroughly, and often laid ambushes or prepared surprise attacks. Such careful operations were the undoing of many of their less organized enemies—and it is important to note that most warlords' forces were indeed badly organized, which is why the few exceptions became famous. Consequently, a warlord who could not establish absolute control over his ambitious

The battle of Okita Nawate

After stopping the Otomo advance into Hyuga, the Shimazu turned their attention to Chikugo and Higo. Conveniently, on the Shimabara peninsula far to the north-west in Hizen, Arima Harunobu requested the support of the Shimazu. Arima was a Christian warlord harassed by the Ryuzoji; and although the Shimazu were extended by the task of managing the unstable province of Higo, they agreed to an alliance. In 1584 Shimazu Yoshihisa overruled the objections of his retainers and sent Iehisa with 3,000 soldiers to Shimabara, crossing the Ariake Sea. In March, enraged by Arima's rebellion, Ryuzoji Takanobu advanced to Shimabara with 50,000 men.

The two armies came face to face at Okita Nawate. Ryuzoji divided his forces into three: the mountain, centre and coastal divisions. Ryuzoji Masaie and Nabeshima Naoshige led the centre and Takanobu himself advanced with the mountain division. Correspondingly, the Shimazu army was also divided into three. Arima Harunobu's main force occupied the coastal flank, with arquebus companies lying in ambush in the pinewoods. Akaboshi Nobuie, supported by Shimazu Iehisa, led the central division; and on the mountain flank Iehisa deployed another ambush force led by Sarutake Nobumitsu.

In front of the Shimazu camp the ground was swampy, crossed by a narrow road leading from the Ryuzoji camp. Shimazu Iehisa had a strong gate built across the road and protected both flanks with palisades; he intended to lure the larger Ryuzoji army on to ground where it could not manoeuvre freely, thus negating its advantage in numbers.

On 24 March, Ryuzoji Takanobu changed his position on seeing the weakness of the Shimazu enemy; doubtless tempted by his Christian devil, he wanted to destroy this doomed opponent with his own hands, and redeployed his army towards the centre. At 8 o'clock in the morning the Ryuzuji army began to advance along the single road through the soft terrain, approaching the Shimazu roadblock. Suddenly, they came under fierce arquebus fire and a storm of arrows from three directions, and as losses mounted the vanguard wavered. As they did so the gate opened, and 50 enraged samurai of the Akaboshi family charged into them— the Akaboshi thirsted for revenge for their hostage families, killed with great cruelty on Takanobu's orders.

The head of the Ryuzoji column became fatally disorganized as those at the front tried to flee and those behind pressed forward. Observing the confusion, Takanobu sent a messenger to find out what was going on; but somehow his message was misunderstood as a simple order to advance. Desperate soldiers were still fighting bravely, but when they tried to deploy to the flanks they bogged down in the swampy ground each side of the road and, helplessly trapped, they were slaughtered by the Shimazu archers and gunners placed for that purpose.

retainers faced tactical defeat—which further threatened his authority, often with dire consequences for himself.

(In 1587, when Toyotomi Hideyoshi's forces attacked Takajo, Yamada Arinobu was again in command of the defense, at the head of 1,500 men. This time, however, he was besieged by 80,000 troops led by Hashiba Hidenaga, a retainer of the great conqueror Hideyoshi. On 10 April, Shimazu Yoshihiro executed a night raid on the fortress at Shiranezaka; but, in expectation of attack, the defenders had laid booby-traps to protect the approaches. Hampered by these traps, Yoshihiro could not take the castle during the hours of darkness; and with the dawn came Hidenaga's reinforcements. Yoshihiro and Yoshihisa were forced to retreat; even the Shimazus' coordinated operations did not work against Hideyoshi's well-prepared troops.)

Returning to 1584: after their defeat at Takajo, the Otomo influence in Chikugo and Higo began to dwindle. Although most of the local warlords were under Ryuzoji control, the Shimazu and Otomo were always trying to undermine their unity. From the earliest times, mutual loyalty among Japanese warlords was based on short term advantage; once the balance began to tip towards the other side their unity was easily broken. True loyalty and steadfast alliance between the samurai rarely survived for long amid a thousand treacheries.

At the appropriate moment the Shimazu samurai opened the gate and launched an all-out charge on the dispirited enemy. They penetrated the Ryuzoji front, second and third lines. The Ryuzoji leader's bodyguard could not stand against this onslaught. In the midst of hand-to-hand fighting a Shimazu retainer cut his way to Ryuzoji Takanobu, and told him: 'My name is Kawakami Tadatoshi, and I've come to take your head!'. He was as good as his word.

On learning of Takanobu's death all the Ryuzoji forces retreated to their own domain. The Shimazu returned Takanobu's severed head after viewing it in the usual post-battle ceremony; but the Ryuzoji family refused to receive it. Thus the man who had been called 'The Bear of Higo' was destroyed, unmourned, by the Shimazu of Satsuma.

* * *

The death of Ryuzoji Takanobu and the destruction of the Otomo force at Takajo brought the Shimazu an unexpected opportunity to conquer the whole of Kyushu. Although Otomo power had been weakened by the defeat in 1568, Otomo Sorin still ruled Bungo and Hozen. In 1585 a Shimazu army, divided into two forces, began to advance into Bungo; one marched from Hyuga, led by Shimazu Yoshihisa, and the other from Higo, led by Yoshihiro. Otomo Sorin and his retainers defended their domain courageously, but could not stop the rising power of the Shimazu. Otomo and his family travelled to Kyoto and asked Toyotomi Hideyoshi for help. It became a race to see if the Shimazu could conquer all of Kyushu before

Hideyoshi's forces arrived. The Shimazu believed that they would have the necessary respite, since Hideyoshi had been involved in a battle at Komaki-Nagakute against Tokugawa Ieyasu. But Hideyoshi quickly concluded peace with Ieyasu, and turned his army towards Kyushu.

In 1586, Otomo Sorin's retainer Takahashi Soun, with just 763 soldiers, held Iwaya Castle against a Shimazu army of 50,000 which advanced into Hizen. With abundant powder, shot, arrows and food, the garrison held out for 13 days against Shimazu assaults; in the end all of the samurai defenders died, 50 by their own hand. The Shimazu lost 3,000 killed and 1,500 wounded at Iwaya—and much precious time. Now Hideyoshi's vanguard under Kobayakawa Takakage landed in Kyushu.

It is not too much of an exaggeration to say that the Shimazu ambition to conquer Kyushu was shattered by Otomo Sorin's two retainers Takahashi Soun and his son Tachibana Muneshige. Amongst many Otomo retainers who deserted him, they were loyal to their master until the end. Sorin died of illness in his domain of Tsukumi.

Hideyoshi's expeditionary force advanced in the opposite direction to the Shimazu, marching to Satsuma with 100,000 men. A conqueror who knew how to consolidate his conquests had arisen, and the Sengoku period had nearly come to an end.

*In the Sengoku period there were many kinds of reconnaissance,
including, famously, the use of* ninja *scouts or spies. They not only sneaked
into enemy camps to gather information, but also disturbed the enemy
forces by night to create confusion. But the enemy, expecting these tactics,
sometimes set their own* ninja *to intercept enemy scouts and follow them
back to their camp. Before an operation a password was decided; when*
ninja *returned from a reconnaissance the leader used the word without
warning, and his men all stood up, as decided in advance. Anyone who
did not stand was recognized as an enemy infiltrator. (SY)*

THE ARROWS OF CHUGOKU

1498–1571

Peasants taking refuge in a mountain fort to avoid pillaging by an advancing enemy force. This kind of 'hideout' was made by each village in mountainous territory. Some lords permitted these evacuations, but some thought them an insult to their prestige. The angry Oda Nobunaga sent samurai to destroy these refuges; documents record that they killed the unfortunate peasants and stole rice from the villagers. (SY)

One arrow is easily broken, but three together can survive: this was what Mori Motonari taught his sons. From the lowly status of small *kokujin*, Motonari forged a hegemony over the daimyos of the Chugoku region at the southern tip of Honshu. Solidarity was the strongest weapon of the Mori family.

Mori Motonari was born the second son of Hiromoto in 1498. He was named as heir by the recommendation of vassals when his elder brother Okimoto died young. In this period, Chugoku was divided between two powerful daimyo families: the Ouchi in Nagato, and the Kyogoku in Izumo. The deputy *shugo's* family, the Amako, later overthrew the Kyogoku and became rulers of Izumo. Between these powerful clans the smaller Mori, Kikkawa, Takeda, Masuda, and Kobayakawa families were struggling to survive, under the protection of the *shugo* or by becoming retainers of either one or the other great family. The Mori were small but long-established warlords in Aki. In the Muromachi period (14th-15th centuries) Motonari's ancestors served the Ouchi family. During the Onin War of the 1460s-70s Mori Toyomoto, Motonari's uncle, followed the Ouchi and wrested 16 territories from the enemy.

In 1499, when the deposed shogun Ashikaga Yoshitane took refuge with the Ouchi in Nagato, Toyomoto's son Hiromoto sent a letter to the bakufu assuring the regime that he would follow their orders. The bakufu instructed him to attack Yoshitane and Ouchi Yoshioki. While doing so Hiromoto gave over the leadership of the family to his son, Okimoto; and also sent a message to the Ouchi that he was willing to join their side to save the Mori family. While mighty baronies clashed, the weaker gentry were always having to make such difficult decisions in order to preserve their domains. Hedging the bets could occasionally work, however. When the Ouchi and ex-shogun Yoshitane entered Hiromoto's domain with their forces as part of their bid to recover the shogun's position, the bakufu tried to seek peace; the following year the Ouchi and the shogun recovered the bakufu, and young Mori Okimoto was able to follow them.

After Okimoto's return from Kyoto, he made alliances with the Amano, Hiraga, Kobayakawa and Kikkawa families in Aki, and tried to establish stable conditions. However, one powerful baron, Shishiro—who would later become an important retainer under Motonari's rule—resisted Okimoto stubbornly. They fought several times without decisive results; and then Mori Okimoto died at only 24 years of age, through overindulgence in *sake*. His young son Komatsumaru succeeded to the leadership position.

Mori Motonari

If it had not been for the early death of Komatsumaru, Motonari would never have had the opportunity to

Nanbokucho period samurai with tachi *sword. The* ogi *or fan was used not only for its original purpose, but also served as a staff of command and, in emergencies, as a weapon of self-defense.*

distinguish himself. When his father Hiromoto died, Motonari had succeeded to the Yoshida domain; but at that time his position was so weak that his land was stolen from him by a powerful retainer, Motomori. The deaths of Okimoto and Komatsumaru faced the Mori family council with a possibly fatal crisis. If they had no credible successor then the family's legacy would be torn apart by squabbles between their petty samurai. In this desperate moment, Motomori and 15 other retainers gambled on Motonari, and recommended him as the successor to the province in 1523. During the Sengoku period retainers had the status of counselors, and if the leader made a wrong decision—or one unfavorable to his retainers—they could force him to retract it. After he became master of the Mori family Motonari did indeed have to work his way through some domestic quarrels.

At the time of his succession the Mori paid homage to the Amako, but two years later they changed sides to ally themselves with the Ouchi. In 1540, Amako Haruhisa belatedly decided to punish this disloyalty, and against the advice of some of his retainers Amako Kunihisa was sent with 3,000 men towards Yoshida, where Motonari's Koriyama Castle was located. There were two routes of approach to Yoshida: the Bingo road, leading to Yoshida from the west, and the Iwamiji road from the east. The

initial attempt by Kunihisa followed the Bingo route. The ambitious Kunihisa needed to take a key defensive position which lay in his path, Goryu Castle, which was held by a former rival of Motonari's father. Motonari had sent his daughter to be married to Shishido Ietaka, however, and had established a strong alliance. In his father's day the Shishido would undoubtedly have been an Achilles heel of Mori's regional defense, but now they were closely related and reliable allies. Shishido Motoyori defended his castle with booby-traps and stone devices to repel any enemy attempt to climb the walls, and set slingers on the ramparts. His stubborn and skilled resistance inflicted great losses among the Amako force, and Kunihisa retired.

That September, Amako Haruhisa took the Iwamiji route with his main army of 30,000 troops, and reached Yoshida. Motonari had ordered all his local farmers to harvest their rice, and accommodated them in his castle, where nearly 8,000 people were besieged. From Goryu Castle, Shishido Ietaka arrived with 100 more samurai; they were appreciated, since of the total within the walls only 3,000 were soldiers. In spite of being so outnumbered, Mori's people defended Koriyama Castle for many weeks, even making some successful sorties to harass the besiegers. After four months' siege reinforcements sent by the Ouchi arrived at Yoshida led by Sue Fusakata. In January 1541 the Amako forces were beaten again at Aoyama by Mori, and began to retreat in heavy snow. After this miserable defeat they managed to return to their Tomita Castle, but 13 major retainers left the Amako and paid homage to the Ouchi.

The war followed its inevitable course, and Ouchi Yoshitaka invaded Izumo to destroy the Amako family in 1543, with Mori Motonari among his followers. The Amako defended Tomita Castle stubbornly, however; the expedition failed, and during the subsequent retreat Yoshitaka lost his son. After he returned to Yamaguchi he lost the will to be a military leader of the Ouchi family. Motonari was nearly caught and killed by pursuing Amako soldiers, but his double was killed instead (such ruses were not uncommon during the endless wars of the Sengoku). In the aftermath of this failed campaign the Ouchi influence over the Mori began to wane.

In 1550 Motonari killed one of his most powerful retainers, Inoue Motokane, for a number of reasons—he neglected orders, failed to pay his taxes to Mori, did not come to help repair the family's castles, and so forth. In this period any daimyo's authority was dependent on his *kokujin*, the samurai land-holders within his domain, who combined in an *ikki* or league. When relations between the lord and his samurai retainers were co-operative, the province prospered; but they sometimes opposed his wishes. The powerful *kokujin* sat on a family council; as mentioned above, Motonari only became the heir of Mori

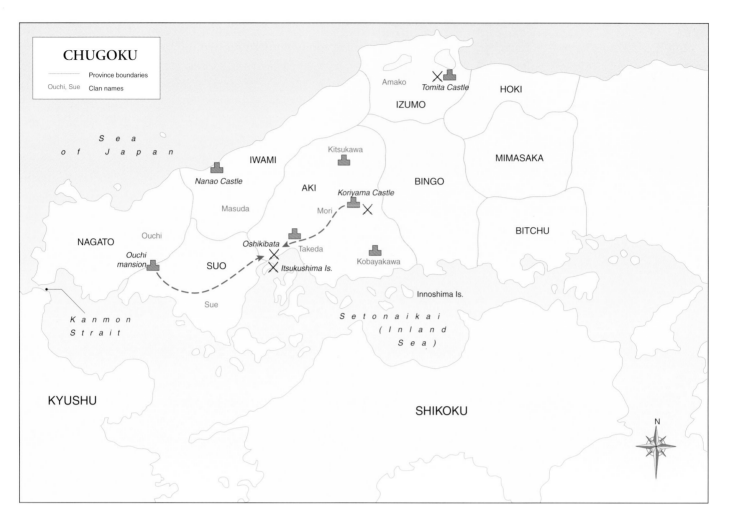

with the consent of this group. Under these circumstances it was natural that some retainers should rely unwisely on the belief that Motonari's power depended solely on their approval. Inoue's arrogant disregard for his daimyo was not such unusual behavior that he would have believed himself to be in any particular danger. Inoue misjudged both his man and his times, however. The family council recognized that collective survival depended upon a powerful leader who could suppress the retainers' chronic tendency toward eternal feuding amongst themselves; and Motonari recognized that only a daimyo who successfully dominated his retainers could survive in those bloody and chaotic times. It is not surprising that when he presented his *kokujin* with a document confirming that they had no objection to his killing Inoue, most of them signed it without protest.

Sue Harukata, a leading retainer of Ouchi Yoshitaka, had been worried for some time about his master's incompetence as a military leader. Though Yoshitaka was a man of letters, a musician, a scholar, and a patron of fine arts, these qualities definitely would not ensure the position of the Ouchi family in an age of endemic warfare. Even worse, Yoshitaka relied too much on one particular retainer, and the unity of his counselors began to disintegrate. It was thus unfortunate that Yoshitaka imposed a heavy tax to pay for his artistic luxuries. Sue Harukata's response was to plan rebellion.

Being a relative of the Ouchi, Sue had been the leading figure in the council of retainers. It is unclear exactly when he decided to rise against his master, but by 1550 he was already holding secret talks about border issues with the Mori, whose support he would need when he finally struck. When the New Year festival came around in 1551 Sue did not visit his master but stayed in his domain at Hagi. Under the conditions of that world such a failure to appear was universally considered as a sign of rebellion; but Yoshitaka took no action to prevent further offense. It is not clear if he was simply a very optimistic man, or if he wanted to punish Sue Harutaka but lacked the military strength to do so. In August 1551, Harukata occupied Itsukushima Island; he then advanced to Yamaguchi, and destroyed the Ouchi family. After this Harukata offered his homage to a new lord from the Otomo family over the straits in Kyushu.

Mori Motonari was not the kind of man to overlook the possibilities offered by a quarrel next door. He stretched out his hand to Bingo and the west of Aki, and secured them both during the confusion between Ouchi and Sue. At first Motonari had deceived Sue Harukata by giving consent to his plan for rebellion; but this was just a prelude to his longer term agenda. In 1554, 3,000 Mori soldiers advanced south to take Kanayama Castle, after which he moved up to the border of the Sue domain. A Sue counterattack was checked severely by Motonari's forces at Oshikibata; he then crossed the sea and took Itsukushima Island, where he constructed a castle. On this island stands an ancient and very sacred shrine for samurai, a centre of religion in the Inland Sea. Sue Harukata had become obsessed with this shrine, and every time he went to war he used to visit it first to pray to the god. Apart from its religious importance, Itsukushima was a key point in the maritime trade of the Inland Sea. Motonari chose it as the field of his decisive battle against Sue—he knew that if he took Itsukushima, Sue would not be able to resist coming to recover it.

The Inland Sea

The Inland Sea was a very important route from the Asian mainland to the east coast of Japan and thus to Osaka and Kyoto. In calm weather these sheltered waters assured safe navigation. However, the straits between Aki in Southeast Honshu and Iyo in northern Shikoku were scattered with many islands and offered convenient lairs for pirates. These pirates sometimes resisted the government in Kyoto (e.g. the Sumitomo rebellion), but in general they were not organized enough to be a serious problem to the regime. Because of the complexity of the channels and currents, merchantmen and missionary ships from China and Korea needed pilots to pass through safely; and the pirates were often satisfied to provide them, levying tolls for safe passage.

In the Kamakura period, the Kobayakawa family was ordered by the bakufu to pacify the pirates in this area; they did so, but then made themselves the leaders and controllers of this trade. When Motonari had his third son adopted by the Kobayakawa in 1544 he obtained a powerful sea-going ally. But the Kobayakawa did not have the only fleet; there were also three major sea-bandits based on Innoshima, Noshima and Kurushima Islands, which were ruled by three brothers from the Murakami family. Mori Motonari had connections with the Innoshima fleet through the Kobayakawa, and could rely upon it. It was important, however, to find out how the other two fleets at Noshima and Kurushima would respond his request to destroy Sue's navy.

As well as family considerations, a conflict between the island fleets and Sue over the issue of the taxation of the merchants and people of Itsukushima Island influenced the attitude of the Murakami. When Sue Harutaka had seized the Ouchi domain in 1552 he made dangerous enemies by terminating the right of the Murakami family to impose such levies.

Motonari's intention was to lure the Sue forces out to Itsukushima Island, and then cut them off there by means of his allies' fleets. To win he needed overwhelming sea power—the basic strength of the Sue army so far exceeded that of his own that he did not want to fight a pitched battle on land. But if Sue did not respond to Motonari's bait at Itsukushima, then the Mori cause was doomed.

Retainer wearing a do maru kawazutsumi yoroi—*a* do maru *cuirass covered with leather.*

To reinforce his plot, Motonari had Katsura Motozumi, one of his retainers whose castle lay on the border, send a letter to the Sue saying that if Harutaka crossed the sea to Itsukushima to attack the Mori castle there, and if Motonari also crossed to defend it, then Motozumi would switch sides and attack the Mori home base at Yoshida. Motonari also made contact with a most formidable Sue retainer, Era Yoshifusa. Although he invited Yoshifusa to change sides and join the Mori, negotiations over the question of reward could not be brought to a conclusion. Once Motonari knew that negotiations had failed, he made Yoshifusa's treacherous correspondence known; Yoshifusa was duly killed by his master at Kohakuin temple. Finally, Motonari allowed enemy spies to learn that he now regretted building

Top & above: *The way an arquebusier attached his sword in the Kamakura period. In the Sengoku period samurai carried the* katana *tip pointing downwards, but gunners reversed it so that the tip did not touch the ground when they kneeled to shoot.*

his castle on Itsukushima, because its defenses were too weak to withstand a Sue siege. Such thorough preparation inevitably brought Sue Harutaka's forces out to the island.

On 21 September 1555, 20,000 Sue troops embarked on 400 ships and landed on the beach west of Mori's castle. When he learned of the Sue landing on Itsukushima, Motonari left Yoshida on the 27th and marched to his harbor. While preparing to cross he sent word to the Murakami family via Kobayakawa Takakage, requesting that they join his forces. Sue Harutaka also invited them to join his side, but he would now pay for his termination of their taxation rights over Itsukushima the previous year.

Motonari's forces divided into three. The first squadron would make landfall at Tsutsumigaura and its troops would cross the mountains, attacking the rear of the Sue camp. The second squadron would disembark its soldiers on the beach in front of the enemy camp; the third would attack the Sue fleet to paralyze the enemy's supply route. At the castle, the defenders would open the gates and join the other Mori forces in their attack.

The assault was executed in the early morning while it was still dark. The Kurushima ships landed in front of the

Opposite & over page: *In the Sengoku period, samurai were particularly anxious to be noticed for their prowess in battle by their master; they tended towards extremes of display in the personal emblems mounted like flags on the back of the cuirass. Although these were made of light materials, one might think they would still be encumbering in combat; however, the samurai persisted in these displays, which they often came to believe brought them good luck.* (SY)

Black fur balls

Peacock feathers

Prayer flag

Arrow

Tied cotton sheaf

Food sack

Feather fan

Rice pestle

Turnip

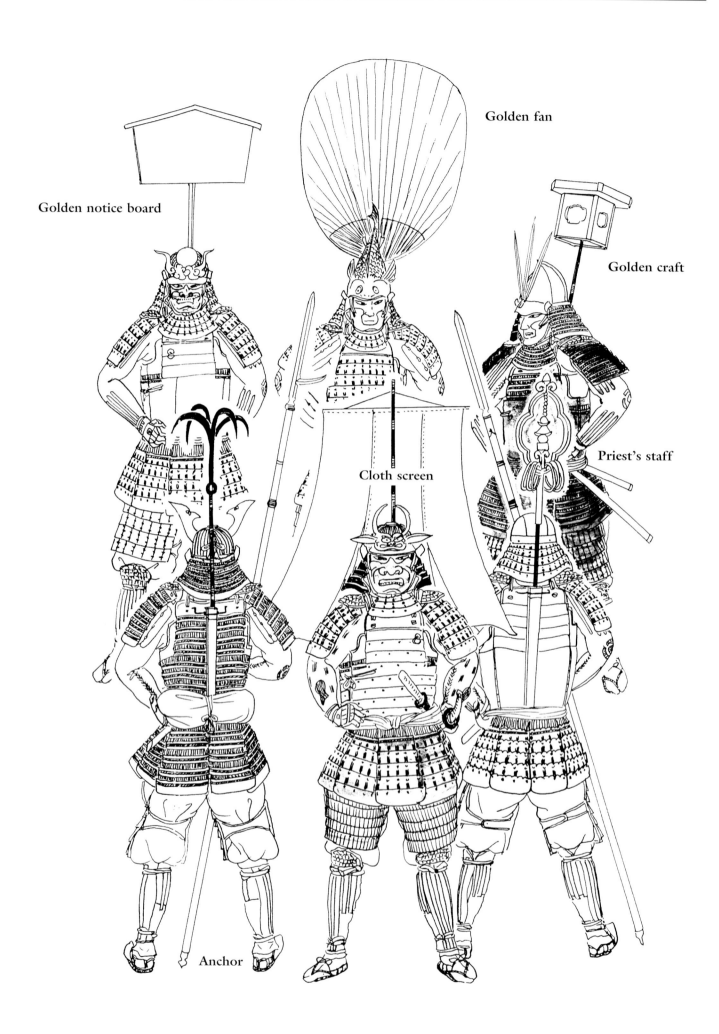

Golden notice board

Golden fan

Golden craft

Golden craft

Cloth screen

Priest's staff

Anchor

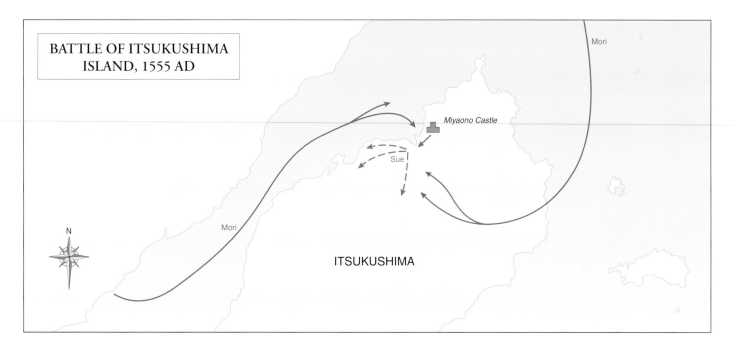

BATTLE OF ITSUKUSHIMA
ISLAND, 1555 AD

Mori

Miyaono Castle

Sue

Mori

N

ITSUKUSHIMA

Sue camp, approaching without war cries in pretense that they were bringing Sue reinforcements. The Kurushima fleet had connections with the Ouchi, and it was not surprising that the Sue forces were deceived. A sudden, coordinated attack from three directions—sea, mountain and castle—tore the Sue camp apart. Harutaka escaped to the western coast where his navy was supposed to wait for him, but his fleet never came; it had been destroyed by Mori's navy. It was there that Sue Harutaka committed suicide.

* * *

In 1557, after Mori Motonari had combined the Ouchi and Sue domains under his rule, he wrote a letter to his three sons in which he said: 'Never mind our other provinces; even in my own lands nobody is friendly to us. Therefore you must all be very co-operative with one another, otherwise the Mori will be destroyed'. Legend has it that Motonari showed one arrow to his sons and snapped it easily, but then showed them how hard it was to break three together.

Always conscious of the danger of treachery among his *kokujin*, Motonari had conducted a patient and cunning campaign to destroy his enemies within his domain. His letter to his sons may have overstated the danger, but at least his words attracted their attention. His eldest son, Takamoto, was already becoming famous as a good military leader. The second, Motoharu, was adopted by his mother's family, the Kikkawa; and the third, Takakage, was adopted by the Kobayakawa. Motoharu and Takakage both came to power in these families, and helped Motonari.

In the process of incorporating the Ouchi domain it was inevitable that Mori and Otomo forces should clash. After the deaths of Ouchi and his retainer Sue's death, Mori claimed that their lands in Kyushu should pass to him. After some skirmishing, Otomo and Mori were reconciled by the shogun in Kyoto; Motonari had asked the shogun to sponsor these negotiations, because he did not want to get involved in simultaneous operations on two fronts, against both the Amako and the Otomo. His attention was now directed on the Amako of Izumo province, where his forces had been defeated along with the rest of the Ouchi army in 1543. Circumstances were now very different, however. By destroying the Ouchi and Sue, Motonari had become the most powerful daimyo in the Chugoku region; his retainers, and his allies the Kikkawa and Kobayakawa, were brimming with aggressive energy.

Motonari conducted a general assault on Toda Castle in April 1565, after surrounding it and cutting it off completely from outside help. It was not an easy task even for this supremely cunning general; the main castle was defended by a strong network of outer works. Nevertheless, after a long siege Amako Yoshihisa surrendered to Mori. As the vanquished, Yoshihisa requested that he be allowed to commit *harakiri* in return for the sparing of his retainers' lives, but Motonari rejected his plea. He also accepted the surrender of Yoshihisa's brother—on condition that both should live in the Mori domain thereafter.

This act of mercy, unusual at the time, is a strong reminder of the fact that Motonari was not only a shrewd and cunning warlord but also a keen student of Confucianism. All the Amako retainers were also spared, and served the Mori; and after a few years the Amako brothers were released and given domains. In 1571, Mori Motonari died in his bed in Kohiriyama Castle at Yoshida at the age of 75—a rare accomplishment.

Unsurprisingly, Chugoku was still unstable. In time, remnants of the Ouchi and Amako rebelled. Motonari's grandson Terumoto, Kikkawa Motoharu and Kobayakawa Takakage would soon oppose the most formidable enemies of their age: the unifier Oda Nobunaga, and his retainer Toyotomi Hideyoshi.

WEAPONS OF THE SAMURAI: POLE-WEAPONS

Left: *Muromachi period* ashigaru *with rakes to pull horsemen out of the saddle.*

Right: *From the late 16th century Muromachi period the spear or lance became a main weapon of samurai warfare. Pole-arms with various heads, from 9cm to 74cm long, mounted on hafts ranging from 2m to 7m long, were used as thrusting and striking weapons by* ashigaru. (*Tokyo National Museum*)

Opposite: *Kamakura period foot soldiers with* naginata. *They wear straw sandals over the divided-toe* tabi *socks; in this period many common soldiers went barefoot.*

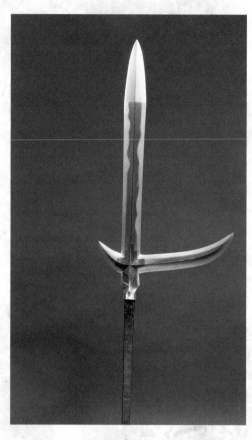

The *naginata* or 'pole-sword' developed from the sword. From battle experience, samurai learned to have the sword hilt lengthened so as to extend their reach. Unlike a sword, the hilt was made from a lacquered wooden pole. The lower class samurai preferred the *naginata* when involved in close combat; not only did its length protect them by keeping the enemy at a distance, but the extra leverage of the long pole allowed them to deliver heavier blows. The blade was broad and curved noticeably at the point. A similar weapon called a *nagamaki* had a longer, slimmer blade; this was developed from the long sword, and like a sword its hilt was covered with sharkskin overlapped with braided cord to prevent it getting slippery with blood in combat. Early examples of the *naginata* had blades about 2ft (60cm) long, but later longer blades appeared. An example with a 9.8ft (3m) pole and 5.9ft (1.8m) blade is exceptional, however; common weapons had poles as long as the distance from a man's foot to his ear. In the Edo period the *naginata* was regarded as a woman's weapon and the daughters of samurai were encouraged to practice with it. (Some of them actually fought on the battlefield in the final stages of the samurai period, against the overwhelming firepower of the Meiji imperial army.)

The *yari* or long thrusting spear evolved in the Nanbokucho period, at the height of the 14th century. In ancient times there were thrusting weapons called *hoko*, which were wielded with one hand in conjunction with a shield (though some ancient warriors probably used both hands, of course). Today the *hoko* and *yari* are regarded as the products of different lines of development. When a samurai used the *yari* he thrust it with his right hand, giving it a screwing motion to pierce the enemy's armor; the left hand was used solely to support the pole. Accordingly the pole of the *yari* was painted with lacquer and had a smooth surface to allow it to revolve. When longer *yari* were later introduced as a defense against cavalry charges they were used as a 'pushing' weapon by formed units of *ashigaru* foot soldiers, like a Macedonian phalanx armed with long pikes.

The shapes of the spearheads differed, as did their length, but the longest known measures 3.3ft (1m) long. The pole of the *yari* became longer in the climactic Sengoku period, commonly increasing to 13ft (4m), but mounted samurai preferred shorter hafts for ease of handling.

* * *

Apart from the main weapons described in these pages, in actual combat soldiers used many others according to availability or circumstances. These included slings; iron rakes to dismount an enemy or grapple a boat; large axes and heavy wooden hammers to smash through gates, etc.— but these were regarded as special purpose weapons, and never became common.

UESUGI KENSHIN & TAKEDA SHINGEN
MID-16TH CENTURY AD

Uesugi Kenshin was born in Echigo in 1530, a son of a deputy *shugo* named Nagao Tamekage. His given name was Torachiyo—born in the Year of the Tiger—and his adult name was Nagao Kagetora. The *shugo* of Echigo was Uesugi Sadazane, but the real power was held by Tamekage. Ojo Sadanori, an uncle of Sadazane, helped him to destroy Tamekage, and internal conflict broke out in Echigo.

In all parts of Japan at this period, numbers of small independent samurai attached to the land—*kokujin*, or 'men of the province'—held considerable influence; and as we have already seen, no baron could govern without their support. In Echigo the *kokujin* split into two factions, and the conflict seemed as if it would last forever. In 1534 Tamekage's forces defeated the Sadanori; but within the year Tamekage died of illness. Due to the unsettled conditions, the seven-year-old Kagetora attended his father's funeral wearing armor. Since his eldest brother Harukage headed the Nagao, Kagetora was admitted to Rensenji temple and studied Zen. It may be true that his spirit and character were molded by his years in the temple.

When Kagetora turned fifteen, his brother Harukage summoned him and sent him to Tochio Castle to supervise the vassal who held it. In 1544 the regionally powerful *kokujin* families who were hostile to Harukage attacked the castle with 1,300 samurai. Kagetora and the master of the castle, Honjo Saneyori, successfully beat them off, and the young man's name became feared among his family's enemies.

His brother Harukage lacked the gifts to control the confused situation in his province. The following year a minister of Uesugi, Kuroda Hidetada of Kurotaki Castle, rebelled and killed one of Harukage's brothers. Instantly, Kagetora moved to Kasugayama Castle to support Harukage. The rebel Kuroda, frightened by Kagetora's reputation, begged peace in return for becoming a monk; his plea was granted, and Kagetora returned to Tochio Castle. However, the next year Hidetada again entered Kurotaki Castle and raised the standard of rebellion. On the orders of the *shugo* Uesugi Sadazane, Kagetora attacked the castle and destroyed the Kuroda family.

His growing fame and prowess aroused the unease of his brother Harukage, who had a tendency to illness. On the other hand, conflict between the two brothers made the *shugo* Uesugi's position fragile. Uesugi persuaded Harukage to retire after taking Kagetora as a son-in-law. Though unwilling, Harukage accepted the reconciliation. The nineteen-year-old Kagetora succeeded to the position of deputy *shugo*, and entered his late father's castle of Kasugayama at last.

* * *

South of Echigo in central Honshu there is a region called Kai, long famous for raising good horses and thus the strongest armies in Japan. Mountains surround Kai in what is now called the Kofu Basin; the climate is hot in summer and bitterly cold in winter.

To judge from their excavated skeletons, Japanese horses averaged 51in (130cm) from the ground to the shoulder. When a short samurai was mounted he looked like a taller man in the mass of foot soldiers. Horsemen were unable to break through an enemy front line by shock attack, nor to by-pass an enemy force and attack from the rear, without the support of foot soldiers. When a lord called his samurai for service, they arrived at the appointed place, variously armed, to be allocated to tactical units according to the orders of an officer called the *furejo* or *chakutojo*. A lord's forces were assembled from such small individual groups that they had never been trained to maneuver en masse; an independent force of cavalry never existed in the armies of the Sengoku period. Therefore it is not appropriate to describe the Takeda forces from Kai as a true cavalry corps. Why, then, were they reputed to be invincible? Apart from the tough breed of the soldiers from Kai, the answer probably lay in their unrivaled transport resources—the ample provision of good horses gave the Takeda forces superior mobility. In any case, the strongest Takeda would soon meet a formidable adversary in Uesugi Kenshin.

Long before, Kai had been ruled by Takeda Yoshikiyo, son of Shinra Saburo; he had been living at Takeda in Hitachi, present Ibaragi prefecture, when he was expelled to Kai because of his rude behavior. Thereafter his descendants took Takeda as a family name. When Nobutora, father of Takeda Shingen, was growing up, Kai had been disputed in a rebellion by his uncle; Nobutora supported his father and averted the danger to the province. After succeeding his father Nobutora moved his base from Isawa to Kofu,

Opposite top: The forces of Uesugi Kenshin and Takeda Shingen confronted one another at Kawanakajima five times, though they did not always fight engagements. In August 1561, at the last pitched battle between their main forces, Kenshin's surprise attack on Shingen's camp led to single combat between them. Kenshin rode at Shingen three times, slashing with his sword, but Shingen fended off the blows with his iron fan. In this reconstruction Kenshin wears a white hood over his armor—he had become a priest.

Opposite below: Uesugi ashigaru ready to attack during a re-enactment of the fourth battle of Kawanakajima, 1561. (Isawa)

Takeda's forces defending their position against the wheeling onslaught of the Uesugi. (Isawa)

founding Kofu city, which is still today the capital of Yamanashi prefecture. Nobutora's harsh rule and absolute attitude towards his retainers became unpopular among the *kokujin*, however.

Takeda Shingen was born in 1521 and was given the adult name Nobuharu. At first he supported his father, but as time went by Nobuharu's retainers and *kokujin* began to plot a coup to install him in his father's place. Their discontent under the dictatorship of Nobutora was real; but they may also have supposed that his son would be easy to control. In 1541 Nobutora and his son attacked and defeated the Unno family in Shinshu, returning to Kofu in June. During an intermission of the conflict, Nobutora visited his daughter's husband Imagawa Yoshimoto in Suruga, little imagining that he would never be able to come home. In his absence Nobuharu took power in a bloodless coup with the assistance of his father's major retainers—and of his brother-in-law Imagawa Yoshimoto. Nobutora died in exile at the age of 81.

Whatever the retainers' intentions, Nobuharu became a strong leader. In 1542 his forces invaded Suwa; this rapid mobilization was intended to divert any dissatisfaction among the family's retainers over the coup, uniting them in loyalty against an outside enemy.

The origins of the Suwa family dated back to the legendary period. Suwa Shrine was dedicated to Takeminakata-no mikoto, who escaped from the sun goddess Amaterasu omikami to Suwa. He had been worshiped as a war god, and the shrine was very important to the people of the age of battles, especially for Nobuharu. Suwa Yorishige, husband of a sister of Takeda Nobuharu, was high priest of the shrine as well as being a warrior. Suwa

Shrine was at that time divided into two, the Upper and the Lower. The Upper Shrine supervised both; but the Kanasasi family who were in charge of the Lower Shrine were dissatisfied with Suwa rule, and rebelled. Takeda Nobuharu took advantage of the internal conflict to intervene. Takato Yoritsugu, from one of the Suwa families, supported Nobuharu because he hoped to succeed to the shrine.

After the complete encirclement of Kuwabara Castle, where Suwa Yorishige had taken his stand, Nobuharu offered to discuss peace. Although Suwa Yorishige had been determined to fight, when he was suddenly offered terms he accepted them. If he thought that he would be safe because he was Nobuharu's brother-in-law he was disappointed: Yorishige was taken prisoner, sent to Kofu, and ordered to commit *harakiri*.

The Suwa domain was now divided in two, and Takato Yoritsugu was given half; but he was dissatisfied with his reward. He had expected the position of high priest of Suwa Shrine, but this was abolished and Nobuharu took half of the land. Later that same year Takato Yoritsugu invaded Suwa and occupied both shrines, but these were instantly counterattacked by Nobuharu's forces. Nobuharu declared the son of Suwa Yorishige as the leader of the pacification forces; he knew that the samurai of the Suwa domain would respect a direct ancestor of the Suwa family. As a result, influential samurai failed to rally to the rebels, and Takato Yoritsugu fled to Ina after the battle of Ankokuji.

The pursuing Takeda forces entered the Ina Basin by way of the Tsuetsuki Pass and laid siege to Fukuyo Castle, which was surrendered to them by Takato's ally Fujisawa Yorichika. In 1544, in spite of his previous failure, Yorichika again rebelled, supported by Takato Yoritsugu. Nobuharu reacted promptly and advanced into Ina again, besieging Yorichika's Kojinyama Castle; however, when threatened by Takato Yoritsugu's forces they had to retreat.

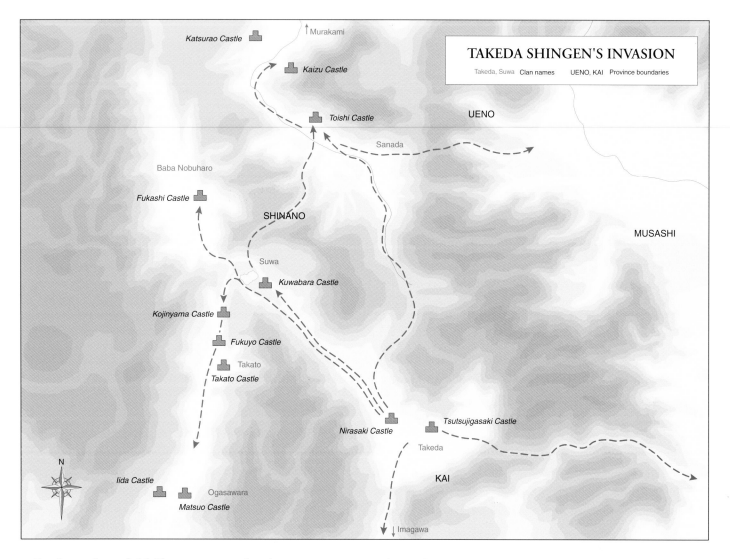

In the spring of 1545, as soon as the thaw was over, Nobuharu organized another advance on Ina. Reinforced by troops of Imagawa Yoshimoto from Suruga, he successfully attacked Takato, Ryugasaki and Fukuyo castles. By this campaign the upper Ina fell into Nobuharu's hands, but the lower Ina was still dominated by Ogasawara Nobusada; it would take ten years to wrest control of the lower Ina from the Ogasawara family.

In September 1543, Oi Sadataka of Saku had rebelled against the Takeda with the support of Murakami Yoshikiyo; the rising was crushed, and Sadataka was killed by Nobuharu. Two years later Sadataka's son Sadakiyo mounted a brief rebellion, but soon surrendered to Nobuharu. Another baron of the Saku, Kasahara Kiyoshige of Shiga Castle, resisted Takeda's forces stubbornly, since he expected reinforcement by Uesugi Norimasa from Kozuke (Upper Kanto). Uesugi Norimasa's force, led by Kanai Hidekage, crossed the Usui Pass to Saku with 3,000 men. Leaving 2,000 men to continue the siege, 3,000 Takeda troops marched east to meet the Uesugi expedition, and annihilated them at Odaihara. Despairing of rescue, Kasahara's garrison now made a desperate sortie from Shiga Castle, and were wiped out. The women and children left in

the castle were taken to Kofu and sold cheaply as slaves.

Naturally, Murakami Yoshikiyo, in Katsurao Castle located north-west of Saku, was alerted to Takeda's expansion to the west. In February 1548 he advanced south to meet Nobuharu's forces marching north; the two armies, with about 7,000 men each, met at Uedahara on 14 February. At first Takeda's centre penetrated Murakami's centre; but Itagaki Nobukata advanced too recklessly, and was encircled and killed by Murakami's troops. A long march to the field in cold weather had weakened the Takeda forces. Now Murakami counterattacked, pushing the Takeda troops back. In the confusion Takeda Nobuharu became involved in hand-to-hand combat with the lance, and was wounded in the left arm. Several of his generals fell in this action. Gradually the battle became a stalemate; and in spite of great losses, neither army would withdraw from the ground. They faced each other for no less than 20 days, unable to gain a decision; but finally the Takeda forces retreated from the field, and returned to Kofu without any gain. This was the first defeat ever suffered by Takeda Nobuharu.

Another powerful dynasty in Shinano was the Ogasawara family; influential daimyos, who became *shugo* in the Muromachi period, they were not strong enough to rule

the entire region. Ogasawara Nagatoki supported Takato Yoritsugu and Fujisawa Yorichika when Nobuharu invaded Ina in 1544. After the defeat of Nobuharu by Murakami Yoshikiyo at Uedahara, they organized anti-Takeda samurai and invaded Suwa in April 1548. An Ogasawara force occupied the Shiojiri Pass and awaited Nobuharu's response. In July, Nobuharu's forces approached the pass and, to Ogasawara's puzzlement, halted for six days. On the seventh night Nobuharu organized an assault group and advanced in the middle of the night. The horses' hooves were muffled with grass sandals, and the soldiers' *kusazuri*—hanging skirt-armor plates—were folded and tied so as not to make any noise. They did not launch their assault in darkness, to avoid confusion among their own men, but got into position and waited for dawn. When the sky paled, and before the enemy samurai had put on their armor, Nobuharu's troops charged the enemy position, killing many of them and driving the rest back to Hayashi Castle in panic.

Two years later, Nobuharu attacked this castle; unable to resist the assault, Ogasawara fled to the domain of Murakami Yoshikiyo in northern Shinshu. Relentlessly, Nobuharu advanced north, and laid siege to Toishi Castle in the mountains along the Chikuma River. Taking this castle would give Takeda an advanced base for an attack on the main Murakami stronghold. After thorough preparation, including attempts to persuade the Murakami samurai to change sides, a general assault was launched on 9 September. After eight days of intensive fighting, however, Nobuharu still could not take Toishi Castle. Even worse, Murakami Yoshikiyo—who was supposed to be defending the castle—appeared in the Takeda army's rear and began to attack. Takeda Nobuharu's troops gave up the siege and began to withdraw on 1 October. They were

The fourth battle of Kawanakajima was fought on a river bank. Trapping an enemy army against a river, and driving them in to drown, was not an uncommon tactic of successful samurai generals.

attacked during their retreat by pursuing Murakami forces, and only a furious defense by the rearguard enabled them to escape. This was Nobuharu's second defeat.

The following year Toishi Castle unexpectedly fell to one of Nobuharu's vassals, Sanada Yukitaka. Now Nobuharu had a secure forward base for an attack on the northern part of Shinshu. In 1553 he finally drove Murakami Yoshikiyo out of the province, and Yoshikiyo escaped to take refuge in the domain of Uesugi Kenshin (Nagao Kagetora) in Echigo.

The aggressive expansion of Takeda Nobuharu now presented an unmistakable threat to Uesugi Kenshin, who moved his own forces into northern Shinshu. This was the beginning the famous series of battles at Kawanakajima. At this time Takeda Shingen Nobuharu was 33 years old and Nagao Kagetora Kenshin was ten years younger.

The two generals confronted each other at Kawanakajima on five occasions over eleven years. When two great daimyos faced each other across a border, war was the natural and inevitable result. Less understandable are the reasons why they joined battle at the same place so many times, and why none of these battles had a decisive result. Factors to be considered are that Takeda Shingen's battle strategy was to avoid losses rather than seeking outright victory; and that Uesugi Kenshin had little ambition for territorial expansion.

The first encounter occurred in August 1553, when Takeda Shingen drove Murakami Yoshikiyo from Shinshu. The course of the battle is not known today. It is obvious that Kenshin felt threatened by the Takeda move into

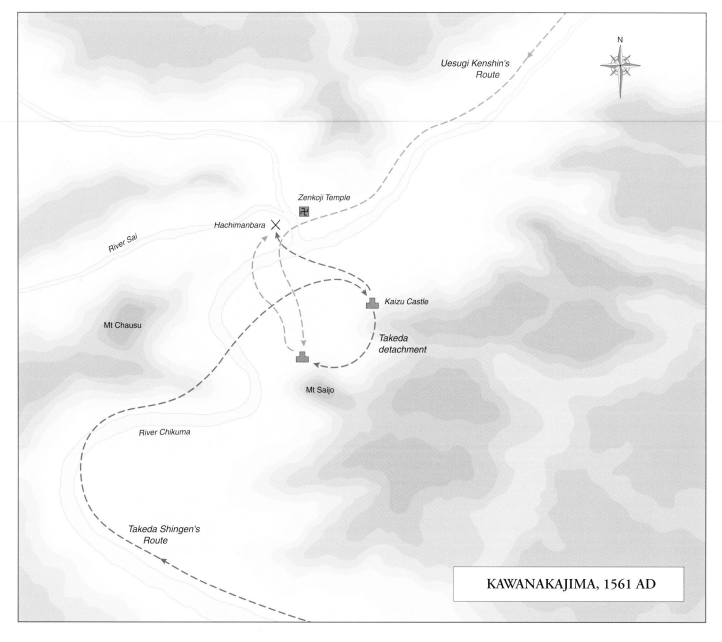

Uesugi Kenshin's
Route

N

Zenkoji Temple

Hachimanbara

River Sai

Kaizu Castle

Mt Chausu

Takeda
detachment

Mt Saijo

River Chikuma

Takeda Shingen's
Route

KAWANAKAJIMA, 1561 AD

Shinshu; and, being a man of honor, when Kenshin accepted Murakami Yoshikiyo as his ally he tried to help him recover his domain.

The second and third battles of Kawanakajima occurred in 1555 and 1557 respectively. Again, events are not known in detail; but it seems that in these encounters the main corps were never actually engaged.

The fourth battle of Kawanakajima

On August 14, 1561, Uesugi Kenshin started to march on Kawanakajima with 18,000 men. He advanced to the Zenkoji Plain and made camp on Saijo Mountain. Informed by smoke signals, Takeda Shingen marched to Chausu Mountain and finally entered Kaizu Castle. (However, another report states that Shingen marched to Kaizu first, and Kenshin only reached Mt. Saijo later.) Whatever the exact sequence of events, for twenty days both armies occupied their camps without fighting. As the stalemate

continued, Uesugi Kenshin enjoyed the pleasures of poetry and dancing in his camp, apparently uncaring of the enemy's presence.

Based in Kaizu Castle, Takeda Shingen divided his forces in two. On the night of 9 September he sent one detachment of 12,000 samurai towards the rear of Kenshin's camp on Mt. Saijo. Shingen's main body advanced to the field of Hachimanbara, awaiting their chance to take the enemy in the flank when Uesugi's forces tried to retire in the face of the attack on their camp. Another goal of Takeda's advance was to attack Uesugi's supply base at Zenkoji temple. The attack on the rear of Kenshin's camp was supposed to be a diversionary action; it was called 'Operation Woodpecker'—the pecking by which the worm would be lured out. Whatever Takeda Shingen's true intentions, they were thwarted.

Uesugi Kenshin descended Mt. Saijo in the early morning, leaving only 1,000 men behind as a rearguard;

undetected by their enemies, and shielded by the morning mist, they moved north and crossed the River Chikuma. It has been said that he was warned of Takeda's impending assault by the greater than usual amount of smoke rising from cooking fires in the enemy camp.

When the main armies clashed, Uesugi Kenshin maneuvered his forces like a turning wheel. Today this is termed *kurumagakari*, 'wheel attack,' but in fact the way it actually worked remains unclear; historians can only speculate. The most likely explanation is that Kenshin's forces marched to Zenkoji temple in three columns along the left bank of the River Chikuma, where Takeda's forces were waiting. When the shrouding mist suddenly cleared, Kenshin's right hand column saw the enemy and turned to the right to charge; successively, the second and third columns engaged in battle one after another. The right column attacked Takeda's left wing, and at short time intervals the other columns also made turns to their right to engage; this looked like the continuous turn of a wheel.

The initiative having been taken by Uesugi Kenshin, Takeda's left wing was severely beaten by the Kakizaki and Shibata groups; his brother Nobushige repulsed three waves of attack but was eventually killed. The right wing of the Takeda army was defended by Morozumi and Hajikano, but they too were killed. Only the centre and far left wing of the Takeda force remained intact. The Takeda headquarters was harassed, and Takeda Shingen himself was wounded in the confusion. Kenshin's headquarters also came under attack, from Shingen's son Yoshinobu, and Kenshin had to fight hand-to-hand. After some hours of fighting Takeda's army faced complete disintegration. In the nick of time his diversionary force arrived on the battlefield, and the balance shifted, though the action still raged for another six hours. Finally, Uesugi Kenshin's army was forced to withdraw across the River Sai, and by evening the fighting faded out. Uesugi Kenshin collected his remaining troops, numbering about 4,000, and returned to his castle; Takeda Shingen remained in possession of Hachimanbara battlefield. Takeda's forces had suffered the loss of 88 per cent of their

Iroiro odoshi haramaki, *meaning a* haramaki *armor laced with braid of many colors. This Sengoku period piece is attributed to Uesugi Kenshin. The* suji kabuto *has a multi-layered* shikoro, *with a hanging defense beneath the horizontal 'parasol.' The frontal crest or* maedate *is a Buddha with a fox. (Uesugi Shrine)*

men; Kenshin's had lost 77 per cent. The outcome of this fourth battle of Kawanakajima was indecisive; Takeda secured the land south of the River Sai and controlled northern Shinshu, but his further expansion was blocked by the continuing determined resistance of Uesugi Kenshin.

In 1564 the fifth and last contest between the two armies occurred; but during 60 days of maneuvering for position no major engagement took place.

Uchigatana *attributed to Uesugi Kenshin.(Tokyo National Museum)*

CHAOS IN KANTO
15TH–16TH CENTURIES AD

The organization of the 14th century Muromachi bakufu consisted of three divisions; *kanrei*, *Kamakurafu* and others. *Kanrei* or ministers supported the Ashikaga shogunate at Muromachi. At provincial level the Oshu *tandai*, Usho *tandai*, Kyushu *tandai* and *shugo* were all governors who exercised executive powers over the samurai class. Within this executive organization, Kamakura was regarded as special; its government was called the *Kamakurafu*, under a chief executive entitled the *kubo*. Ashikaga Motouji was appointed to this position; he was succeeded by his descendants, who increasingly became more independent of the Muromachi bakufu.

A steward of the *kubo* who called himself a *kanrei* began to oppose him, and was supported by the bakufu. Since both were responsible for governing eight provinces in Kanto, Kai and Izu, this factional struggle soon involved all the samurai of this region. *Shugo* and *jito* also took sides, but their territories were comparatively smaller.

In Kanto, samurai who were related to the *kubo* in Kamakura, the family of the *kanrei* Uesugi, various *shugo* and other free samurai started to contest power. The Uesugi family itself was divided into three factions: the Yamanouchi Uesugi, the Inukake Uesugi, and (later) the Ogigayatsu Uesugi.

The shogun Yoshinori sent forces to punish the defiant *kubo* Mochiuji in 1423. It appeared that Yoshinori's displeasure had been mollified by an apology from Mochiuji, but repeated rebellion cost the latter his life. In 1439, Mochiuji was defeated by the *kanrei* Uesugi Norizane supported by the shogun, and committed suicide. Although the destruction of the *kubo* in Kamakura might have brought peace in Kanto, the death of the shogun Yoshinori plunged the region into more confusion.

Ashikaga Shigeuji, a son of Mochiuji, was approved as *kubo* by the shogun; but by 1450 Shigeuji and the Uesugi had started another war. Into this chaos the shogun Yoshimasa sent his brother Masatomo to Kamakura to replace Shigeuji as the *kubo*. Unfortunately, Masatomo was unable to enter Kamakura in the face of strong opposition from Shigeuji's faction. He had to stay at Horigoe in Izu, and hence was called the Horigoe *kubo* (1457).

Into this endless conflict between the *kubo* (who moved his base to Koga) and the Uesugi, a new factor was introduced. Nagao Kageharu, who became powerful at Hachigata in Kanto, rebelled against his master Uesugi Akisada. His forces attacked the Akisada base at Ikakko, and

In the late Muromachi period the amount of service expected from a samurai was strictly calculated according to payments from his lord. The fee was measured in kan, *equal to about five* koku; *one koku was equal to about 180 liters of rice, and the* kan *was the unit of conversion from rice into money. Though the number of soldiers which a samurai had to provide differed depending on his masters, it was considered that if he received 100* kan *he should provide one mounted samurai. This illustration shows the arrival at the assembly of a samurai who is paid 50* kan *by his master, of the Hojo family: one mounted samurai, one banner, one arquebus carrier, two lance carriers and a horse-holder (the arquebus and lances are for the use of the samurai, not the attendants). This is equal to the requirement from a samurai of 250-*koku *rank in the Edo period. In battle the flag was attached to the* gattari, *a bracket at the top rear of the samurai's cuirass. (SY)*

then dispersed—this was significant. Until this period, rebellions had usually been attempted by dissatisfied factions exploiting another family claimant such as their master's brother. But Kageharu's rebellion had the simple aim of destroying Uesugi Akisada. This trend, which would become common during the Sengoku period, was given a name: Gekokujo—'the lower overthrow the higher.'

The rebellion was finally put down by an Uesugi minister, Ota Dokan, who was based at Edo (Tokyo). In this process, the *kubo* based at Koga and the *kanrei* Uesugi began to reconcile themselves to the emergence of a new power. In 1482, reconciled by Uesugi Fusasada in Echigo,

Nanbokucho period samurai; his cape protects his back from stray arrows, by entangling them. Later this was developed into the balloon-shaped horo, *which puffed out as the horse ran, thus giving the rider a kind of air cushion on his back.*

the Koga *kubo* Narishige and the shogun made peace. This time it seemed that the struggle was completely settled. But when Uesugi Sadamasa killed his minister Ota Dokan, and his son appealed for help to Uesugi Akisada, the flames broke out again; and this time the samurai war in northern Kanto would last for 18 years. Meanwhile, in Kyoto, the *kanrei* Hosokawa Masamoto, supporting Ashikaga Yoshitaka, attempted a coup against Ashikaga Yoshiaki. Yoshitaka was a son of the Horigoe *kubo* Ashikaga Masatomo, and Yoshitaka's brother Chachamaru had succeeded to that office. This was the bafflingly complex situation of Kanto in the chaotic aftermath of the Onin War, when Hojo Soun emerged onto the stage of history.

The adventurer: Hojo Soun

Ise Shinkuro Sozui (who later claimed descent from the Hojo, and adopted the Buddhist name Soun) left Ise for Suruga in 1487 with six retainers, to help his nephew in the matter of the Imagawa succession. In Japanese histories, Soun is said to have become a powerful daimyo in Kanto from a start as a very low class samurai or masterless *ronin*

(he was supposed by some to be a model for a character in Kurosawa's film *The Seven Samurai*). This legend has now been corrected by research: he was born into the Ise family in Okayama, and his elder sister married Imagawa Yoshitada in Suruga. He was, however, a soldier of fortune with few resources other than his wits and courage. When his brother-in-law Yoshitada was killed Soun travelled to Suruga from Kyoto to help his nephew Ryumaru (later Imagawa Ujichika). It is not known whether or not Soun was involved in the death of Imagawa Norimitsu; but as a result of that death Ryumaru became the Imagawa heir. Soun was given a castle, presumably as a reward for helping his nephew.

Soun now turned his gaze towards Izu. In Izu, Ashikaga Chachamaru had succeeded to the position of Horigoe *kubo* by killing his stepmother and brother-in-law. The shogun Yoshitaka supported the *kanrei* Hosokawa Masamoto in his desire for revenge on Chachamaru. Soun's assault on the Horigoe *kubo* was probably linked with the feuds currently raging in Kyoto. In 1493, Soun attacked Chachamaru, and after two years' fighting destroyed him. His invasion was supported not only by the Imagawa but also by the Ogigayatsu Uesugi, the latter being involved in a struggle against the Yamanouchi Uesugi. Soun exploited the utter confusion in Kanto, and expanded his power in Izu.

By 1505, Soun had taken Odawara from the Omori family and became ruler. He then began to invade Kanto, which had been suffering the continuous internecine war between the two Uesugi factions. In 1506 Soun marched to Edo to attack the castle there, but was counterattacked by Uesugi Akisada and obliged to retreat to Odawara. Opportunities to intervene in Kanto were not hard to find, however. In 1512, while the Ogigayatsu and Yamanouchi factions of the Uesugi were locked in conflict, Soun rapidly advanced east and attacked the Miura family, finally defeating them on 11 September. By seizing power over the Miura peninsula he became a daimyo in Sagami province. Without pausing, Soun then crossed Tokyo Bay and intervened in the war between the Takeda and Hara in Chiba. With peace in Chiba he seems to have lost his ambition to expand his territory any further. Soun turned over leadership to his son Ujitsuna, and retired to Nirayama Castle, where he died the following year.

Return to Kamakura: Hojo Ujitsuna

Ise Shinkuro Ujitsuna was born in 1487, the eldest son of Soun. His first appearance in documents dates from 1512, when he co-signed with his father a letter of thanks to his retainers. This letter proves that he had already been accepted as his father's successor. His main castle was supposed to be at Odawara. Although Soun carried out the first *kenchi* or land survey (predating that of Toyotomi

Hideyoshi), Ujitsuna put in hand a new one in the Odawara and Izu area. He was aware of the importance of an economic base to support his campaigns. His attention was directed mainly eastwards, and at this time the main target was the Ogigayatsu Uesugi Tomooki, who held Edo Castle. In about 1522, Ujitsuna changed his family name from Ise to Hojo, recalling the image of the old Hojo regency under the Kamakura bakufu of 200 years before. The reason for this change of name was his ambition to establish a bakufu in support of the *kubo*, with himself as regent.

In 1524 Ujitsuna's forces marched to Edo, but were checked by Uesugi troops at Takanawa near Shinagawa. The Uesugi force was by-passed and attacked from the rear, and Tomooki retreated to Edo Castle. From inside the castle Tomooki's minister Ota Suketada held secret communications with Ujitsuna, and opened the gate. The betrayed Tomooki escaped to Itabashi and then Kawagoe. By obtaining Edo Castle, which lay in the centre of the Kanto plain, Ujitsuna had acquired a base for large scale intervention throughout the region, and had also demonstrated his power over the *kanrei* Uesugi. To remove the *kanrei*, Ujitsuna married off his daughter to the son of the Koga *kubo*. After securing the Edo area he returned to Odawara.

The vengeful Uesugi Tomooki and Ujitsuna fought more than ten battles over 17 years. In 1526 the tide turned against Ujitsuna when Tomooki and Norihiro, a son of Norifusa in Hachijo, invaded Sagami. At the end of this busy year, Satomi Sanetaka invaded Kamakura by crossing Tokyo Bay from Chiba. In the course of this campaign Kamakura was burned down and the Tsurugaoka Hachimangu shrine reduced to ashes.

In due course, away in Suruga, Imagawa Ujiteru died and was succeeded by Yoshimoto. The Imagawa had been the masters of the Hojo; but now Imagawa Yoshimoto became friendly with Takeda Nobutora, and the alliance with the Hojo came to an end. War between the Imagawa and Hojo followed, especially for the territory north of the Fuji River. In 1535, Hojo Ujitsuna invaded Kai to punish Takeda Nobutora for his support of Uesugi Tomooki. While he was absent, Tomooki invaded Sagami and Ujitsuna had to return. That same year Ujitsuna sent the combined forces of Sagami, Izu, Shimofusa and Kazusa to punish Tomooki, and defeated him at Iruma in Saitama. In 1537 Uesugi Tomooki died in Kawagoe Castle, to be succeeded by his son Tomosada. Hearing of the death of his old rival, Ujitsuna advanced on Kawagoe. Finally, the Hojo forces triumphed over the Uesugi and captured Kawagoe Castle. The defeat of the Ogigayatsu Uesugi faction meant that Kanto fell into Ujitsuna's hand.

In 1540, Ujitsuna advanced to Konodai in Shimofusa and defeated Ashikaga Yoshiaki and Satomi Yoshitaka. After this battle Shimofusa, too, fell under the Hojos' sway.

After its destruction in 1526 Ujitsuna had carried out rebuilding work in Kamakura. Since the city had been a

Hojo samurai of the Sengoku period sally out from the castle at Odawara. Their leader wears mogami do kebiki odoshi *armor, of horizontal plates laced together.*

symbol of samurai rule since Minamoto Yoritomo's Kamakura bakufu, the task of reconstructing it obviously had political resonance. In 1540 Kamakura was reborn; and the next year Hojo Ujitsuna died of illness at the age of 55.

The complete commander: Hojo Ujiyasu

In spite of the old saying that a rich family crumbles away in the third generation (as was indeed the case with the Minamoto), the third master of the Hojo family was far from a worthless man. Today Hojo Ujiyasu is regarded as thoughtful, a good administrator and a clever commander.

He was born in 1515. When his father changed his name from Ise to Hojo, Ujiyasu did not immediately follow suit, and stayed in Ise for two years. Ujitsuna was given a position as Kanto *kanrei* by the Koga *kubo*, and after his death Ujiyasu succeeded to it. When Ujitsuna died the situation in Kanto was unstable because of the conflict between the Hojo, the Ogigayatsu Uesugi faction, the Yamanouchi Uesugi and the *kubo*. Ujiyasu had to fight not only against them but also against the Takeda in Kai, Imagawa in Suruga and Uesugi in Echigo.

Above & above right: When Toyotomi Hideyoshi attacked the Hojo family at Odawara in 1590, a Tokugawa force also made a coordinated attack on Hachigata, one of the Hojo castles. Japanese armies deployed wooden cannon to set fire to castles, shooting at the largely wooden structures with paper capsules containing oil and gunpowder—this had a far more lethal outcome than firing individual iron balls at the garrison.

As soon as Ogigayatsu heard news of the death of Ujitsuna in 1541, he marched to Kawagoe to retake the castle; he also attacked Edo Castle—but Ujiyasu defended both successfully. In 1545, the Ogigayatsu Uesugi Tomosada and the *kanrei* Uesugi Norimasa moved once again on Kawagoe Castle, which was defended by Hojo Tsunashige. The *kubo* Ashikaga Haruuji, after sitting on the fence, finally joined the attacking side. They laid siege with 85,000 men; isolated, Tsunashige and his 3,000 soldiers defended the castle until the following year. In April 1546, Ujiyasu marched to Kawagoe to relieve Tsunashige with 8,000 troops. The first thing to be done was to send a messenger to Tsunashige letting him know that a rescue force was approaching. A young samurai was chosen to carry out the mission. He boldly passed through the enemy siege lines during a lull in the action, entered the castle and delivered the welcome news. The messenger was Tsunashige's brother.

The Hojo chronicles describe the battle as follows (although this kind of document, written much later than the events, is not always credible). Supposedly, Hojo Ujiyasu sent an envoy to Ashikaga Haruuji saying that if the defenders' lives were spared he would take them and retire to Odawara, leaving Kawagoe Castle to the besiegers. Confident of victory, the enemy refused this offer. After the peace talks Ujiyasu sent *ninja* into the enemy camp. When they returned with the information that the enemy thought that the battle was as good as over, and discipline had slackened, Ujiyasu decided to chance a night attack. At midnight on 1 April he and his 8,000-odd soldiers charged

the enemy position; by pre-arrangement, Tsunashige's forces sortied from the castle at the same time, and both forces attacked Uesugi's and Haruuji's troops fiercely. Taken by surprise, the besiegers began to retreat. In the confusion Uesugi Asatomo was killed; Norimasa fled back to Ueno Hirai Castle, and the *kubo* returned to Koga. Some 8,000 men had defeated 85,000; and Ujiyasu was able to drive the Uesugi family from Kanto.

* * *

In 1564, internal conflict within the Takeda family in Kazusa brought Ujiyasu to the battlefield once again. The Takeda had invited the Koga *kubo's* brother Ashikaga Yoshiaki to Kazusa, and supported him; displeased, the *kubo* tried to attack Yoshiaki. Meanwhile a quarrel divided the Takeda brothers, Nobutaka and Nobumasa; the Hojo supported Nobutaka, and the Satomi family in Awa allied themselves with Nobumasa.

Receiving a report that Satomi forces had advanced to Ichikawa but were unable to march further because of lack of supplies, Hojo Ujiyasu summoned his retainers; his orders are preserved in a document: 'Tomorrow afternoon, on 5 January, our forces depart from Odawara. Retainers should assemble at Odawara with supplies transported on packhorses. You should wear armor. If you are unable to obtain enough supplies you can rent them here in Odawara. It will be a short battle, so do not take porters or laborers. As soon as your soldiers arrive, mount up, pick up your lances and ride here.'

On 7 January the two armies confronted one another at Konodai Hill in Ichikawa; this time Ujiyasu's forces totalled some 20,000 and Satomi's only about 8,000 samurai. When they first confronted the enemy the Satomi troops retreated. Seeing their withdrawal, Ujiyasu's front line charged—into

Opposite: Takigawa Kazumasu, who first pacified northern Ise for Nobunaga, and was then sent to Kai, where he destroyed Takeda Katsuyori. He was finally defeated in Kanto by the Hojo family.

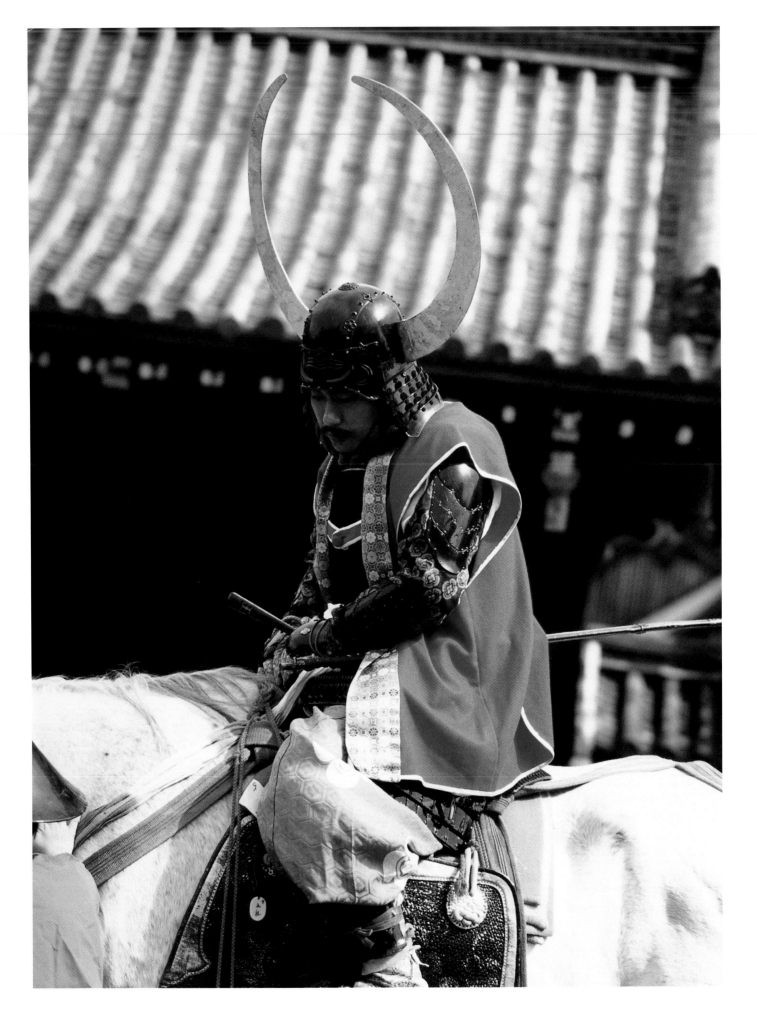

a planned ambush, which cost the Hojo army many powerful samurai. Ujiyasu is quoted as saying that he fought 36 battles in his life, and lost none of them. On this occasion, as often elsewhere, he organized a pincer movement. Hojo Ujimasa, Ujiyasu's son, and Tsunashige, his brother, by-passed Konodai Hill and attacked the enemy from the rear. The Satomi forces, encouraged by their successful ambush, were not alert. In the confusion Satomi Yoshihiro had to fight his way out through the Hojo lines, sword in hand; while he was doing so his 15-year-old son Chokuro was killed by Hojo's retainer Matsuda Yasuyoshi. (After the battle Matsuda Yasuyoshi did not go home; regretful over killing the boy, he became a priest.)

The sinews of war

How did the Hojo family manage to mount almost continuous campaigns? The question applies equally to all 'Sengoku daimyos', whose lives—whether long or short—involved constant warfare. As mentioned already, in 1506 Hojo Soun had made a detailed survey of his domains, and by Ujiyasu's generation the internal taxation system was settled. Not only the farmers but also artisans, merchants and townspeople were integrated into this system. In the late Sengoku period tax was calculated on the amount of rice production. When Hojo Soun carried out his *kenchi* the tax was paid in money. Basically, the village headman declared the cultivated acreage, and a land register was filled in accordingly. Three kinds of taxes were imposed on farmers in the provinces: on agricultural fields, rice paddies, and pressed labor. The Hojo tax on fields was first introduced in 1550 by Ujiyasu, and represented 6 per cent of the income from the field; this compared with 8 per cent imposed on the income from rice paddies. Before this system was introduced various different taxes were collected by the lord, so introduction of the new system lightened the burden of farmers. It was not only land which was taxed; the farmers' houses were also assessed. Generally the Hojos' taxation was relatively lenient. Of course, this does not mean that they were unnecessarily generous to the people of their domain. By 1559 it was suspected that agriculture in the Hojo domain was approaching collapse as a result of continuous warfare. However, the Hojo organization of a 'war economy' succeeded in stabilising the life of the farmers.

Today the Japanese word *hyakusho* means 'farmer', but it is interesting to note that from the Muromachi to Edo periods it had meant 'people not in a specific town'. The term therefore embraced not only peasants but also artisans, carriers, villagers and the people of small towns. By mistranslation of the word, such non-agricultural workers in the provinces have become neglected by history. Of course, townspeople, traders, merchants and fishermen were also taxed individually; in fact, it was taxation by occupation which practically fixed an individual's position in society.

According to the assessment of Professor Owada Tetsuo of Shizuoka University, the comparative rice production figures of the three great families in Echigo province—the Hojo, Takeda and Uesugi—were similar, at about one million *koku*. In this period, although tax was paid in currency, it is misleading to compare family wealth by a straightforward conversion from *koku* of rice to money value. The biggest difference between the families was that the Hojo territory did not include major gold mines. Uesugi Kenshin (Nagao Kagetora) depended on his gold mines on Sado Island, and when he died his son-in-law inherited a huge amount of gold lodged in Kasugayama Castle.

The last years of Uesugi Kenshin and Takeda Shingen

Yet even though Kenshin possessed this great wealth in gold, he still could not grasp absolute power in his province. The *kokujin* maintained an independent attitude, and if Kenshin had fallen they would immediately have torn his domain apart by feuding amongst themselves. Presumably, this was the reason for his invading Kanto on several occasions. He needed to satisfy the hunger of his samurai for riches by invading enemy territories. Kenshin was often praised as righteous warrior who would never refuse if asked for help, but in fact his decisions to get involved in campaigns were quite calculated. When the Takeda invaded Odawara, the Hojo asked Kenshin to attack Takeda lands from the rear to draw off the threat; but in spite of an alliance he did not move. According to Professor Fujiki Hisashi of Rikkyo University, Kenshin always invaded Kanto in wintertime, because he needed to feed the farmers in his province by looting enemy territories after the harvest. At other seasons the farmers of neighboring provinces had little to fear from him. After Kenshin's death the *kokujin* families betrayed Kenshin's son Katsuyori and drove him to destruction.

In Kai, Takeda Shingen Nobuharu suffered from the same problem. Although he was an excellent military leader, his relatives kept independent authority over their lands. Therefore, neither of these two great daimyos were ever able to rise to absolute pre-eminence over their contemporaries, as such things were judged in their world.

In 1560, Uesugi Kenshin invaded Kanto and advanced to attack Hojo Ujiyasu at Odawara. He had been appointed to the position of Kanto *kanrei* by Uesugi Norimasa, who had been defeated by Hojo Ujiyasu at Kawagoe 15 years earlier. Kenshin's army left Kasugayama Castle with only 8,000 men; but on the way to Odawara he absorbed into his forces the former vassals of Uesugi Norimasa, and by the time he arrived and laid siege to Odawara his army had grown to some 113,000. Faced by this whirlwind invasion, Ujiyasu decided to settle down to defend his castle; with vast

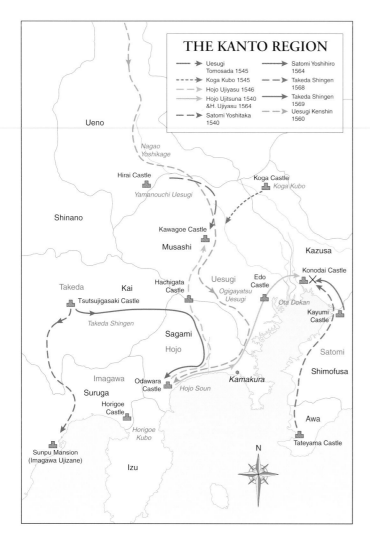

THE KANTO REGION

→	Uesugi Tomosada 1545	→	Satomi Yoshihiro 1564
→	Koga Kubo 1545	→	Takeda Shingen 1568
→	Hojo Ujiyasu 1546	→	Takeda Shingen 1569
→	Hojo Ujitsuna 1540 & H. Ujiyasu 1564	→	Uesugi Kenshin 1560
→	Satomi Yoshitaka 1540		

Ueno

Nagao Yoshikage

Hirai Castle

Koga Castle
Koga Kubo

Yamanouchi Uesugi

Shinano

Kawagoe Castle

Musashi

Kazusa

Konodai Castle

Takeda   Kai

Hachigata Castle

Uesugi
Ogigayatsu Uesugi

Edo Castle

Tsutsujigasaki Castle

Ota Dokan

Kayumi Castle

Takeda Shingen

Sagami

Hojo

Satomi

Shimofusa

Imagawa

Odawara Castle

Hojo Soun

Kamakura

Suruga

Horigoe Castle

Awa

Horigoe Kubo

Tateyama Castle

Sunpu Mansion
(Imagawa Ujizane)

Izu

N

stockpiles of supplies inside, he simply waited for Kenshin's army around his walls to become hungry. Kenshin's supply route from Echigo stretched too far for efficiency; and he had to rely upon it, rather than upon local foraging, because as he had advanced on Odawara he had laid waste to the countryside in a short-sighted 'scorched earth' strategy. After a month he was obliged to withdraw to Echigo.

Takeda Shingen, allied to the Hojo, commented on how difficult it was to destroy Hojo Ujiyasu. For his part the Hojo daimyo learnt lessons from the Uesugi invasion which would benefit him in the future. So did the samurai who had followed Kenshin in Kanto: they soon returned to the Hojo fold, reckoning that Kenshin, although a brave warrior, was not a far-sighted leader in whose service they could prosper. After the invasion the shogun Ashikaga Yoshiteru mediated between Kenshin and Ujiyasu in Kyoto and brought about a reconciliation. Kenshin needed the peace because he was troubled by rebellion among his own retainers.

In 1568, Takeda Shingen left Tsutsujigasaki mansion to lead an army south into Suruga. After Imagawa Yoshimoto was killed by Oda Nobunaga at the battle of Okehazama eight years before, his son Ujizane had inherited the domain. The exact reasons why Takeda invaded Suruga are unclear. Possible factors are that Shingen needed access to

the sea, especially to secure his salt supply; that he wanted to prevent Matsudaira Motoyasu (Tokugawa Ieyasu) from taking over the Imagawa domain from the east; or that Oda Nobunaga urged him to do it. Since 1565 Shingen had been in correspondence with Nobunaga, who needed to secure his rear when he moved on Kyoto. By dangling the bait of Suruga province in front of Shingen, Nobunaga could leave Mino in safety. Whatever the true reason, Shingen's forces invaded Suruga, and the weak resistance of the Imagawa samurai allowed them to advance swiftly. Ujizane and his wife—a daughter of Hojo Ujiyasu—had to flee from their house on foot to save their lives.

Naturally, Hojo Ujiyasu and his son Ujimasa considered this a violation of the peace treaty between them, and tried to cut Shingen's supply route. Afraid of being isolated from his own domain, Shingen once again had to withdraw his forces to Kai.

Now it was obvious that his most dangerous rivals in the region were the Hojo; unless Takeda Shingen could take the Hojo off the board he would not be able to seize Suruga. The following year, in September, his forces marched southeast once more towards Odawara. On the way they attempted to take the Hojo castles in Kanto, such as Hachigata and Takiyama, but met with no success. The Hojo followed their usual tactics, defending Odawara Castle. After only four days' siege the Takeda force began to retreat to Kai yet again; not only were their supply lines in danger, but this time Hojo field forces which had followed them from Hachigata and Takiyama represented a real threat of encirclement in enemy territory. Forces under Hojo Ujikuni from Hachigata and Hojo Ujiteru from Takiyama ambushed the Takeda army at Mimasu Pass; but they failed to trap it, and in fact suffered heavy losses themselves.

The struggle between Takeda Shingen and Hojo Ujiyasu continued until 1571 when the Hojo lord died of illness. Before Ujiyasu died he advised his son Ujimasa that since Uesugi Kenshin was an unreliable man, he should make alliance with Takeda Shingen. This agreement between the Hojo and Takeda ensured that the old rivalry over northern Kanto between the Hojo and the Uesugi would flare up once more.

In October 1572, Takeda Shingen, his rear secured by this alliance, set off to Suruga once again at the head of 25,000 soldiers. He sent the shogun Ashikaga Yoshiaki a letter saying that he would ally himself with the Asai and Asakura and destroy Oda Nobunaga. His first target was Matsudaira Motoyasu in Mikawa, and Takeda forces took Motoyasu's castles one after another. As an obedient ally of Oda, Motoyasu tried to resist the Takeda invasion, relying on Hamamatsu Castle.

Advancing south, the Takeda army came into sight of Motoyasu's forces encamped at Saigake cliff—whereupon

the invaders turned to the north-west and began to retreat. This was a trap to lure Motoyasu's troops out into the open. Pursuing the Takeda force, Motoyasu's 8,000 men tried to keep at a sufficient distance not to get sucked into a large scale battle. At Mikatagahara the Takeda army turned on their pursuers, and their slingers began to harass Motoyasu's samurai with showers of stones. The provocation worked: driven to fury, Motoyasu's men began to engage the enemy. The invincible Takeda army charged down on them, with a howling north wind and a snowstorm at their backs, at about 4 o'clock on a short February afternoon. The charge tore the centre out of Motoyasu's smaller army; dusk fell over the mass of struggling men, amid shouts, the rattle of armor, the shrieking clash of swordblades, the roar of gunfire and the groans of the maimed and dying. With the survivors, Matsudaira Motoyasu fled back to Hamamatsu Castle. No doubt the man who would become Tokugawa Ieyasu learned from this defeat, and remembered.

After the battle of Mitakagahara, Takeda Shingen did not follow up his victory to attack Hamamatsu Castle, but directed his forces to the west. When he left his province of

A Hojo samurai leader receives a report from a messenger. The messenger's right hand is behind his back grasping his sword scabbard, to show he has no intention of assassinating the lord—this was the normal position for a courier to adopt.

Kai he had already been suffering from illness. Now his condition became steadily more serious, and his officers began to march the Takeda army back to their homeland. Unable to reach Kai, Takeda Shingen died on the way home in April 1573, at the age of fifty-three. His death was concealed until the entire army had returned home.

* * *

The long, chaotic struggle for the three Kanto provinces would now be brought to an end by Oda Nobunaga's ambition for hegemony, which was of an entirely different order to the competitive greed of his contemporaries.

Oda Nobunaga appeared in the skies of the late Sengoku period like a comet, and got a long way towards terminating the feudal thinking of his day. A cold, cunning personality of great intelligence and vision, he established absolute power in his domains by taking able retainers into his service, and suppressing the powers of the troublesome *kokujin*. He began to dream of uniting the separated provinces into one power in the course of the war which was eliminating the competing Sengoku daimyos one by one. This was not merely the old urge to expand a warlord's territory, but an ambition to create something quite new— the ambition, perhaps, to be a king of Japan.

In the course of building his new road to power he slighted the last Ashikaga shogun, Yoshiaki, and brought the bakufu to an end in 1573. Being a man who clung to the old-fashioned ways and respected the authority of the old system, Uesugi Kenshin detested Nobunaga's ambition. Kenshin made alliance with his old enemies of the Ikko-shu sect on the basis of their shared hostility to Nobunaga, and began to advance westwards towards Kyoto.

In 1577, Kenshin laid siege to the Cho family's Nanao Castle in Noto with an army of 20,000 men. The Cho sent to ask help from Oda Nobunaga. Although Nobunaga could not respond to this plea promptly, hampered as he was by the anti-Nobunaga movement around Kyoto, his forces set off from Azuchi Castle in September. It was too late; learning of the fall of Nanao Castle to Uesugi Kenshin, Oda Nobunaga decided to retreat; but soon Kenshin's forces had come up and began harassing his rear division. Trapped by the high waters of the Tetori River, the Oda troops were butchered; more than 1,000 were killed in this action, and Nobunaga fled back to Azuchi. The first and last battle between Uesugi Kenshin and Oda Nobunaga—the old sort of samurai and the new—ended in complete victory for the former. It was not to prove an omen.

Kenshin called off the pursuit of Nobunaga's fleeing soldiers and returned to Kasugayama Castle; he needed to settle matters in Kanto before he could concentrate his forces to destroy Oda. In 1578 Uesugi Kenshin summoned his vassals to invade Kanto; but they never marched. On 13 March the 'dragon of Echigo' was struck down by apoplexy, and died at the age of forty-eight.

CHRONOLOGY

The dates are given as A.D.

792   Nara government abolishes provincial corps and founds *kondeisei* system.

Early Heian Period

794   Kanmu Emperor moves court to Kyoto.

935   Taira Masakado kills his uncle Kunika and seizes power in Kanto.
Fujiwara Sumitomo rebels in Kyushu.

940   Masakado killed in battle.

1028   Taira Tadatsune rebels in Kanto.

1031   Minamoto Yorinobu puts down Tadatsune's revolt.

1035   Conflict between the warrior monks of Enjo and Enryaku temples.

1036   Conflict between the Todai and Kofuku temples.

1051   Abe family in Mutsu revolts against imperial court— the start of the Zenkunen-no-eki, or Nine Years' War.

1056   Minamoto Yoriyoshi appointed *shogun* to pacify Mutsu.

1062   Minamoto Yoshiie finally crushes Abe revolt.

1083   Yoshiie intervenes in internal feuding of Kiwohara family in Dewa.

1086   Former emperor Shirakawa opens *In* (cloistered office) at imperial court.

1091   Minamoto Yoshiie refused entry to Kyoto with his forces.

1095   *Hokumen-no bushi* appointed to guard *In*.

1129   Taira Tadamori suppresses pirates of Inland Sea.

Late Heian Period

1156   Hogen insurrection in Kyoto put down.

1159   The Heishi acquire military supremacy over the Minamoto family.

1167   Taira Kiyomori appointed *daijodaijin* (court prime minister).

1180   Minamoto Yoritomo and Kiso Yoshinaka rise against the Heishi; beginning of the Genpei War.
Yoritomo founds *monchujo* (financial court) as departments of *bakufu* in Kamakura.

1183   Kiso Yoshinaka defeats Heishi and enters Kyoto.

1184   Minamoto Yoshitsune defeats the Heishi at Ichinotani.
Minamoto Yoritomo founds *kumonjo* (secretariat).

1185   Taira family perish in sea battle of Dan-no-ura.

Kamakura Period

1192   Minamoto Yoritomo appointed as shogun.

1202   Yoriie becomes second shogun.

1203   Hojo Tokimasa assassinates Yoriie at Shuzen temple.

1204   Minamoto Sanetomo became third shogun.

1205   Hojo Tokimasa becomes regent.

1219   Assassination of Sanetomo ends Minamoto Yoritomo's blood-line.

1221   Retired emperor Go-Toba's plot against Kamakura bakufu fails.

1232   Regent Hojo Yasutoki proclaims *gosei baishi kimoku* (samurai code).

1268   Envoys from Kublai Khan arrives at Dazaifu in Kyushu.

1274   Yuan/Mongol army lands in Kyushu and is repulsed (*Bunei-no-Eki*).

1281   Yuan/Mongol army's second invasion fails (*Kouan-no-Eki*).

1297   Bakufu decrees cancellation of debts to aid impoverished provincial samurai.

1321   Go-Daigo Emperor abolishes *In* office and governs by himself.

1331   Go-Daigo Emperor raises army to destroy Kamakura bakufu.

1333   Fall of Kamakura bakufu.

1334   New imperial government established (*Kenmu-no-shinsei*).

1335   Ashikaga Takauji revolts against new government.

Muromachi Period

1336   Kusunoki Masashige defeats Takauji who flees to Kyushu. Takauji strikes back, defeats Masashige at Minatogawa. Takauji establishes bakufu in Kyoto and sets Komyo on throne, beginning Nanbokucho —age of rival courts in Kyoto and Yoshino.

1338   Ashikaga Takauji appointed shogun.

1368   Ashikaga Yoshimitsu becomes third shogun.

1378   Yoshimitsu moves bakufu to Muromachi in Kyoto.

1392   Two rival courts integrated by Yoshimitsu.

1402   Relations established between Yoshimitsu and Ming Chinese emperor.

1428   First *ikki* revolt by disaffected poorer classes.

1429   Ashikaga Yoshinori becomes shogun.

1441   Akamatsu Yoshisuke assassinates Yoshinori.

1457   Ota Dokan constructs Edo Castle in Tokyo.

1467   Beginning of Onin War in Kyoto.

1471   Rennyo opens halls for Buddhist sect *Jodo-shin-shu* or *Ikko-shu*.

1477 End of Onin War.

1485 *Ikki* seize control in Yamashiro.

1488 *Ikki* rising in Kaga.

1495 Hojo Soun takes Odawara and seizes power in Kanto region.

1496 Rennyo starts building Ishiyama Honganji temple at Osaka.

1504 *Tokusei-ikki* riots in Kyoto demanding revocation of debt.

1531 *Ikko-ikki* forces defeat warlord Asakura Norikage.

1543 Portuguese bring firearms to Japan.

1549 St. Francis Xavier's Christian mission to Nagasaki.

1553 Takeda Shingen and Uesugi Kenshin fight first battle at Kawanakajima.

1555 The Mori destroy the Sue family.

1560 Oda Nobunaga kills Imagawa Yoshimoto at battle of Okehazama.

1563 *Ikko-ikki* in Mikawa.

1568 Oda Nobunaga enters Kyoto with shogun Ashikaga Yoshiaki.

1570 Nobunaga defeats Asai and Asakura families at Anegawa.

1571 Nobunaga attacks *Ikko-ikki* in Nagashima; and destroys Enryaku temple.

1572 Takeda Shingen defeats Tokugawa Ieyasu at Mikatagahara.

1573 Fall of the Muromachi bakufu.

1575 Oda/Tokugawa allied army defeats Takeda Katsuyori at Nagashino.

1576 Nobunaga starts building Azuchi Castle.

Momoyama Period

1582 Akechi Mitsuhide kills Oda Nobunaga at Honnoji temple.
Hashiba (Toyotomi) Hideyoshi defeats Akechi at Yamazaki.

1583 Hideyoshi defeats Shibata Katsuie.

1584 Tokugawa Ieyasu submits to Hideyoshi after battle of Nagakute.

1585 Hideyoshi pacifies Shikoku.

1586 Hideyoshi becomes *daijodaijin*.

1587 Hideyoshi pacifies Kyushu; orders expulsion of Christian missionaries from Japan.

1590 Hideyoshi destroys Hojo family in Odawara and unites Japan.

1592 Hideyoshi's forces invade Korea.

1597 Second invasion of Korea.

1598 Hideyoshi dies; army withdrawn from Korea.

1600 Tokugawa Ieyasu defeats Ishida Mitsunari at Sekigahara.

Edo (Tokugawa) Period

1603 Ieyasu becomes shogun and establishes bakufu at Edo.

1614 Ieyasu attacks Osaka Castle.

1615 Second Osaka campaign; Ieyasu destroys Toyotomi family.

1616 Ieyasu dies; Tokugawa Hidetada becomes second shogun.

1623 Tokugawa Iemitsu becomes third shogun.

1637 Christian rebellion in Shimabara starts.

1639 Bakufu prohibits visits by Portuguese shipping.

1641 Bakufu transfers Dutch trading post to Dejima in Nagasaki.

1736 Russian ship appears in Chiba.

1793 Russian delegate arrives in Hokkaido.

1796 English ship visits Japan.

1801 Russian delegate visits Nagasaki to request trading rights.

1825 Bakufu orders that foreign ships are to be fired upon.

1853 US Navy Cdre. Perry calls at port in Hiraga.

1854 Treaty of Kanagawa

1860 Commercial treaty signed with USA.

1863 Chochu Han fires on British squadron off Shimonoseki.

1864 British, Dutch, French, & US ships bombard Shimonoseki.
First bakufu punitive campaign against Choshu Han.

1866 Failure of second punitive expedition against Choshu.

1867 Abdication of shogun Keiki and restoration of imperial regime under Meiji Emperor.

1868 Satsuma and Choshu army defeats Keiki's bakufu army at Toba-Fushimi.
New government army defeats Aizu Han rebels.

Meiji Period

1869 New government established in Edo, which is renamed Tokyo.

1877 Saigo Takamori dies as leader of failed samurai rebellion in Kyushu.

GLOSSARY

Technical terms for parts of armor, weapons etc. are not listed here, but are explained in context where they occur e.g. in captions throughout this book.

Akuto Bandit or landless samurai, warrior monk, and thief in late Kamakura and Muromachi periods. They appeared in Kyoto and Nara, where there were many *shoen* or manorhouses belonging to major temples.

Ashigaru Common foot soldier.

Bakufu Field headquarters of commanding general; by extension, the institution of government under the shogunate.

Daimyo A feudal baron in the Japanese provinces.

Do-ikki Movement of rebellious farmers demanding cuts in taxes, mainly occurring in Kinki district. In some cases the rebels expelled the provincial governor or baron.

Gekokujo 'The lower overthrow the higher'—the time of social turmoil beginning in the 1480s during the Muromachi period and more or less coincident with the early *Sengoku*—'the age of the country at war.'

Gokenin Samurai who held land by direct feudal connection with shogunate of Minamoto Yoritomo or the Kamakura bakufu—'franchised samurai.'

Gosho The imperial residence, or the court.

Ho-o A 'cloistered emperor' (see *Joko*), not living in a temple but having special apartments in the emperor's court. From these offices he might issue laws, and wield as much influence as the emperor himself.

In The apartments of the *Ho-o* or *Joko* at court.

Jito Provincial governor, appointed by the regime, in charge of collecting taxes, management of land and maintaining peace and order.

Joko A retired emperor, often the father of the present emperor. He might live in 'cloistered' retreat; or be simultaneously a *Ho-o*—see above.

Kokujin Vassals of a *daimyo*, holding land in his province and owing his family military service.

-no- In Japanese this postposition is often inserted between the family and the personal name, meaning 'of' or 'from' e.g. Minamoto-no-Yoshiie, 'Yoshiie from the Minamoto family.' It is sometimes not pronounced, and has been omitted from male names in this text for simplicity.

Ronin Masterless, and thus landless, samurai outside the system of feudal fiefs; soldiers of fortune.

Samurai 'In service.' Initially a professional fighting man, later a member of the feudal military class. Used in this text as both singular and plural.

Shogun Originally, temporary commander-in-chief of expeditionary army; later, hereditary military dictator governing through regime parallel to imperial court.

Shugo Provincial governor, appointed by the regime, in charge of policing and military duty.

Shugo-daimyo A governor who became a powerful landowner in his own right.

Tokusei-ikki A revolt to demand the revocation of all debt by order of the bakufu. A *tokusei* was formerly a bakufu decree cancelling the debts of the *gokenin* to relieve them of this burden after the Mongolian invasion. However, during the Muromachi period farmers and the lower classes rose to compel the bakufu to issue such decrees.

Wako Japanese pirates of the Muromachi period. They intruded in Chinese and Korean territory and throughout south-east Asia.

Opposite: Kamakura period samurai in hunting clothes.

BIBLIOGRAPHY

Akuto no seiki, Arai Takashige; Yoshikawa Kobunkan, 1997

Botshin senso, Sasaki Suguru; Chuko Shinsho, 1997

Bunroku-Keisho no eki, Che Guan; Kodansha, 1994

Bushi no seiritsu, Bushizo no soshutsu, Takahashi Masaaki; Tokyo daigaku, 1999

Bushi no tanjo, Seki Yukihiko; NHK books, 2000

Chuusei buke no saho, Futaki Kenichi; Yoshikawa Kobunkan, 1999

Edojidai no mikataga kawaruhon, Amino Yoshihiko et al; Yosensha, 1998

Genpei kassen no Kyozo wo hagu, Kawai Yasushi; Kodansha, 1996

Hideyoshi no yabo to gosan, Kasaya Kazuhiko et al; Buneido, 2000

Hideyoshi to Momoyama bunka, Watanabe Takeshi et al; Osakajo Tenshukaku Museum, 1997.

Ikusa, Fukuda Toyohiko; Yoshikawa Kobunkan, 1993

Jidai shozoku; Kyoto shoin, 1995

Kamakura bushi monogatari, Konno Nobuo: Kawade shobo shinsha, 1991

Kassen engi emaki, Yoshida Seiichi et al; Heibonsha, 1979

Katchyu no subete, Sasama Yoshihiko; PHP kenkyujo, 1997

Moko shurai ekotoba, Komatsu Shigemi; Chuokoronsha, 1990

Moko shurai, Amino Yoshihiko; Shogakukan, 1992

Moko shurai, Kaitsu Ichiro; Yoshikawa Kobunkan, 1997

Nagashino-Shitaragahara kassen no shijitsu, Nawa Yumio; Yuzankaku, 1999

Nazotoki chuseishi, Imatani Akira; Senyosha, 1997

Nihon chuseishizo no saikento, Amino Yoshihiko et al; Yamakawa shuppan, 1998

Nihon kassen zenshu, Kuwata Tadachika; Akiyama shoten, 1990

Nihon kassen zuten, Sasama Yoshihiko; Yuzankaku, 1997

Nihon no bijutsu no.146, Miya Tsugio; Shibundo, 1946

Nihon no kassen bugu jiten, Sasama Yoshihiko; Kashiwa shobo, 1999

Nihon no katchyu; Kyoto Museum, 1987

Nihon no rekishi, Ienaga Saburo; Horupu sha, 1982

Nihon rekishi; Gakken, 1991

Nihon senjin saho jiten, Sasama Yoshihiko; Kashiwa shobo, 2000

Nobunaga no sengoku gunjigaku, Fujimoto Masayuki; Yosensha, 1997

Onin no ran, Takano Kiyoshi et al.; Gakken, 1994

Osakanojin, Takano Kiyoshi et al.; Gakken, 1994

Sekigahara kassen, Kasaya Kazuhiko; Kodansha, 1994

Sekigahara kassen, Owada Tetsuo et al; Shinjinbutsu oraisha, 2000

Sekigahara, Nakai Hitoshi et al.; Gakken, 2000

Sengoku kassen no joshiki ga kawaru hon, Fujimoto Masayuki; Senyosha, 1999

Sengoku kassen no Kyojitsu, Suzuki Naoya; Kodansha, 1998

Sengoku kassen, honto wa kodatta, Fujimoto Masayuki; Yusenshya Mook,1996

Teppo denrai, Udagawa Takehiko; Chuko shinsho, 1997

Teppo to Nihonjin, Suzuki Masaya; Yosensha, 1997

Toyotomi Hideyoshi kassen soran, Yasui Hisayoshi et al; Shinjinbutsuorai sha, 1986

Toyotomi Hideyoshi, Nagaoka Keinosuke et al; Gakken, 1996

Toyotomi Hideyoshi, Yasui Hisayoshi; Shinjinbutsuorai Sha, 1996

Yoroi to kabuto, Yamagami Hachiro et al; Colour books

Yumiya to token, Kondo Yoshikazu; Yoshikawa Kobunkan, 1997

Zohyo tachino senjo, Fujiki Hisashi; Asahishinbun sha, 1996